Learning Ext JS
Fourth Edition

Create powerful web applications with the new and improved Ext JS 5 library

Carlos A. Méndez

Crysfel Villais

Armando Gonzalez

PUBLISHING

BIRMINGHAM - MUMBAI

Learning Ext JS
Fourth Edition

First published: November 2008

Second edition: October 2010

Third edition: January 2013

Fourth edition: July 2015

Production reference: 1290715

Published by Packt Publishing Ltd.
Livery Place
35 Livery Street
Birmingham B3 2PB, UK.

ISBN 978-1-78439-438-7

www.packtpub.com

Credits

Authors

Carlos A. Méndez

Crysfel Villa

Armando Gonzalez

Reviewers

Davor Lozić

Olivier Pons

Juris Vecvanags

Commissioning Editor

Ashwin Nair

Acquisition Editor

Shaon Basu

Content Development Editor

Akashdeep Kundu

Technical Editor

Menza Mathew

Copy Editors

Vikrant Phadke

Angad Singh

Ameesha Smith-Green

Project Coordinator

Milton Dsouza

Proofreader

Safis Editing

Indexer

Tejal Daruwale Soni

Production Coordinator

Manu Joseph

Cover Work

Manu Joseph

About the Authors

Carlos A. Méndez is a freelance developer and graphic designer living in México, with expertise in web development since 2000 and Windows development since 1998. He has also worked with Ext JS since version 2.x up to the present day. Since 1998, he has developed and designed administrative applications for accounting, payroll, inventory, human resource control, restaurants, hotels, and much more—applications that are in production and up to date.

Trying to explore creativity with a deep passion, Carlos has created many Ext JS components and VB components for private companies and was also involved in graphic design, such as illustrations and small animations used for interactive presentations by some companies in México. He always has a passion for creating and learning new things on the Web.

He is the founder and development manager of the company administrationonline.com, which is focused on administrative applications. Carlos is involved in many projects around the world and also provides support and maintenance to many Ext JS projects ranging from 2.x to 5.x.

> First of all, I would like to thank my mother and brother for their support and help in realizing this project. Thanks to my best friend, Nacir Garcia Junior, for his support and friendship over these last years. Also, thanks to my father and uncles, whose challenges, work pressures, and work and personal knowledge were passed on through all these years in matters of design and business logic. These have brought me where I am today. Without all you guys, I would not have been able to accomplish many achievements and goals. Thanks, everybody!

Crysfel Villa is a software engineer with more than 8 years of experience with JavaScript. He started his career as a web developer working with HTML and basic JavaScript in the late 1990s but then started focusing on server-side technologies, such as PHP and Java J2EE.

Before he started working with the Ext JS library, he loved to work with MooTools, but in late 2007, he started learning about an awesome new library that was emerging as an open source project. At that time, version 2.0 of the Ext JS library had just been released, and Crysfel started using this new library for medium-to-large projects in the agency that he used to work for.

In early 2010, he started working as a freelancer. He began training teams on Ext JS for private companies; writing a blog with tutorials, tips, and tricks; developing custom components on Ext JS for his clients; and working on open source projects to share his knowledge with the world.

More recently, Crysfel has been getting into new technologies such as Angular JS and React Native. If you want to find out more about his work, you can follow him on Twitter (`@crysfel`) or download his open source projects from GitHub (`crysfel`).

Writing this book was very hard, especially when you are a busy person and really like to get involved in exciting things. I want to give special thanks to my wife, Hazel, who supported me in every step of the process. Without her, this wouldn't have been possible. She read all the scripts before I submitted them. She usually found some mistakes or things to clarify. Her work on this project is priceless.

Thanks to my parents and brothers, who used to keep asking me very often about the project and provided me with the moral support to work and complete this dream. Also, I want to thank all my closest friends for the moral support that they gave me. Special thanks to my best friends, Carlos and Gina, who often pushed me to continue working on this project.

About the Reviewers

Davor Lozić is a senior software engineer interested in many subjects, especially computer security, algorithms, and data structures. He creates web applications in CakePHP and Ext JS, and in his spare time, he reads books about modern physics, graph databases like Neo4j, and related subjects. You can check out his website at http://warriorkitty.com, where you can contact him. He likes cats because cats are great! If you would like to talk about any aspect of technology, or if you have great and funny pictures of cats, feel free to contact him.

Olivier Pons is a senior developer who has been building websites since 1997. He's a teacher at the University of Sciences (IUT) of Aix-en-Provence, France. In ISEN (Institut Supérieur de l'Électronique et du Numérique) and École d'Ingénieurs des Mines de Gardanne, he teaches state-of-the-art web techniques, such as the MVC fundamentals, Symfony, Wordpress, PHP, HTML, CSS, jQuery, jQuery Mobile, Node.js, AngularJS, Apache, NoSQL, Linux basics, and advanced VIM techniques. He has already done some technical reviews, including Packt Publishing's *Ext JS 4 First Look*, *jQuery Hotshots*, *jQuery Mobile Web Development Essentials*, *Wordpress Complete*, and *jQuery 2.0 for Designers Beginner's Guide*, among others.

In 2011, Olivier left a full-time job as a Delphi and PHP developer to concentrate on his own company, HQF Development (http://hqf.fr). He currently runs a number of websites, including http://krystallopolis.fr, http://artsgaleries.com, http://www.battlesoop.fr, http://www.livrepizzas.fr, http://www.papdevis.fr, and http://olivierpons.fr, which is his own web development blog. He's currently learning Unity and building a game on his own. He works as a consultant, teacher, and project manager and sometimes helps major companies as a senior/highly skilled developer.

Juris Vecvanags started a career in the IT field in early 90s. At that time, he had the chance to work with a broad range of technologies and share his knowledge with Fortune 500 companies as well as private and government customers.

Before moving to Silicon Valley, he owned a well-established web design start-up in Europe. Juris is currently employed as a solutions architect at Sencha, where he helps customers write better apps for both desktop and emerging mobile platforms. He contributes to the Ext JS framework as well as dedicates his time to write custom components and add new features.

When it comes to web technologies, this invaluable experience serves as his ground to be a trusted advisor and competent reviewer. When Juris is away from the office, you can find him speaking at meetups in the San Francisco Bay Area, Chicago, and New York. Among the topics he covers are Node.js, Ext JS, and Sencha Touch.

He is passionate about cutting-edge technologies and everything related to JavaScript.

www.PacktPub.com

Support files, eBooks, discount offers, and more

For support files and downloads related to your book, please visit www.PacktPub.com.

Did you know that Packt offers eBook versions of every book published, with PDF and ePub files available? You can upgrade to the eBook version at www.PacktPub.com and as a print book customer, you are entitled to a discount on the eBook copy. Get in touch with us at service@packtpub.com for more details.

At www.PacktPub.com, you can also read a collection of free technical articles, sign up for a range of free newsletters and receive exclusive discounts and offers on Packt books and eBooks.

https://www2.packtpub.com/books/subscription/packtlib

Do you need instant solutions to your IT questions? PacktLib is Packt's online digital book library. Here, you can search, access, and read Packt's entire library of books.

Why subscribe?
- Fully searchable across every book published by Packt
- Copy and paste, print, and bookmark content
- On demand and accessible via a web browser

Free access for Packt account holders

If you have an account with Packt at www.PacktPub.com, you can use this to access PacktLib today and view 9 entirely free books. Simply use your login credentials for immediate access.

Table of Contents

Preface

Over the past few years, Ext JS has become a popular and powerful JavaScript framework for desktop application development. For an Ext JS developer, the learning curve is not very easy/fast and I have seen cases where developers learning this framework find it to be a slow process. While writing this book I was thinking about the easiest and most comprehensible points so that you can understand the basics, just as I would have liked to learn about the framework if I was in your place.

This book is intended for developers who have the desire to learn and begin using this framework for their applications, and also for developers who have not started using the current version. It is written as an easy-to-follow guide that will help you understand the basics and fundamentals of the framework. If you have experience with previous versions of the framework, this book may clear many of your doubts about upgrading and how things happen in version 5.x.

This book covers all of the basic information you need to know to start development with this nice and powerful framework.

What this book covers

Chapter 1, *An Introduction to Ext JS 5*, covers an explanation of how to start by getting the framework (downloading the file) and setting up the basic requirements you need in order to begin coding. This chapter also provides an explanation of how the framework is structured, how to set up some required tools, and gives a quick peek at the product, Sencha Architect.

Chapter 2, *The Core Concepts*, is about the framework's class system, and tells you how to use object-oriented programming with Ext JS. Also, this chapter explains how to extend classes, how to inherit properties, and the use of the Loader system in order to define and require dependencies in a dynamic way.

Chapter 3, *Components and Layouts*, explains how components work, how they are created, their life cycle, and how to take advantage of all this. Here, you also learn about types of containers and the layout system, which will help you create amazing UIs with little effort.

Chapter 4, *It's All about the Data*, explains how the framework handles and manipulates data to display information using data-aware widgets or components.

Chapter 5, *Buttons and Toolbars*, shows you how to make use of component events; listen to events; (mainly) create buttons, toolbars, and menus; and set the most basic configurations for these components.

Chapter 6, *Doing It with Forms*, talks about the form component, the available fields that we can use in our forms, and how to collect and submit data.

Chapter 7, *Give Me the Grid*, covers the basics of the most popular component, the Grid panel, in the framework, how to implement it, its column model, and custom data renderers for displaying data. We also see how to listen to events in the Grid panel and look at some plugins and features (specific capabilities) that can be implemented in the grid.

Chapter 8, *DataViews and Templates*, explains how to make use of DataViews and templates to create data-aware views, implement a nice organization of our data, and set styles and custom logic for the representation of data.

Chapter 9, *The Tree Panel*, covers the use of the tree panel component and its implementation. It also explains how to create stores and data for this component.

Chapter 10, *Architecture*, is one of the most important chapters in the book. It shows how to create an application using the MVC and MVVM patterns. This is done in order to create applications that can be scalable and easy to maintain. The MVVM pattern, which is a powerful pattern for reducing code, is introduced in version 5.

Chapter 11, *The Look and Feel*, demonstrates how to create new themes inside the framework and applications by giving our applications a new look and some color changes (themes). Also, you learn how to create specific component-style UIs using Compass and Sass.

Chapter 12, *Responsive Configurations and Tablet Support*, explains how we can use touch screen themes and how to set responsive configurations in components in order to make those components responsive-aware.

Chapter 13, From Drawing to Charting, talks about the basics of drawing and chart creation. We see how to create charts by the use of the SVG/VML engines. This chapter also explains how to add the Chart package to applications and the theme engine introduced in version 5.

Chapter 14, Finishing the Application, covers how to prepare our application for the production environment and deployment, covering the most essential parts for final production.

Chapter 15, What's Next?, shows you where to get more feedback and resources such as forums, other useful resources to get information tutorials from, and so on. This chapter also gives a sneak peek into some useful plugins (commercial and free).

What you need for this book

The web browsers recommended for use are as follows:

- Google Chrome: `http://www.google.com/chrome`
- Firefox: `https://www.mozilla.org/en-US/firefox/new/`
- Firefox for developers: `https://www.mozilla.org/en-US/firefox/developer/`

These browsers come in handy because they come with debugging tools for easy development.

For a web server with PHP support, use this:

- Xampp: `https://www.apachefriends.org/index.html`

For the database, use the following:

- MySQL: `http://dev.mysql.com/downloads/mysql/` (this also comes bundled in Xampp)

For Sencha Cmd and the required tools, use these:

- Sencha Cmd: `http://www.sencha.com/products/sencha-cmd/download`
- Ruby 1.8 or 1.9: `http://www.ruby-lang.org/en/downloads/`
- Sass: `http://sass-lang.com/`
- Compass: `http://compass-style.org/`

- Java RTE (version 1.7.0): http://www.oracle.com/technetwork/java/javase/downloads/java-se-jre-7-download-432155.html

- Apache ANT: http://ant.apache.org/bindownload.cgi

- Ext JS (of course): http://www.sencha.com/products/extjs/

We will use Ext JS 5.1.1 in this book.

Who this book is for

If you are new developers who are beginners in Ext JS, developers familiar with Ext JS who want to augment the skills of creating better applications, or developers who haven't yet used version 5.x and want to know more about it, this is the book for you.

Users should possess a basic knowledge of HTML/JavaScript/CSS/Sass/Compass, and an understanding of JSON, XML, and any server-side language (such as PHP, ASP, JAVA, and so on) is required.

Conventions

In this book, you will find a number of styles of text that distinguish between different kinds of information. Here are some examples of these styles, and an explanation of their meaning.

Code words in text are shown as follows: "Inside the app/view folder, we remove all existing files (the initial skeleton), and proceed to create the initial view our application will have."

A block of code is set as follows:

```
Ext.define('myApp.model.modulesModel', {
    extend: 'Ext.data.Model',
    requires: [
        'Ext.data.field.String',
        'Ext.data.field.Boolean',
        'Ext.data.field.Integer'
    ],
    fields: [
```

```
            {type: 'string', name: 'description'},
            {type: 'boolean', name: 'allowaccess'},
            {type: 'int', name: 'level'},
            {type: 'string', name: 'moduleType', defaultValue: ''},
            {type: 'string', name: 'moduleAlias', defaultValue: ''},
            {type: 'string', name: 'options'}
        ]
    });
```

When we wish to draw your attention to a particular part of a code block, the relevant lines or items are set in bold:

```
Ext.define('myApp.store.modulesTreeDs', {
    extend: 'Ext.data.TreeStore',
    requires: [
        'myApp.model.modulesModel',
        'Ext.data.proxy.Ajax'
    ],
    constructor: function(cfg) {
        var me = this;
        cfg = cfg || {};
        me.callParent([Ext.apply({
            storeId: 'mymodulesTreeDs',
            autoLoad: true,
            model: 'myApp.model.modulesModel',
            proxy: {
                type: 'ajax',
                url: 'serverside/data/menu_extended.json'
            }
        }, cfg)]);
    }
});
```
Any command-line input or output is written as follows:

```
sencha -sdk /path/to/ext generate app myApp /path/to/myApp
```

New terms and **important words** are shown in bold. Words that you see on the screen, in menus or dialog boxes for example, appear in the text like this: "Try to write something in the **Customer ID** field and you will see that it is read-only."

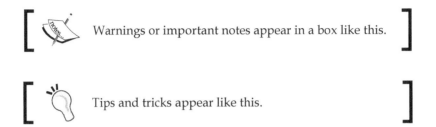

Warnings or important notes appear in a box like this.

Tips and tricks appear like this.

Reader feedback

Feedback from our readers is always welcome. Let us know what you think about this book—what you liked or may have disliked. Reader feedback is important for us to develop titles that you really get the most out of.

To send us general feedback, simply send an e-mail to feedback@packtpub.com, and mention the book title via the subject of your message. If there is a topic that you have expertise in and you are interested in either writing or contributing to a book, see our author guide on www.packtpub.com/authors.

Customer support

Now that you are the proud owner of a Packt book, we have a number of things to help you to get the most from your purchase.

Downloading the example code

You can download the example code files for all Packt books you have purchased from your account at http://www.packtpub.com. If you purchased this book elsewhere, you can visit http://www.packtpub.com/support and register to have the files e-mailed directly to you.

Errata

Although we have taken every care to ensure the accuracy of our content, mistakes do happen. If you find a mistake in one of our books—maybe a mistake in the text or the code—we would be grateful if you would report this to us. By doing so, you can save other readers from frustration and help us improve subsequent versions of this book. If you find any errata, please report them by visiting http://www.packtpub.com/submit-errata, selecting your book, clicking on the **errata submission form** link, and entering the details of your errata. Once your errata are verified, your submission will be accepted and the errata will be uploaded on our website, or added to any list of existing errata, under the Errata section of that title. Any existing errata can be viewed by selecting your title from http://www.packtpub.com/support.

Piracy

Piracy of copyright material on the Internet is an ongoing problem across all media. At Packt, we take the protection of our copyright and licenses very seriously. If you come across any illegal copies of our works, in any form, on the Internet, please provide us with the location address or website name immediately so that we can pursue a remedy.

Please contact us at copyright@packtpub.com with a link to the suspected pirated material.

We appreciate your help in protecting our authors, and our ability to bring you valuable content.

Questions

You can contact us at questions@packtpub.com if you are having a problem with any aspect of the book, and we will do our best to address it.

An Introduction to Ext JS 5

When learning a new technology such as Ext JS, some developers face a hard time to begin with, so this book will give you the best possible way to start to understand this technology more than any other source. We have to go from the library documentation to blogs and forums looking for answers, trying to figure out how the library and all the components work together. Even though there are tutorials in the official learning center, it would be great to have a guide to learn the library from the basics to a more advanced level; this is the main goal of this book.

Ext JS is a state of the art framework to create **Rich Internet Applications (RIAs)**. The framework allows us to create cross-browser applications with a powerful set of components and widgets. The idea behind the framework is to create user-friendly applications in rapid development cycles, facilitate teamwork (MVC or MVVM), and also have a long-term maintainability.

Ext JS is not just a library of widgets anymore; the brand new version is a framework full of new exciting features for us to play with. Some of these features are the new class system, the loader, the new application package, which defines a standard way to code our applications, and much more awesome stuff.

The company behind the Ext JS library is Sencha Inc. They work on great products that are based on web standards. Some of the most famous products that Sencha also have are **Sencha Touch** and **Sencha Architect**.

In this chapter, we will cover the basic concepts of the framework of version 5. You'll learn how to set up the library or SDK and create our first program, get to know the available tools to write our code, and take a look at some of the new features in Ext JS 5.

- Considering Ext JS for your next project
- Getting started with Ext JS—our first program

- Tools and editors
- What's new in Ext JS 5?

Considering Ext JS for your next project

Ext JS is a great library to create RIAs that require a lot of interactivity with the user. If you need complex components to manage your information, then Ext is your best option because it contains a lot of widgets such as the grid, forms, trees, panels, and a great data package and class system.

Ext JS is best suited for enterprise or intranet applications; it's a great tool to develop an entire CRM or ERP software solution. One of the more appealing examples is the Desktop sample (`http://dev.sencha.com/ext/5.1.0/examples/desktop/index.html`). It really looks and feels like a native application running in the browser. In some cases, this is an advantage because the users already know how to interact with the components and we can improve the user experience.

Ext JS 5 came out with a great tool to create themes and templates in a very simple way. The framework for creating themes is built on top of **Compass** and **Sass**, so we can modify some variables and properties and in a few minutes we can have a custom template for our Ext JS applications. If we want something more complex or unique, we can modify the original template to suit our needs. This might be more time-consuming depending on our experience with Compass and Sass.

Compass and Sass are extensions for CSS. We can use expressions, conditions, variables, mixins, and many more awesome things to generate well-formatted CSS. You can learn more about Compass on their website at `http://compass-style.org/`.

The new class system allows us to define classes incredibly easily. We can develop our application using the object-oriented programming paradigm and take advantage of the single and multiple inheritances. This is a great advantage because we can implement any of the available patterns such as **MVC**, **MVVM**, Observable, or any other. This will allow us to have a good code structure, which leads us to have easy access for maintenance.

Another thing to keep in mind is the growing community around the library; there are lots of people around the world that are working with Ext JS right now. You can even join the meeting groups that have local reunions frequently to share knowledge and experiences; I recommend you to look for a group in your city or create one.

The new loader system is a great way to load our modules or classes on demand. We can load only the modules and applications that the user needs just in time. This functionality allows us to bootstrap our application faster by loading only the minimal code for our application to work.

One more thing to keep in mind is the ability to prepare our code for deployment. We can compress and obfuscate our code for a production environment using the Sencha Cmd, a tool that we can run on our terminal to automatically analyze all the dependencies of our code and create packages.

Documentation is very important and Ext JS has great documentation, which is very descriptive with a lot of examples, videos, and sample code so that we can see it in action right on the documentation pages, and we can also read the comments from the community.

Getting started with Ext JS

So, let's begin with Ext JS! The first thing we should do is download the framework from the official website, `http://www.sencha.com/products/extjs/`. The version available at the time of writing this book is 5.1.1.

There are three types of license:

- **The open source license**: If you are creating or want to develop an open source application compatible under the GNU GPL license v3 (`http://www.gnu.org/copyleft/gpl.html`).

- **The commercial license**: You need to buy this if you are planning/wanting to develop a closed source project and want to keep the source code as your own property. Usually used by corporations, banks, or enterprises.

- **The commercial OEM**: If you want to use Ext JS to create your own commercial SDK or web application builder, or use it as frontend for some embedded device, then this comes into the picture. As this type of license can vary, it's customized for each customer.

You can see more detailed information about this subject at `http://www.sencha.com/products/extjs/licensing`.

Downloading Ext JS

If you download Ext JS directly from `http://www.sencha.com/products/download/`, this will be a 30-day trial version of Ext JS and you will also be required to enter some personal information in order to get the trial. To obtain the GPL version, you can get it from `http://www.sencha.com/legal/GPL/`. We can also use the available **Content Delivery Network (CDN)**, as shown in the following table, so that we don't need to store the library on our own computer or server:

Theme	Links
Classic	• CSS file: `http://cdn.sencha.com/ext/trial/5.1.1/packages/ext-theme-classic/build/resources/ext-theme-classic-all.css` • JavaScript file: `http://cdn.sencha.com/ext/trial/5.1.1/build/ext-all.js`
Neptune	• CSS file: `http://cdn.sencha.com/ext/trial/5.1.1/packages/ext-theme-neptune/build/resources/ext-theme-neptune-all.css` • JavaScript file: `http://cdn.sencha.com/ext/trial/5.1.1/build/ext-all.js` • Theme JS Overrides: `http://cdn.sencha.com/ext/trial/5.1.1/packages/ext-theme-neptune/build/ext-theme-neptune.js`
Crisp	• CSS file: `http://cdn.sencha.com/ext/trial/5.1.1/packages/ext-theme-crisp/build/resources/ext-theme-crisp-all.css` • JavaScript file: `http://cdn.sencha.com/ext/trial/5.1.1/build/ext-all.js` • Theme JS Overrides: `http://cdn.sencha.com/ext/trial/5.1.1/packages/ext-theme-crisp/build/ext-theme-crisp.js`

Setting up and installing Ext JS 5

After you download the Ext JS Library (ZIP file), extract the contents to a working folder. For the first time, you will probably get overwhelmed by the size of the ZIP file and by the number of files and folders, but don't worry, the purpose of each file and the content of each folder will be explained shortly.

Sencha Cmd

Besides the Ext JS library, we need to download the Sencha Cmd (command tool). This tool is intended to be a cornerstone for building applications, creating workspaces, and new themes, and the ability to minify and deploy our applications to a production environment.

Download this tool at `http://www.sencha.com/products/sencha-cmd/` and also check that the following requirements are met in order for Sencha Cmd to work properly:

- JRE Sencha Cmd requires **Java Runtime Environment** version 1.7 to support all functionality, however, most features will work with 1.6 (the minimum supported version).
- Ruby differs by OS:
    - Windows: Download Ruby from `http://rubyinstaller.org`. Get the `.exe` file version of the software and install it.
    - Mac OS: Ruby is preinstalled. You can test whether Ruby is installed with the Ruby `-v` command.
    - Linux-based OS: Use `sudo apt-get install ruby 2.0.0` to download Ruby.

Run the Sencha Cmd setup, follow the instructions, and after installing Sencha Cmd, we need to verify the installation. Proceed to open the command line and type the following command:

`sencha`

 On Windows environments, it's recommended that you restart the system after installation in order to get the proper environment variables applied.

After typing the command `Sencha`, we should see the following output:

```
cmd - Shortcut

C:\>sencha
Sencha Cmd v5.0.1.231
Sencha Cmd provides several categories of commands and some global switches. In
most cases, the first step is to generate an application based on a Sencha SDK
such as Ext JS or Sencha Touch:

    sencha -sdk /path/to/sdk generate app MyApp /path/to/myapp

Sencha Cmd supports Ext JS 4.1.1a and higher and Sencha Touch 2.1 and higher.

To get help on commands use the help command:

    sencha help generate app

For more information on using Sencha Cmd, consult the guides found here:

http://docs.sencha.com/ext-js/4-2/#!/guide/command
http://docs.sencha.com/ext-js/4-1/#!/guide/command

http://docs.sencha.com/touch/2-2/#!/guide/command
http://docs.sencha.com/touch/2-1/#!/guide/command
```

Why so many files and folders?

This is a natural question when you look at the downloaded files and folders for the first time, but every file and folder is there for a purpose and now you're going to learn it:

- The `build` folder contains compiled files of the SDK and is ready to be used. This folder is very useful to start with in Ext JS without the need to use Sencha Cmd. From version 5, this folder also contains examples and ready-to-use Ext JS themes located in packages (folder).

- The `examples` folder contains the source code of the examples. These examples are built to show what we can do with the library. However one significant change in version 5 is that this folder needs to be compiled using Sencha Cmd in order to be deployed/compiled into the build folder.

- The `overrides` folder contains JavaScript files used to add extra functionality and behavior to components and widgets and they are also used when an application or code is compiled.

- The `packages` folder is where the styles and images are located; we can also find the Sass files to create our custom theme in here. Sass is an extension of CSS3 to improve the language; we can use variables, mixins, conditionals, expressions, and more with Sass. From version 5 onward, this folder also contains more folders, which are `Locales`, `Ext JS Core`, `Charts`, `Aria`, and many more.

- The src folder contains the source code files that are part of the framework. Each file represents a class/object so we can read it easily, and every folder corresponds to the namespace assigned to the class. For example, the Ext.grid.Panel class is in a file called Panel.js, which in a folder called grid (src/grid/Panel.js).

- The welcome folder contains the styles and images that are shown when we open the index.html file in the root folder.

  If you look at the root folder, you can also see other JavaScript files. Basically, they are the compressed, debug, and development versions of the library.

- The bootsprap-*.js files contain information about the framework; these files are used by ext*.js files in order to load the required files (the src folder or packages folder).

- The ext-all.js file loads the complete library with all the components, utilities, and classes.

- The ext-all-debug.js file is the same as the ext-all.js file. The difference is that this file will show console logs and we can use this file to debug our application.

- The ext.js file is the core and foundation layer for Ext JS. If we use this file, we're not loading the whole library; this file contains only the class system, the loader, and a few other classes. We can use the Ext.Loader class to load just the required classes and not the entire framework.

Folders that changed in version 5 from previous versions

Developers that use previous versions of Ext JS may find the new folder structure confusing, and may notice that some of folders disappeared in version 5. The significant changes to folders are listed below. The builds folder no longer exists; instead, we should use the build folder.

- The locale folder has been moved to the packages/ext-locale folder. In version 5, Locales have a more complex folder structure and we also now have the ext-locale-language.js file and ext-locale-language-debug.js file. By default, the components are displayed in English, but you can translate them to any other language.

- The jsbuilder folder was removed, now in version 5 we will use Sencha Cmd to build and compress our source code.

- The ext*-dev.js file was removed in version 5, as according to Sencha, there was much confusion about the use of these files. On Sencha Touch these files were merged and following the same pattern as Sencha Touch on Ext JS. *-dev.js files and ext*-debug.js files were merged into one.

- The resources folder was removed, so now we need to use the packages folder.

- The docs folder was removed, so as of version 5, developers should check the documentation and guides at http://docs.sencha.com/. Also, there is an alternative to download the offline documentation selection (offline docs) from the link in the documentation menu:

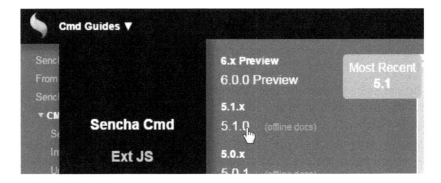

Now that you have a basic understanding of the downloaded files and folders, we can advance to the next step of "getting started."

Looking at the whole picture

Before we start writing code, you need to learn and understand a few concepts first. Ext JS is divided into three layers, as shown in the following screenshot. The purpose of these layers is to share code with Sencha Touch, a framework to create mobile web applications.

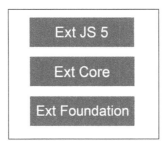

In the **Ext Foundation** layer, the `Ext` object is created, as well as some useful utilities and the class system that allows us to extend classes, override methods and properties, add mixins and configurations to classes, and many more things.

> To understand more about mixins, see `http://docs.sencha.com/extjs/5.1/5.1.1-apidocs/#!/api/Ext.Mixin.`

The **Ext Core** layer contains the classes that manage the **Document Object Model (DOM)**, the setting and firing of events, support for Ajax requests, and classes to search the DOM using CSS selectors. Also now, part of `Ext.Core` is the data package (classes related to data such as fields, store, and so on). As of version 5.1, Ext JS Core will have common shared code with Sencha Touch (the next major release).

Finally, the **Ext JS 5** layer contains all the components, widgets, and many more features that you're going to be learning about in this book.

Our first program

We need to set up our workspace to write all the examples of this book. Let's create a folder named `learning-ext-5`. For now, we don't need a web server to host our examples, but in the following chapters we are going to use Ajax; therefore, it's a good idea to use your favorite web server to host our code from these first examples.

In our new folder, we are going to create folders that contain the examples for each chapter in this book. At this point, we have a folder called `chapter_01` that corresponds to this chapter and other called `extjs-5.1.1` that contains the Ext JS framework. Both folders are located on the same level.

Inside the `chapter_01` folder, we're going to create a file called `myfirstapp.html`, where we need to import the `Ext` library and create a JavaScript file called `app.js` that will contain our JavaScript code:

Open the `myfirstapp.html` file in your favorite editor and type the following code:

```
<!doctype html>
<html>
<head>
  <meta http-equiv="X-UA-Compatible" content="IE=edge">
  <meta charset="utf-8">
  <title>My first application</title>
    <!-- Importing the stylesheet (theme neptune) -->
    <link rel="stylesheet" type="text/css" href="../
      ext-5.1.1/build/packages/ext-theme-neptune/build/resources/
        ext-theme-neptune-all.css">
    <!-- Importing the Extjs library -->
    <script src="../ext-5.1.1/build/ext-all.js"></script>
    <!-- Importing overrides Js code special for theme neptune -->
    <script src="../ext-5.1.1/build/packages/ext-theme-neptune/build/
      ext-theme-neptune.js"></script>

    <!-- Importing our application -->
    <script type ="text/javascript" src="app.js"></script>
```

```
</head>
<body> </body>
</html>
```

Writing the Ext JS code

The previous code shows how to import the library for a development environment. First, we import the stylesheet that is located at `ext-5.1.1/build/packages/ext-theme-neptune/build/resources/ext-theme-neptune-all.css`. The second step is to import the whole library from `ext-5.1.1/build/ext-all.js`. The third step is to import a JavaScript file that contains overrides so the theme can work properly (specific adjustments on this theme).

Now we're ready to write our code in the `app.js` file.

Before we can start creating widgets, we need to wait until the DOM is ready to be used and Ext JS is loaded and parsed. Ext JS provides a function called `Ext.onReady`, which executes a callback automatically when all the nodes in the tree can be accessed. Let's write the following code in our `app.js` file:

```
Ext.onReady(function(){
  alert("This is my first Extjs app !");
});
```

An alternative to this code can also be:

```
Ext.application({
    name : 'MyFirstApplication',
    launch : function() {
        Ext.Msg.alert("Hello"," my first Ext JS app");
    }
});
```

One of the advantages of using Ext JS is that the library only uses one single object in the global scope called `Ext` to allocate all the classes and objects within the framework.

If you open the HTML file in your favorite browser, you will see something like the following screenshot:

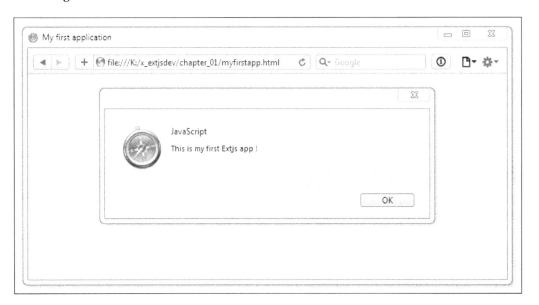

 Feel free to use your favorite browser to work through the examples in this book. I recommend you use Google Chrome because it has more advanced developer tools and it's a fast browser. If you are a Firefox fan, you can download the Firebug plugin; it's a powerful tool that we can use for debugging in Firefox.

If for some reason we can't see the alert message in our browser, it's because we haven't defined the correct path to the `ext-all.js` file. If you look at the JavaScript console, we'll probably see the following error:

Uncaught ReferenceError: Ext is not defined

This means that the `ext-all.js` file is not imported correctly. We need to make sure everything is correct with the path and refresh the browser again.

Adding interaction to the program

Now that we know how to execute code when the DOM is ready, let's send an alert message from the Ext library. Using the `Ext.MessageBox` alias `Ext.Msg` object, we can create different types of messages such as an alert, confirmation, prompt, progress bar, or even a custom message:

```
Ext.onReady(function(){
    //alert("This is my first Extjs app !");
    Ext.Msg.alert("Alert","This is my first Ext js app !");
});
```

The output for the preceding lines of code is shown in the following screenshot:

 If you're not getting any errors in the JavaScript console but still you can't see the message on the screen, as seen in the preceding screenshot, make sure you have inserted the stylesheet correctly.

In this case, we're using the `alert` method of the `Ext.Msg` object. The first parameter is the title of the message and the second parameter is the content of the message. That was easy, right? Now let's create a confirmation dialog box:

```
Ext.onReady(function(){
    Ext.Msg.alert("Alert","This is my first Ext JS app !");
    Ext.Msg.confirm("Confirm","Do you like Ext JS 5?");
});
```

We use the `confirm` method to request two possible answers from the user. The first parameter is the title of the dialog box and the second parameter is the question or message we want to show to the user:

Before the confirmation dialog box appeared, there was an alert that didn't show up. One important thing to keep in mind is that the messages and alerts from the Ext library don't block the JavaScript loop, unlike the native browser dialog box. This means that if we add another alert or custom message after the `confirm` method is called, we will not see the confirmation dialog box anymore.

So far, we have shown a confirmation dialog box requesting two possible answers from the user, but how can we know the user's response in order to do something according to the answer? There's a third parameter in the confirmation dialog box, which is a callback function that will be executed when the user clicks on one of the two answers:

```
Ext.onReady(function(){
  Ext.Msg.alert("Alert","This is my first Ext JS app !");
  Ext.Msg.confirm("Confirm","Do you like Ext JS 5?",
    function(btn){
      if (btn === "yes") {
        Ext.Msg.alert("Great!","This is great!");
      } else {
        Ext.Msg.alert("Really?","That's too bad.");
      }
  });
});
```

The callback function is executed after the user clicks on the **Yes** or **No** button or closes the confirmation dialog box. The function receives the value of the clicked button as a parameter, which is **Yes** or **No**; we can do whatever we want inside the callback function. In this case, we're sending a message depending on the given answer. Let's refresh our browser and test our small program to watch our changes. Confirmations are usually asked when a user wants to delete something, or maybe when they want to trigger a long process, basically anything that has only two options.

Tools and editors

Before we go any further, it's important we use some tools in order to be more productive when building our code and our applications. There are many editors in the market we can use to write code. Let's review some of them that will be useful in this book.

XAMPP or WAMP

XAMPP is an open source distribution of Apache that contains MySQL, PHP, and Perl, and is easy to install and easy to use. XAMPP can provide us with a local web development environment that is easy to handle without the need to test on a public server or hosting.

XAMPP is available for Windows (32-bit), Linux, and OS X versions and you can download XAMPP at `https://www.apachefriends.org/index.html`.

WAMP is another free package containing Apache, MySQL, and PHP, especially designed for the Windows OS. You can get it at `http://www.wampserver.com/en/`. WAMP comes in 32-bit and 64-bit versions according to your Windows OS.

In order to test the code or review some Ext JS examples, we will need a web server (Apache) or IIS to get the proper functionality and AJAX responses that the examples and code require.

Aptana

The **Aptana** editor is an IDE from Appcelerator. It's based on Eclipse but optimized for web applications. It's an open source project and free of charge.

Among other IDEs, Aptana contains an autocomplete functionality for JavaScript and Ext JS, a JavaScript validator, a CSS and HTML validator, a JavaScript debugger, Bundles, and more:

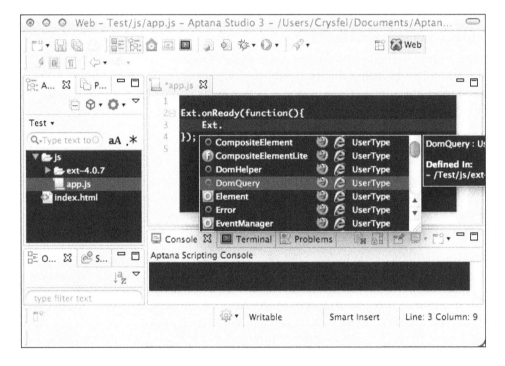

Aptana is a great tool when working with Python, Ruby, or PHP as the backend of our projects. It contains tools to work with those out-of-the-box languages and also contains tools to deploy your application in the cloud using Heroku or Engine Yard.

Sencha Architect

The **Sencha Architect** desktop application is a tool that will help you design and develop an application faster than coding it by hand. The idea is to drag and drop the components into a canvas, and then add the functionality. The Sencha Architect desktop application is a product from Sencha Inc. that aims to help developers define components with a few clicks. We can create an Ext JS or Sencha Touch project. We can get a free trial from the official website of Sencha. We can also buy the license there.

 The current Sencha Architect version is 3.1.0. This works for Ext JS versions 4.x and 5.x. Previous versions of Sencha architect, such as 2.x will not work for Ext JS 5.

One of the advantages that Architect has is that you can drag-and-drop components into the work zone and this tool will create (generate) the basic code of the components and/or the part(s) you are working with.

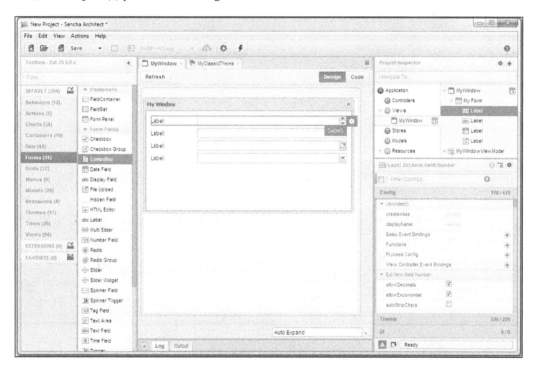

Also, you can switch to the code view and see the results so far (some parts of the Ext JS classes/components can be edited but not all of them). You can see the **code** view in the following screenshot:

The intention of this book is not to teach you about Sencha Architect, it's for you to understand and learn Ext JS and create applications without the need to use Sencha Architect. Later, if you feel you need to use Sencha Architect or want to give a try, it may be easier once you know the basics and essentials that are covered in this book.

What's new in Ext JS 5?

Ext JS 5 introduces a great number of new features, and most of them will be covered in the upcoming chapters when we have a closer look, but for the moment we will briefly mention some of the significant additions in version 5:

- **Tablet support and new themes**: This has introduced the ability to create apps compatible with touch-screen devices (touch-screen laptops, PCs, and tablets). The Crisp theme is introduced and is based on the Neptune theme. Also, there are new themes for tablet support, which are Neptune touch and Crisp touch.

- **New application architecture – MVVM**: Adding a new alternative to MVC Sencha called MVVM (which stands for Model-View-ViewModel), this new architecture has data binding and two-way data binding, allowing us to decrease much of the extra code that some of us were doing in past versions. This new architecture introduces:
  - Data binding
  - View controllers
  - View models

- **Routing**: Routing provides deep linking of application functionality and allows us to perform certain actions or methods in our application by translating the URL. This gives us the ability to control the application state, which means that we can go to a specific part or a direct link to our application. Also, it can handle multiple actions in the URL.

- **Responsive configurations**: Now we have the ability to set the `responsiveConfig` property (new property) to some components, which will be a configuration object that represents conditions and criteria on which the configurations set will be applied, if the rule meets these configurations. As an example:

```
responsiveConfig: {
    'width > 800': { region: 'west' },
    'width <= 800':{ region: 'north' }
}
```

- **Data package improvements**: Some good changes came in version 5 relating to data handling and data manipulation. These changes allowed developers an easier journey in their projects, and some of the new things are:
  - Common Data (the Ext JS Data class, `Ext.Data`, is now part of the core package)

- ° Many-to-many associations
- ° Chained stores
- ° Custom field types

- **Event system**: The event logic was changed, and is now a single listener attached at the very top of the DOM hierarchy. So this means when a DOM element fires an event, it bubbles to the top of the hierarchy before it's handled. So Ext JS intercepts this and checks the relevant listeners you added to the component or store. This reduces the number of interactions on the DOM and also gives us the ability to enable gestures.

- **Sencha Charts**: Charts can work on both Ext JS and Sencha Touch, and have enhanced performance on tablet devices. Legacy Ext JS 4 charts were converted into a separate package to minimize the conversion/upgrade. In version 5, charts have new features such as:

  - ° Candlestick and OHLC series
  - ° Pan, zoom, and crosshair interactions
  - ° Floating axes
  - ° Multiple axes
  - ° SVG and HTML Canvas support
  - ° Better performance
  - ° Greater customization
  - ° Chart themes

- **Tab Panels**: Tab panels have more options to control configurations such as icon alignment and text rotation. Thanks to new flexible Sass mixins, we can easily control presentation options.

- **Grids**: This component, which has been present since version 2.x, is one of the most popular components, and we may call it one of the cornerstones of this framework. In version 5, it got some awesome new features:

  - ° **Components in Cells**
  - ° **Buffered updates**
  - ° **Cell updaters**
  - ° **Grid filters** (The popular "UX" (user extension) has been rewritten and integrated into the framework. Also filters can be saved in the component state.)
  - ° **Rendering optimizations**

- **Widgets**: This is a lightweight component, which is a middle ground between `Ext.Component` and the Cell renderer.

- **Breadcrumb bars**: This new component displays the data of a store (a specific data store for the tree component) in a toolbar form. This new control can be a space saver on small screens or tablets.

- **Form package improvements**: Ext JS 5 introduces some new controls and significant changes on others:
    - **Tagfield**: This is a new control to select multiple values.
    - **Segmented buttons**: These are buttons with presentation such as multiple selections on mobile interfaces.
    - **Goodbye to TriggerField**: In version 5, TriggerField is deprecated and now the way to create triggers is by using the Text field and implementing the triggers on the TextField configuration. (TriggerField in version 4 is a text field with a configured button(s) on the right side.)

    - **Field and Form layouts**: Layouts were refactored using HTML and CSS, so there is improvement as the performance is now better.

- **New SASS Mixins** (`http://sass-lang.com/`): Several components that were not able to be custom-themed now have the ability to be styled in multiple ways in a single theme or application. These components are:
    - `Ext.menu.Menu`
    - `Ext.form.Labelable`
    - `Ext.form.FieldSet`
    - `Ext.form.CheckboxGroup`
    - `Ext.form.field.Text`
    - `Ext.form.field.Spinner`
    - `Ext.form.field.Display`
    - `Ext.form.field.Checkbox`

- **The Sencha Core package**: The core package contains code shared between Ext JS and Sencha Touch and in the future, this core will be part of the next major release of Sencha Touch. The Core includes:
  - Class system
  - Data
  - Events
  - Element
  - Utilities
  - Feature/environment detection

Summary

In this chapter, you learned how to set up and install Ext JS 5 and Sencha Cmd too. You also learned about the content of the folders included in the Ext JS 5 SDK, and the differences between folders in version 4 and version 5. We mentioned some useful tools that will be essential for this book; however, many developers may not like them or may not feel comfortable with these tools, so feel free to use your favorite tools and editors.

Through the course of this book, you are going to learn about the use of Ext JS 5, and we will cover the most important parts, features, and components, and many more classes and tools. At the end of this book, we will complete a small real-world application so you can get an idea of how to implement Ex JS for your next and future projects.

In the next chapter, we will focus on the Ext JS 5 core concepts and DOM manipulation.

2
The Core Concepts

In this chapter, you're going to learn about the class system, which was first introduced in Ext JS version 4. You are also going to learn how to load classes dynamically and how to interact with the **Document Object Model (DOM)** to modify the structure of the DOM tree for our convenience.

You should know that JavaScript is classless (prototype-oriented); however, we can emulate it using the `prototype` object and other techniques. One of the major features of Ext JS is that since version 4, all the code in the framework was developed with a class-based structure. Along with naming conventions, it's easy to learn and understand, and keep the code organized, structured, and easy to maintain.

Knowing and understanding the concept of the **Object-Oriented Programming System (OOPS)** is very important. This book may not be a focused guide on the concept of OOPS, but you are going to learn how we can use and implement this concept in Ext JS.

The following are the main topics in this chapter, which you need to understand well before moving on to other parts of the library:

- The class system
- Loading classes on demand
- Working with the DOM

The class system

In version 4, the class system was completely redesigned and new features were added. It became a more powerful way to extend and create classes. And Ext JS 5 keeps the same structure and consistency as version 4.

In order to create classes, Ext JS uses the `Ext.ClassManager` object internally to manage the associations between the names, aliases, or alternate names we define. And all classes (existing and new) use `Ext.Base` as the base code.

It's not recommended to use these classes directly; instead we should use the following shorthands:

- `Ext.define`: This shorthand is used to create a new class, extend a class, or whenever we need to apply some override(s) in a class.

- `Ext.create`: This shorthand creates a new instance of a class, using either the `fullname` class, the `alias` class, or the `alternate name` class. Using any of these options, the class manager handles the correct mapping to create the class. We can also use this shorthand to create objects from an existing class.

- `Ext.widget`: This shorthand is used to create a widget using the `xtype` (alias) property or a configuration object.

> Alias is a short name for a class, which is usually easy to remember and handle in code, for example, `Ext.grid.column.Action` has an alias that is `actioncolumn`. The full list can be found here: `http://docs.sencha.com/extjs/5.1/5.1.1-apidocs/#!/api/Ext.enums.Widget`.

Naming conventions

Ext JS uses consistent naming conventions throughout the framework. This allows you to have classes, namespaces, filenames, and so on, to keep an organized structure. As part of the coding conventions used by Sencha, there are some basic rules:

- Names may use alphanumeric characters, and you can use numbers, but as a convention, rule numbers may be used for technical terms. The use of underscores or hyphens may not be used as a convention rule, but it is not impossible to use them. For example:
    - `MyApp.utils-common.string-renderers` (not good)
    - `MyApp.utils.Md5encyption` (good)
    - `MyApp.reportFormats.FM160` (good)

- Names should be grouped into `packages/namespaces`, spaced using object dot-notation as `(namespace).(namespace).(class)`. You cannot repeat the top-level namespace followed by the class name. For example:

  ◦ `MyApp.EmployeeApp` (good)

  ◦ `MyApp.EmployeeApp.EmployeeClass` (not good; also this will be interpreted as a property rather than a class)

- The name for the top-level classes should be camel-cased. The groups and namespaces grouping of the top-level class should be in lowercase (again as a convention but not forbidden). For example:

  ◦ `MyApp.`**`grids`**`.EmployeesGrid`

  ◦ `MyApp.`**`data.clients`**`.SalesReport`

- As a rule and also to avoid possible errors, classes that are not part of the framework should never use `Ext` as the top-level namespace, unless you are creating an `Ext.ux` component. However, as a rule if you are using plugins or third-party components, be sure that the name(s) you are using do not collide or interfere with these plugins/components.

Writing your first class

So now let's create our first class using the first shorthand in the preceding list. In a new file called `classes_01.js`, we need to write the following code:

```
Ext.define('Myapp.sample.Employee',{
  name: 'Unknown',
  constructor: function (name){
    this.name= name;
    console.log('class was created - name:' + this.name);
  },
  work: function(task){
    alert(this.name + ' is working on: ' + task);
  }
});
var patricia = Ext.create('Myapp.sample.Employee', 'Patricia Diaz');
patricia.work('Attending phone calls');
```

In this code, we defined the name of the class as a string `'Myapp.sample.Employee'` as the first parameter of the `Ext.define` function. Then we set the `name` property and two methods: `constructor` and `work`.

When a new class is created, Ext will use the `constructor` method as a callback and it will be executed each time a new instance is created, giving us the chance to apply the initial configurations to the class. If constructor is not defined, Ext will use an empty function and also the initial properties of the class will be the default values.

We now have the class already defined in the code, and a new instance of the class is created in the following code:

```
var patricia = Ext.create('Myapp.sample.Employee','Patricia Diaz');
```

We are telling Ext JS to create a new instance of the `Myapp.sample.Employee` class and passing a one-string parameter, `Patricia Diaz`, right after the execution of the code where the constructor method will be executed:

```
constructor: function(name){
  this.name = name;
  console.log('class was created - name:' + this.name);
},
```

Finally, we invoke the `work` method, which will make an alert appear in the browser:

So far we have been handling one value in the class, and the usual way for most developers to do this is that we handle multiple values when creating classes, so let's change the code as shown in the following sample:

```
Ext.define('Myapp.sample.Employee',{
  name: 'Unknown',
  lastName: 'Unknown',
  age: 0,
  constructor: function (config){
    Ext.apply( this, config || {} );
```

```
        console.log('class created - fullname:' + this.name + ' ' +
          this.lastName);
      },
      checkAge:function(){
        console.log( 'Age of ' + this.name + ' ' + this.lastName + ' is:'
          + this.age );
      },
      work: function( task ){
        console.log( this.name + ' is working on: ' + task);
      }
    });
    var patricia = Ext.create('Myapp.sample.Employee',{
      name:'Patricia',
      lastName:'Diaz',
      age:21
    });
    patricia.checkAge();
    patricia.work('Attending phone calls');
```

Let's review the changes. The parameter in the `constructor` method was changed to `config`, so now we will pass an object as a parameter to the `constructor` method. `Ext.apply(this, config || {});` will allow us to copy all the properties of the `config` parameter to the class properties.

In order to run the example, we need to create an HTML page containing the following code snippet, and import the Ext JS library and the client class file (`classes_01.js`), and after that we can execute the preceding code.

```
<!doctype html>
<html>
<head>
<meta http-equiv="X-UA-Compatible" content="IE=edge">
<meta charset="utf-8">
<title>My first ExtJS class</title>
<script src="../ext-5.1.1/build/ext-all.js"></script>
<script type ="text/javascript" src="classes_01.js"></script>
</head>
<body> </body>
</html>
```

Open the HTML file in your favorite browser and the JavaScript console by pressing *Ctrl + Shift + I* (shortcut for Windows users) or *Cmd + Option + I* (shortcut for Mac users) to open the developer tools in Google Chrome.

If you're using Firefox, the shortcut to show the JavaScript console is *Ctrl + Shift + K* (for Windows users) or *Cmd + Option + K* (for Mac users). We should see two log messages in the JavaScript console as shown in the following screenshot:

The first message is printed in the console by the `constructor` method that is executed when the `Employee` class is created. The second message is printed when we have called the `checkAge` method and accessed the `age` property. Finally after we have called the `work` method, the third message will appear.

Once we have the instance of the `Employee` class, we can modify its properties by assigning the new value. If we refresh our browser, we will see a new message in the console and it will have the new value. We can create as many instances as we want from our class and every one of them will have the same properties and methods. However, we can change their values individually or even pass an object to the constructor with the properties that we want to change.

Simple inheritance

When we create a class using the `Ext.define` method, we're extending from the `Ext.Base` class. This class contains abstract methods that will be inherited by all the subclasses so we can use them at our convenience.

In our previous example, the Employee class extends from the Base class. We didn't have to do anything special to accomplish that. By default, if we don't configure a class to extend from any other class, it extends from the Base class, and we should keep this in mind.

Most of the classes in the Ext library extend from the Ext.Base class, however there are a few core classes that don't. The following screenshot shows the inheritance tree for the Button and Model components:

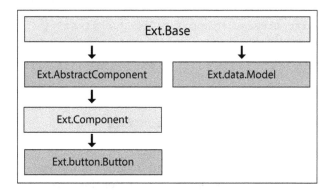

As we can see in the previous image, the root of the tree is the Ext.Base class, which means that the Button and Model components share the same methods defined in the Ext.Base class.

In order to extend from any other class, we need to define the extend property to our new class as follows; this will allow us to inherit all the methods and properties from the parent.

```
Ext.define('Myapp.sample.Supervisor',{
extend: 'Myapp.sample.Employee',
constructor: function ( config ){
  Ext.apply(this, config || {});
  console.log('class B created - fullname:' + this.name +
    ' ' + this.lastName);
},
supervise: function( employee ){
  var employeefullname = employee.name + ' ' +
  employee.lastname;
  console.log( this.name + ' is supervising the work of '
+ employeefullname );
}
});
```

Here we have created a class that extends from the `Myapp.sample.Employee` class just by adding the `extend` property and assigning the name of the superclass in `extend:'Myapp.sample.Employee'`. Also, we added a new method called `supervise`, which will be available only to the `Supervisor` class.

Let's make a duplicate of the files in the first example, and rename the HTML file to `classes_02.html` and the JavaScript file to `classes_02.js`. Now, change the `script` tags that point the `src` property to the new JavaScript file instead. At the end of the code in the `classes_02.js` file, add the following code:

```
var robert = Ext.create('Myapp.sample.Supervisor',{
  name: 'Robert',
  lastName: 'Smith',
  age: 34
});
robert.checkAge();
robert.work( 'Administration of the office' );
robert.supervise( patricia );
```

We used the `Ext.create` method to create an instance of the `Supervisor` class. In this example, we're passing new parameters. After the `Supervisor` class is created, we run the same methods from `Employee` class, and we also run the new method `supervise`.

Let's open the HTML file in our browser and look at the JavaScript console. We should see the new logs from the `Supervisor` class.

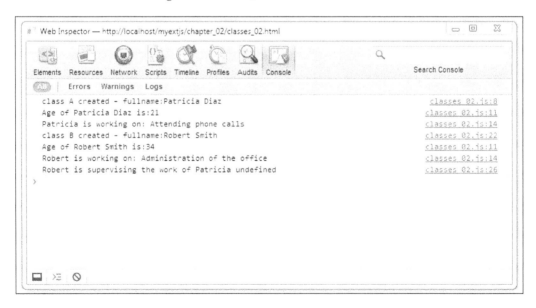

As we can see in this inheritance example, this property is also useful when we want to extend classes/widgets such as Ext.panel.Panel and create our own panel while giving special and extra functionality that the panel does not provide.

Preprocessors and postprocessors

Every class in Ext JS is an instance of the Ext.Class class. When we use the Ext.define method to define a class, we are in fact creating an instance of the Ext.Class class.

According to the documentation, the Ext.Class class is a factory. This doesn't mean that our classes extend from the Ext.Class class. As mentioned before, all classes extend from the Ext.Base class. What this really means is that when we use the Ext.create method, Ext runs processes behind the scenes. Each process is a task with a specific purpose in the whole process of creating the class.

A process may be asynchronous or not, for example, we have a preprocessor that loads all the dependencies for our new class if they are not already loaded. When the preprocessor finishes its tasks, the next process is executed until the list is empty and then our new class is created.

A **preprocessor** is a process that runs before the instance of an Ext.Class class is created, or in other words, before our new class is created. Each of the processes defined will change the behavior of our class, if necessary.

A **postprocessor** is a process that runs after our new class is created. There is a process to make our class a singleton, to define alternative names for our class, and for a few other processes.

There are a few processes defined by the Ext library, but we can define our own and add them to the process queue if we want.

The question now is what processes are we talking about? And what do they do? If we want to see the list of registered processes, we can execute the following lines of code:

```
var pre = Ext.Class.getDefaultPreprocessors(),
post = Ext.ClassManager.defaultPostprocessors;
console.log(pre);
console.log(post);
```

By running the previous code in a browser, we should see the following messages in the JavaScript console:

```
["className", "loader", "extend", "privates", "statics",
"inheritableStatics", "platformConfig", "config", "cachedConfig",
"mixins", "alias"]
["alias", "singleton", "alternateClassName", "debugHooks",
"deprecated", "uses"]
```

The following screenshot represents the flow of the class creation with the preprocessors and postprocessors:

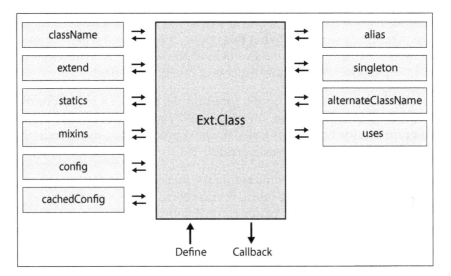

This is what happens when we create a class. All the preprocessors run before the class is ready, modifying the result. The postprocessors on the other hand run when the class is ready to be used.

For example, the `loader` process looks for the dependencies and if they are not present, it tries to load them synchronously. After all the dependencies are ready, it passes the control to the `Ext.Class` class in order to continue with the next process. The following process in the queue is `extend`, which is responsible for copying all the prototype methods and properties from the superclass to the subclass.

The following table shows a brief description of all the preprocessors that may be executed to create a new class:

Preprocessors	Description
className	This defines the namespace and the name of the class
loader	This looks for the dependencies and if they don't exist already, then it tries to load them
extend	This inherits all the methods and properties from the superclass to the new class
statics	This creates the defined static methods or properties for the current class
inheritableStatics	This inherits the static methods or properties from the superclass, if applicable
config	This creates the getters and setters for the configuration properties
mixins	This inherits all the methods and properties from the mixin classes
alias	This sets the alias for the new class

Once the class is created, the following postprocessors are executed:

Postprocessor	Description
alias	This registers the new class to the class manager and its alias
singleton	This creates a single instance of the new class
alternateClassName	This defines alternative names for the new class created
uses	This imports the classes that will be used, along with the new class

Sometimes processes won't run, so if this is the case we need to check out how we have configured and defined our classes. Sometimes, letters in lowercase and uppercase can make a big difference, so keep in mind that class names and property names have to be in the correct uppercase and lowercase syntax; otherwise, these processes or properties will be ignored.

Now that you have a basic understanding of how the class system works, we can advance on to how we can define our classes using the process logic and take advantage of them.

Mixing many classes (the use of mixins)

So far, you have learned about simple inheritance, but we can also mimic multiple inheritances using the `mixins` processor. The concept is really simple: we can mix many classes into one. As a result, the new class will have access to all the properties and methods from the mixed classes.

Continuing with the previous classes, `Employee` and `Supervisor`, let's organize those classes a bit more. Occupations in the company can vary depending on the needs of the organizations; a secretary has different tasks to perform from a manager or an accountant. So we are going to separate the required tasks each occupation has to perform, and this way we will have some different classes with the tasks that people in the company can perform according to the occupation each one has.

The following diagram shows an example:

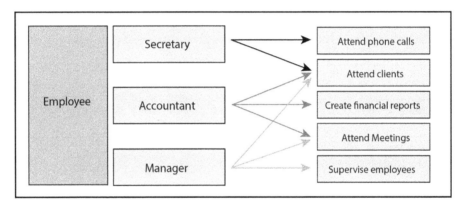

Let's make a duplicate of the `classes_02.js` file and rename it `classes_04.js`; also make a duplicate of the `classes_02.html` HTML file and change the JavaScript file reference to `classes_04.js`. And now we proceed to make some new changes in the `classes_04.js` file. After the code where we defined the employee class, let's write the following code:

```
// Mixins
Ext.define('Myapp.sample.tasks.attendPhone',{
  answerPhone:function(){
    console.log( this.name + ' is answering the phone');
  }
});
Ext.define('Myapp.sample.tasks.attendClient',{
  attendClient:function(clientName){
    console.log( this.name + ' is attending client: ' + clientName);
```

```
  }
});
Ext.define('Myapp.sample.tasks.attendMeeting',{
attendMeeting:function(person){
  console.log( this.name + ' is attending a meeting with ' +
    person);
}
});
Ext.define('Myapp.sample.tasks.superviseEmployees',{
superviseEmployee:function(supervisor, employee){
  console.log( supervisor.name + ' is supervising : ' +
    employee.name + ' ' + employee.lastName);
}
});
```

For the sake of simplicity, we're just sending a log message to the console on each method. But we can do anything else needed. Now let's define the occupation classes, which contain a few methods (tasks) according to what each occupation can do.

As an example, a manager will not answer the phone, as this is the task of a secretary, and a secretary will not supervise any employee, as that is a task for a manager.

```
Ext.define('Myapp.sample.Secretary',{
  extend:'Myapp.sample.Employee',
  mixins:{
    answerPhone: 'Myapp.sample.tasks.attendPhone'
  },
  constructor: function (config){
    Ext.apply(this, config || {});
    console.log('Secretary class created - fullname:' + this.name
      + ' ' + this.lastName);
  }
});

Ext.define('Myapp.sample.Accountant',{
  extend:'Myapp.sample.Employee',
  mixins:{
    attendClient: 'Myapp.sample.tasks.attendClient',
    attendMeeting: 'Myapp.sample.tasks.attendMeeting'
  },
  constructor: function (config){
    Ext.apply(this, config || {});
    console.log('Accountant class created - fullname:' + this.name
      + ' ' + this.lastName);
```

```
    }
  });

  Ext.define('Myapp.sample.Manager',{
    extend:'Myapp.sample.Employee',
    mixins:{
      attendClient:  'Myapp.sample.tasks.attendClient',
      attendMeeting: 'Myapp.sample.tasks.attendMeeting',
      supervisePersons:'Myapp.sample.tasks.superviseEmployees'
    },
    constructor: function (config){
      Ext.apply(this, config || {});//this.name= config.name;
      console.log('Manager class created - fullname:' + this.name +
        ' ' + this.lastName);
    },
    supervise: function(employee){
      console.log( this.name + ' starts supervision ');
      this.mixins.supervisePersons.superviseEmployee(this,
        employee);
      console.log( this.name + ' finished supervision ');
    }
  });
```

Here we created three classes (`Secretary`, `Accountant`, and `Manager`). Each class extends the `Employee` class and on each class, a new configuration has been added: `mixins:{...}`. And lastly, let's insert the following code at the end:

```
// Usage of each class
var patricia = Ext.create('Myapp.sample.Secretary', {
  name:'Patricia', lastName:'Diaz', age:21 } );
patricia.work('Attending phone calls');
patricia.answerPhone();

var peter =  Ext.create('Myapp.sample.Accountant', {name:'Peter',
  lastName:'Jones', age:44 } );
peter.work('Checking financial books');
peter.attendClient('ACME Corp.');
peter.attendMeeting('Patricia');

var robert =  Ext.create('Myapp.sample.Manager', {name:'Robert',
  lastName:'Smith', age:34 } );
robert.work('Administration of the office');
robert.attendClient('Iron Tubes of America');
robert.attendMeeting('Patricia & Peter');
robert.supervise(patricia);
robert.supervise(peter);
```

Once the code is ready, refresh the browser and you should see something like the following screenshot in the JavaScript console:

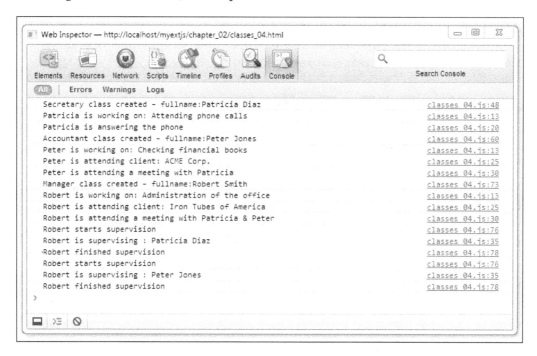

An explanation of mixins

Each class is based on the `Employee` class. We then defined the `employees` tasks (as classes) such as `Myapp.sample.tasks.attendMeeting` and this was incorporated (mixed) into the respective class using the `mixin{...}` configuration.

At the end, we have each class with methods like the ones in the following table:

Classes/Employee type	Methods
Secretary	• work • answerPhone
Accountant	• work • attendClient • attendMeeting
Manager	• work • attendClient • attendMeeting • supervise

Note that the `supervise` method defined in `Manager` uses the next code:

```
this.mixins.supervisePersons.superviseEmployee(this, employee);
```

This code lets us call the correct function defined in `Myapp.sample.tasks.superviseEmployees`. Now let's make validations and perform other operations before we run the `superviseEmployee` function.

Using the mixinConfig property

Using the `mixinConfig` property makes the `mixin` class able to provide `before` or `after` hooks that are not involved in the class (that is, the class we are going to be working with).

An easy way to understand this is that before and after settings can be configured to make some actions linked to the method being called. So the `mixinConfig` settings will be working as a monitor (observable) and when the attached function is called, then will execute the method set on each configuration.

Also, the derived class cannot adjust parameters to the hook methods when these methods are called. In the next example, we are going to create a `mixinConfig` in order to execute methods before and after answering the cell phone (the `Secretary` class).

The following code implements the `mixinConfig` for the `Secretary` class:

```
Ext.define('Myapp.sample.tasks.attendCellPhone',{
  extend: 'Ext.Mixin',
  /* answerCellPhone is the attached function for before and after
  and will execute the method defined in the answerCellPhone
  property on each configuration object (before / after)
  */
  mixinConfig:{
    before:{
      answerCellPhone:'cellPhoneRinging'
    },
    after:{
      answerCellPhone:'finishCall'
    }
  },
  cellPhoneRinging: function(){
    console.log( 'cell phone is ringing you may attend call');
  },
  finishCall: function(){
```

```
      console.log( 'cell phone call is over');
    }
  });
```

Now we need to modify the Secretary class as show in the following code:

```
Ext.define('Myapp.sample.Secretary',{
  extend:'Myapp.sample.Employee',
  mixins:{
    answerPhone: 'Myapp.sample.tasks.attendPhone',
    util:'Myapp.sample.tasks.attendCellPhone'
  },
  constructor: function (config){
    Ext.apply(this, config || {});//this.name= config.name;
    console.log('Secretary class created - fullname:' + this.name
       + ' ' + this.lastName);
  },
  answerCellPhone:function(){
    console.log( this.name + ' is answering the cellphone');
  }
});
```

Refresh the browser and you should see something like the following screenshot in the JavaScript console:

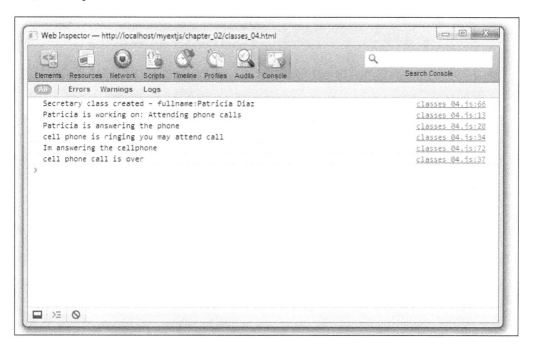

The important thing about mixins is that we can create classes to do specific tasks and then mix those classes into one. This way, we can reuse the same classes over and over again.

In the `Ext` library, classes such as `Ext.util.Observable`, `Ext.util.Floating`, `Ext.state.Stateful`, and others are treated like `mixins`, as each class knows how to do specific things. This is something great for big applications and we should think wisely how we're going to structure our big application before we start coding.

Configurations

Another great feature that started in Ext JS version 4 is the addition of configurations. Usually when we create a class, we set configurations so we can change the values and behavior of our class depending on the input parameters. Since Ext JS 4, this process is really easy by adding a preprocessor to handle the configurations for us.

Here we have an example on how the version prior to version 4 had to define configurations/properties on the classes:

```
Ext.define('Myapp.sample.Employee',{
  name:'Unknown',
  lastName: 'Unknown',
  age: 0,
  constructor: function (config){
    Ext.apply(this, config || {});//this.name= config.name;
    console.log('class A created - fullname:' + this.name +
      ' ' + this.lastName);
  },
  work: function( task ){
    console.log( this.name + ' is working on: ' + task);
  },
  setName: function( newName ){
    this.name = newName;
  },
  getName: function(){
    return this.name;
  }
});
```

In versions prior to version 4, we had to code the `setName` and `getName` methods in order to change properties in the class, which was time-consuming for developers. Since version 4, the `config` property on classes let us avoid all this extra work thanks to the Ext JS preprocessors before the class is created. The features of the configuration are as follows:

- Configurations are encapsulated from other class members.

- Getter and setter methods for every `config` property are created automatically in the class prototype if they are not already defined.

- An `apply` method (for example, `setName`, will change its property name) is also generated for every `config` property. The auto-generated setter method calls the `apply` method internally before setting the value. You may override the `apply` method for a `config` property if you need to run custom logic before setting the value. If `apply` does not return a value, the setter will not set the value.

If you intend/plan to create a new class or component and you are extending the `Ext.Base` class for this, then it's required that you call/use the `initConfig()` method. On classes that are already using the `config` property, you don't have the need to call the `initConfig()` method.

For the next exercise, let's create a new file called `config_01.js` and a HTML called `config_01.html`. Place the necessary reference to the Ext JS library we have made in the previous samples and let's work on the code for the `config_01.js` file, which will be as follows:

```
Ext.define('Myapp.sample.Employee',{
  config:{
    name: 'Unknown',
    lastName: 'Unknown',
    age: 0,
    isOld: false
  },
  constructor: function ( config ){
    this.initConfig( config );
  },
  work: function( task ){
    console.log( this.name + ' is working on: ' + task);
  },
  applyAge: function(newAge) {
    this.setIsOld ( ( newAge >= 90 ) );
    return newAge;
  }
});
```

In the preceding code, we performed the following steps:

1. We wrapped the properties of the `Employee` class in the `config` object.

2. In the constructor method, we changed the old code and set only `this.initConfig(config);`.

3. After creating the class, it will have the setters and getters methods for the properties: `name`, `lastName`, and `age`. Note that by setting up the class this way, we will have four new methods for each property. As an example, the following are the new methods related to `age`:

   ◦ `getAge`

   ◦ `setAge`

   ◦ `applyAge` (this custom method will be launched automatically when `setAge` is invoked)

4. After defining our class with the `config` object as a property, let's place the following code in the `config_01.js` file after the class definition for a test:

```
var patricia = Ext.create('Myapp.sample.Employee',{
  name: 'Patricia',
  lastName: 'Diaz',
  age: 21,
  isOld:false
});

console.log( "employee Name = " + patricia.getName() );
console.log( "employee Last name = " +
  patricia.getLastName() );
console.log( "employee Age  = " + patricia.getAge() );
patricia.work( 'Attending phone calls' );

patricia.setName( 'Karla Patricia' );
patricia.setLastName( 'Diaz de Leon' );
patricia.setAge ( 25 );
console.log("employee New Name=" + patricia.getName() );
console.log("employee New Last name=" +
  patricia.getLastName() );
console.log( "employee New Age  = " + patricia.getAge() );

patricia.work('Attending phone calls');
var is_old='';
is_old= ( patricia.getIsOld() == true)? 'yes' : 'no' ;
console.log( "is patricia old? : " + is_old ) ;
patricia.setAge( 92 );
```

```
is_old='';
is_old= ( patricia.getIsOld() == true)? 'yes' : 'no' ;
console.log( "is patricia old? : " + is_old );
```

As you can see in the highlighted code, we are using the setters and getters methods created automatically by initConfig(config). When we changed the age of the employee using patricia.setAge(92), the applyAge method was invoked that changed the isOld property in the class. Let's take a look at the console:

Statics methods and properties

The statics methods belong to the class and not to the instance; therefore we can use statics methods without an instance. Static members in a class can be defined using the statics config. Again we alter the previous code to the following code:

```
Ext.define('Myapp.sample.Employee',{
  statics:{
    instanceCount: 0,
    payrollId: 1000,
    nextId : function(){
      return ( this.payrollId + this.instanceCount );
    }
  },
  config:{
    name: 'Unknown',
```

```
      lastName: 'Unknown',
      age: 0,
      isOld: false,
      payrollNumber: 0
    },
    constructor: function ( config ){
      this.initConfig( config );
      this.setPayrollNumber( this.statics().nextId() );
      this.self.instanceCount ++;
    },
    work: function( task ){
      console.log( this.getName() + ' is working on: ' + task);
    },
    applyAge: function( newAge ) {
      this.setIsOld ( (newAge >= 90) );
      return newAge;
    },
    getTotalEmployees: function(){
      return this.statics().instanceCount;
    }
});
var patricia = Ext.create('Myapp.sample.Employee', {
  name: 'Patricia',
  lastName: 'Diaz',
  age: 21,
  isOld: false
});
console.log( "patricia payrollId = " +
  patricia.getPayrollNumber());
console.log( "total employees = " + patricia.getTotalEmployees());

var peter = Ext.create('Myapp.sample.Employee', {
  name: 'Peter',
  lastName: 'Pan',
  age: 16,
  isOld: false
});
console.log( "Peter payrollId = " + peter.getPayrollNumber() );
console.log( "total employees = " + patricia.getTotalEmployees());

console.log( "instance(s) of employee class = " +
  Myapp.sample.Employee.instanceCount );
```

Explanation

We created the `statics` configuration in the `Employee` class:

```
statics:{
  instanceCount: 0,
  payrollId: 1000,
  nextId : function(){
    return ( this.payrollId + this.instanceCount );
  }
},
```

These values will be static to all instance classes. In the class `config` property, we added `payrollNumber:0,`; this number will be assigned automatically in the `constructor` method:

```
this.setPayrollNumber(  this.statics().nextId() );
this.self.instanceCount ++;
```

The `instanceCount` will be incremented thanks to the `this.self.instanceCount++` code. When you use the `this.self` code inside the class, keep in mind that we are referring globally to the `Myapp.sample.Employee` class itself.

In this case, we created two instances of the classes `Patricia` and `Peter` so let's refresh the browser and we should see something like the following screenshot in the JavaScript console:

The Singleton class

By definition, a `singleton` class can't be instantiated more than once. It should be the same instance all the time. Ext allows us to create `singleton` classes very easily with one postprocessor.

If we want a class to be singleton, we only need to set the `singleton` property to true. This will fire the correct postprocessor. As practice, we need to change / add the following code at the beginning of the previous file and save it as `singleton_01.js`:

```
Ext.define('Myapp.CompanyConstants',{
  singleton: true,
  companyName: 'Extjs code developers Corp.',
  workingDays: 'Monday to Friday',
  website: 'www.extjscodedevelopers.com',
  welcomeEmployee: function (employee){
    "Hello " + employee.getName() + ", you are now working for " +
      this.companyName;
  }
});
```

As this class will be *the only one and unique* instance in our entire application code, there's no need to create a new instance or use `Ext.create`. We simply call it by its name, for example:

```
alert( Myapp.CompanyConstants.companyName );
// will alert "Extjs code developers Corp."
```

After creating each `Employee` class instance(s) inside the code, let's add the following lines:

```
var patricia = Ext.create('Myapp.sample.Employee', {
  name:'Patricia',
  lastName:'Diaz',
  age:21,
  isOld:false
});
console.log(Myapp.CompanyConstants.welcomeEmployee(patricia));

var peter = Ext.create('Myapp.sample.Employee', {
  name:'Peter',
  lastName:'Pan',
  age:16,
  isOld:false
});
console.log(Myapp.CompanyConstants.welcomeEmployee(peter));
```

Let's save the file and refresh the browser and we should see something like the following screenshot showing the JavaScript console:

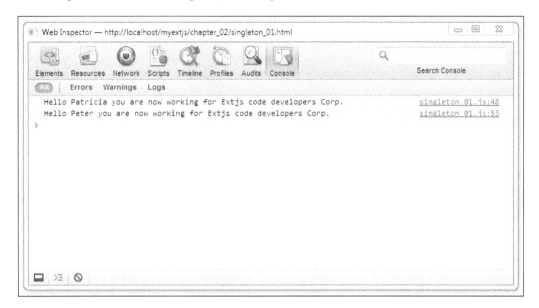

The singleton classes are commonly used to hold constants, configurations, and common functions (commonly referred to as utility classes) for our application such as the base path of our application, the path where the images are located, and things like that.

Aliases

An alias is a short name for a class. The class manager maps /adds the alias name with the actual class object. By convention, an alias should be all in lowercase.

This feature is really useful when using the xtype property to create widgets. Let's create a JavaScript file and name it alias_01.js and place the following code in it:

```
Ext.define('Myapp.sample.EmployeePanel',{
    extend: 'Ext.panel.Panel',
    alias: 'widget.employeePanel',
    alternateClassName: 'mycustomemployeepanel',
    title: 'Employee Panel',
    html: 'Employee content here..!'
});
```

In the previous code, we're setting the `alias` property with a short name. We're also using the `widget` prefix to indicate we're creating a component. A component is a class such as a window, grid, or panel.

Also in the code we defined the `alternateClassName` property, which lets us define other alternative names for our class. This property can be a string or an array object with multiple names, for example, `['employeepanel', 'customEmployeePanel', 'employeeboard']`.

In Ext JS, we have a list of namespaces to use for aliases:

- `feature`: This is used for Grid features
- `plugin`: This is used for plugins
- `store`: This is used for `Ext.data.Store`
- `widget`: This is used for components

Now let's create our class using the `alias` name. We have a few options to do this:

```
Ext.onReady (function(){
  Ext.create('widget.employeePanel',{
    title: 'Employee Panel: Patricia Diaz...',
    height:250,
    width:450,
    renderTo: Ext.getBody()
  });
});
```

As an alternative, we can also use the following code:

```
Ext.onReady (function(){
  Ext.widget('employeePanel',{
  //using the xtype which is employeePanel
    title: 'Employee Panel: Patricia Diaz...',
    height:250,
    width:450,
    renderTo: Ext.getBody()
  });
});
```

Also, create the HTML file named `alias_01.html`. Make the changes to the HTML file so it will look like the following code:

```
<!doctype html>
<html>
<head>
```

```
<meta http-equiv="X-UA-Compatible" content="IE=edge">
<meta charset="utf-8">
<title>Extjs - Alias</title>
   <link rel="stylesheet" type="text/css" href="../ext-5.1.1/build/
packages/ext-theme-neptune/build/resources/ext-theme-neptune-all.css">
   <script src="../ext-5.1.1/build/ext-all.js"></script>
   <script src="../ext-5.1.1/build/packages/ext-theme-neptune/build/
ext-theme-neptune.js"></script>
   <script type ="text/javascript" src="alias_01.js"></script>
</head>
<body style="padding:15px;"></body>
</html>
```

Run the file in your browser and you may have a similar result as shown in the following screenshot:

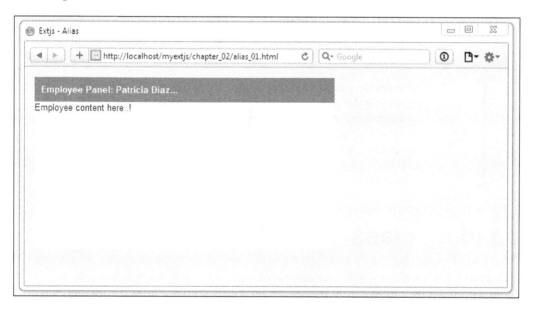

Let's check out the explanation. We defined the new class `Myapp.sample.EmployeePanel` extending the Ext JS class component `Ext.panel.Panel`. As this class is in fact a *widget*, we declared the *alias* as `widget.employeePanel`. As we said previously, `Ext.ClassManager` handles the declaration of our extended class (the internal use of preprocessors and postprocessors) and defines/maps the alias for later use. So when we create a new instance of the new class `Myapp.sample.EmployeePanel`, Ext JS will know how to handle and execute the code properly.

Also, we have other ways to reference the new class:

```
Ext.ClassManager.instantiateByAlias("widget.employeePanel",{
  renderTo: Ext.getBody()
});
// OR
Ext.createByAlias("widget.employeePanel",{
  renderTo: Ext.getBody()
});
```

In this case, `Ext.createByAlias` is the shorthand of `Ext.ClassManager.instantiateByAlias`; they work the same way and usually it's easier to use the second option. Also we can refer to the new class by using its `xtype` property on a configuration object, such as the following code:

```
var win = Ext.create("Ext.window.Window",{
  title: "Window", width:350, height:250,
  items: [{ xtype: "employeePanel" }]
});
win.show();
```

> Remember when extending a class, try to extend the class that gives you the properties and methods you really need in order to create your new class. Sometimes, it's bad practice to extend a class/widget such as `Ext.panel.Panel`, if we are not going to take full advantage of the functionality it can provide us. In this case, perhaps it's more convenient to extend the panel base class, which is the `Ext.container.Container` class.

Loading classes on demand

When we develop large applications, performance is really important. We should only load the scripts we need; this means that if we have many modules in our application, we should separate them into packages so we would be able to load them individually.

Ext JS, since version 4, allows us to dynamically load classes and files when we need them, also we can configure dependencies in each class and the Ext library will load them for us.

You need to understand that using the loader is great for development, that way we can easily debug the code because the loader includes all the classes one by one. However, it's not recommended to load all the Ext classes in production environments. We should create packages of classes and then load them when needed, but not class by class.

In order to use the loader system, we need to follow some conventions when defining our class.

- Define only one class per file.

- The name of the class should match the name of the JavaScript file.

- The namespace of the class should match the folder structure. For example, if we define a class MyApp.customers.controller.Main, we should have the Main.js file in the MyApp/customers/controller path.

Enabling the loader

The loader system is enabled or disabled depending on the Ext file that we import to our HTML file. If we import the ext-all or ext-all-debug file inside the extjs/build folder, the loader is disabled because all the classes in the Ext library are loaded already. If we import the ext-all and ext-all-debug files inside the extjs folder, the loader is enabled because only the core classes in the Ext library are loaded.

If we need to enable the loader, we should do the following at the beginning of the JS file:

```
Ext.Loader.setConfig({
   enabled: true
});
```

The previous code will allow us to load the classes when we need them. Also there's a preprocessor that loads all the dependencies for the given class if they don't exist.

In order to start loading classes, we need to set up the paths where the classes are, and we can do that in two different ways. We can use the setConfig method to define a paths property as follows:

```
Ext.Loader.setConfig({
   enabled:true,
   paths:{
     MyApp:'appcode'
   }
});
```

The `paths` property receives an object containing the root namespace of our application and the folder where all the classes are located in this namespace. So in the previous code when we refer to `Myapp`, Ext JS will look inside the `appcode/` folder. Remember that we can add as many paths or location references as needed.

Once we have enabled and configured the loader correctly, we can start loading our classes using the `require` method:

```
Ext.require([
    'MyApp.Constants',
    'MyApp.samples.demoClass'
]);
```

The `require` method creates a script tag behind the scenes. After all the required files are loaded, the `onReady` event is fired. Inside the callback, we can use all the loaded classes.

If we try to load the classes after the `require` call, we'll get an error because the class won't exist until it's downloaded and created. This is why we need to set the `onReady` callback and wait until everything is ready to be used.

In this case, open the `loader_01.html` file and check that the file has the correct paths (that script tags are correct) to the `ext.js` file instead of `ext-all.js`, and run the file in the browser. If you look at the **Network** traffic tab in the development tools, you will notice the files that were only loaded, which in fact are a few classes (only the classes that Ext JS really need to run the code). Also, the speed of execution of these classes was faster than the previous code samples when we were loading the complete `ext-all.js` file located in the `build` folder.

Working with the DOM

Ext JS provides an easy way to deal with the DOM. We can create nodes, change styles, add listeners, and create beautiful animations, among other things without worrying about the browser's implementations. Ext JS provides us with a cross-browser compatibility API that will make our lives easier.

The responsible class for dealing with the DOM nodes is the `Ext.Element` class. This class is a wrapper for the native nodes and provides us with many methods and utilities to manipulate the nodes.

 Manipulating DOM directly is considered bad practice and none of the DOM markup should be placed in the index file. This example exists only for illustrative purposes.

Getting elements

The Ext.get method let us retrieve a DOM element encapsulated in the Ext.dom. Element class, retrieving this element by its ID. This will let us modify and manipulate the DOM element. Here is a basic example:

```html
<!doctype html>
<html>
<head>
<meta http-equiv="X-UA-Compatible" content="IE=edge">
<meta charset="utf-8">
<title>Extjs - Loader</title>
<link rel="stylesheet" type="text/css" href="../ext-5.1.1/build/
packages/ext-theme-neptune/build/resources/ext-theme-neptune-all.css">
<script src="../ext-5.1.1/ext-all.js"></script>
<script src="../ext-5.1.1/build/packages/ext-theme-neptune/build/ext-
theme-neptune.js"></script>
<script type="text/javascript">
    Ext.onReady(function(){
    var mymainDiv = Ext.get('main');
    var mysecondDiv = Ext.dom.Element.get('second');
  });
</script>
</head>
<body style="padding:10px">
<div id="main"></div>
<div id="second"></div>
</body>
</html>
```

Usually to get an element, we use Ext.get, which is an alias/shorthand for Ext.dom.Element.get.

 When passing an ID, it should not include the # character that is used for a CSS selector.

In the div variable, we have an instance of the Ext.Element class containing a reference to the node that has main as its ID.

We may use the `setStyle` method in order to assign some CSS rules to the node. Let's add the following code to our example:

```
div.setStyle({
    width: "100px",
    height: "100px",
    border: "2px solid #444",
    margin: "80px auto",
    backgroundColor: "#ccc"
});
```

Here we are passing an object with all the rules that we want to apply to the node. As a result, we should see a gray square in the center of our screen:

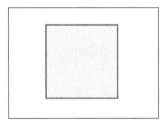

If we want to add a CSS class to the node, we can use the `addCls` method. We can also use the `removeCls` method if we want to remove a CSS class from the node. Let's see how to use the `addCls` method:

```
div.addCls("x-testing x-box-component");
div.removeCls("x-testing");
```

There are a lot of methods we can use to manipulate the node element. Let's try some animations with our element:

```
div.fadeOut()
.fadeIn({
    duration:3000
});
```

The `fadeOut` method slowly hides the element by changing the opacity progressively. When the opacity is zero percent, the `fadeIn` method is executed by changing the opacity by 100 percent in three seconds.

You should take a look at the documentation (`http://docs.sencha.com/`) in order to know all the options we have available, as there we can find examples of code to play with.

Query – how do we find them?

Ext JS allows us to query the DOM to search for specific nodes. The query engine supports most of the CSS3 selector specifications and the basic XPath.

The responsible class that does the job is the Ext.dom.Query class; this class contains some methods to perform a search.

> The Ext.dom.Query class is a singleton class so there is no need to declare it as a new instance to search DOM elements. Also it's important to know about CSS selectors, so this will help us to understand how we may select one or many elements.

The following code is an HTML document that contains a few tags so we can search for them using the Ext.dom.Query class:

```html
<!doctype html>
<html>
<head>
<meta http-equiv="X-UA-Compatible" content="IE=edge">
<meta charset="utf-8">
<title>Extjs - manipulating the DOM </title>
<script src="../ext-5.1.1/build/ext-all.js"></script>
<script type="text/javascript">
Ext.onReady(function(){
  var myElements = Ext.dom.Query.select('#main .menu ul li');
  myElements = Ext.get(myElements);
  myElements.setStyle({
    display: "inline",
    backgroundColor: "#003366",
    margin: "3px",
    color: "#FFCC00",
    padding: "3px 20px",
    borderRadius: "10px",
    boxShadow: "inset 0 1px 15px #6699CC"
  });
  var h1 = Ext.select("#main div[class=content] h1");
  h1.setStyle("color","#003399");
});
</script>
</head>
<body style="padding:10px;">
    <div id="main">
```

```
      <div class="menu">
        <ul>
          <li>Home</li>
          <li>About us</li>
        </ul>
      </div>
      <div class="content">
        <h1>Learning Ext JS 5!</h1>
        <p>This is an example for the DomQuery class.</p>
      </div>
    </div>
  </body>
</html>
```

In order to perform the search, we'll use the `select` method from the `Ext.dom.Query` class, and we pass a CSS selector as the only parameter, `#main .menu ul li`. The `myElements` variable became an array with two elements. `Ext` wraps the nodes into an `Ext.CompositeElementLite` collection.

After that, we convert the collection (each element in the array) to a `Ext.dom.Element` object using the `myElements = Ext.get(myElements);` instruction.

The `myElements.setStyle({...});` instruction takes the action of applying the style (configuration object) to each one of the elements (in the array), using the `Ext.dom.Element` methods to accomplish this. The following screenshot represents the result of the code:

DOM manipulation – how do we change it?

We can create and remove nodes from the DOM very easily. Ext JS contains a `DomHelper` object/class, which provides an abstraction layer and gives us an API to create DOM nodes or HTML fragments.

Let's create an HTML file, import the `Ext` library, and then use the `DomHelper` object to append a `div` element to the document's body:

```
Ext.onReady(function(){
  Ext.DomHelper.append(Ext.getBody(),{
    tag: "div",
    style: {
      width: "100px",
      height: "100px",
      border: "2px solid #333",
      margin  : "20px auto"
    }
  });
});
```

We used the `append` method; the first parameter is where we want to append the new element (or DOM node). In this case, we're going to append it to the document's body.

The second/next parameter is a string or object specifying the element that we are going to append; it's important that we specify the `tag` property, which defines the type/kind of element (DOM element) that we desire to append to the element defined in the first parameter.

In this case, we previously defined a `div` element to be appended in the document's body, but we can define any other tags as defined in the HTML specification. We can define styles, classes, children, and any other property that an HTML element supports. Let's add some children to our previous example:

```
Ext.DomHelper.append(Ext.getBody(),{
  //...
children  : [{
    tag       : "ul",
    children  : [
        {tag: "li", html: "Item 1"},
        {tag: "li", html: "Item 2"}
    ]
  }]
});
```

We have added an unordered list to the main `div` element. The list contains two children that are list elements. We can have as many children as needed.

There's another method that we can use if we want to create a node, but we want to insert it into the DOM later:

```
var h1 = Ext.DomHelper.createDom({
  tag: "h1",
  html: "This is the title!"
});

Ext.getBody().appendChild(h1);
```

When we use the `createDom` method, we create a new node in the memory. We probably append this node to the DOM later on, or maybe not. In this example, we have appended it to the document's body.

We know how to create and append nodes to the DOM, but what if we want to remove elements from the DOM? In order to remove the element from the DOM, we need to use the `remove` method on the `Ext.Element` class:

```
Ext.fly(h1).remove();
```

The previous code is calling the `Ext.fly` method. This method is similar to the `Ext.get` method but the difference is that `Ext.fly` gets the element and does not store this element in memory; really it's for a single use or a one time-reference. The `Ext.get` method stores the element in memory to be reused in other classes or application code.

So `Ext.fly` returns an instance to the `Ext.Element` class containing a reference to the node element. Once we have the node in the wrapper, we can call the `remove` method and the node will be removed from the DOM.

Summary

When using Ext JS, we need to change our mind and see everything as an object or class. We need to think carefully how we're going to organize the classes, as this will help us in the future chapters. Also you learned how to work with OOP with the class system in Ext JS.

You also learned about the loader system to import our classes dynamically, managing dependencies for us, and only loading what we need. At the end of this chapter, you learned about the DOM and how to perform a search in order to manipulate the nodes easily.

In the next chapter, you'll learn about the layout system, a powerful way to create and manage our layouts. Using and combining several types of layouts will help us to create unique interfaces.

3
Components and Layouts

One of the greatest features in Ext JS is the ability to create complex layouts to arrange our components in different ways using the layout system and containers. Since the early versions of the library, Ext JS has had a great layout system. Since Version 4.x, there are new layouts and some other parts have been redesigned in order to have better performance and usability.

In this chapter, you're going to learn about how components work, learn the container types, how to use layouts, and how to make use of nested layouts to achieve complex designs.

We're going to cover the following topics in this chapter:

- Components
- Containers
- The layout system
- Available layouts

The component life cycle

Before we move into the layout systems and widgets, you should know a few concepts about how components work.

Every component in the Ext JS framework extends from the `Ext.Component` class. This class extends from the `Ext.Component`, or by its alternate class name `Ext.AbstractComponent` class, which provides shared methods for components across the framework.

To understand more about component hierarchies, see http://docs.sencha.com/extjs/5.1/ core_concepts/components.html and

When we create components such as panels, windows, grids, trees, and any other, there's a process called "the component lifecycle" that you should understand.

It is important for us to know the things that occur during each of the phases in the lifecycle process. This will help us to create custom components or extend the existing ones.

Basically, there are three phases in the component's lifecycle: the initialization process, the rendering process, and the destruction process.

The initialization phase initializes our new instance and it gets registered on the component manager; then, the rendering phase will create all the required nodes on the DOM, and then the destruction phase will be executed when the component is destroyed, removing listeners and nodes from the DOM:

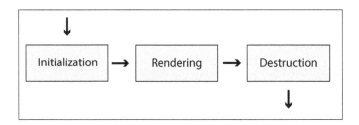

The Ext.AbstractComponent/Ext.Component class directs the lifecycle process, and every class that extends from the Component class will participate in the lifecycle automatically. All the visual components (widgets) extend from these classes and if we're planning to create our own custom components, we should extend from those classes too.

In order to have a better understanding of all three phases, let's create a panel component and see what's going on in each phase step by step:

```
var panel = Ext.create("Ext.panel.Panel",{
  title: "My First panel",
  width: 400,
  height: 250,
  renderTo: Ext.getBody()
});
```

When talking about the width and height of components, the unit measure is handled in pixels.

The initialization phase

The main purpose of this phase is to create the instance of the component according to the configurations that we defined. It also registers our new component in the component manager and a few other things. The following screenshot shows all the steps in this phase:

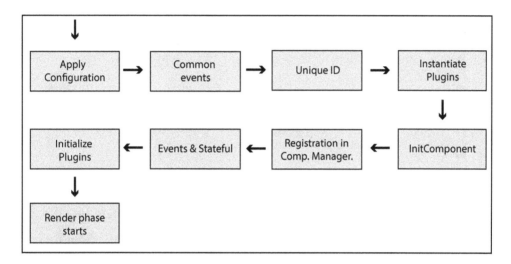

Let's see all the steps in this phase in detail:

1. The first step is to apply the configuration properties to the generated instance of the class that we are creating. In the previous code, the `title`, `width`, `height`, and `renderTo` properties will be copied to the instance of the panel, as well as to any other property that we decide to define.

2. The second step is to define common events, such as enable, disable, or show. These are common events for every component.

3. The next step is to assign an ID to the instance. If we define an ID in the configuration object, then the instance will use that ID. In our example, we didn't specify an ID. In this case, an autogenerated ID is assigned.

Assigning IDs to our components is considered bad practice. We need to avoid doing that because they should be unique. If we work on a big project with other developers, there's a big chance that we may repeat IDs. Duplicating IDs will drive us to unexpected behaviors, because the component's ID is used in the DOM elements when rendering the component, causing one component to maybe disappear.

4. In the fourth step, the creation process verifies whether we have defined plugins in our configuration and tries to create all the required instances for those plugins. A plugin is an additional functionality for our instances. In our previous example, we didn't define any plugin, so this step is skipped.

5. In the fifth step, the initComponent function is executed. We should override this method in our subclasses if we want to execute code when the instance is being created.

There are many more methods that are defined by the Component class. These template methods are intended to be overridden in the subclasses to add specific functionality in different phases of the lifecycle.

6. In this step, the new instance is added to the Ext.ComponentManager object. This means that every component that we create will be stored in the component manager, allowing us to get any reference by using the Ext.getCmp method and passing the ID as a parameter:

```
//getting a component by its ID
var panel = Ext.getCmp("panel-1234");
console.log(panel);
```

The getCmp method is great for debugging applications. We can get the ID of any component by looking at the DOM elements. Then, we can get the instance and inspect the state of our object, but it's not encouraged to use this method in our code. Instead, we may use the Ext.ComponentQuery.query method as an example as follows:

Ext.ComponentQuery.query('panel')

This example will retrieve an array (of xtype panel or Ext.panel. Panel) that exists/is already created.

7. The `Component` class contains two mixins, one for the event management and the other for the state of our components. In this step, the two mixins are initialized by calling their constructor.

8. If we have defined plugins, they should be already instantiated in the previous step, and now they have to be initialized by calling the `init()` method of each plugin and by passing our component instance as a parameter. You will learn how plugins work and how to create one from scratch later in this book.

If the `renderTo` property has been defined in the configurations, the rendering phase starts in this step, which means that all the required nodes that visually represent our component will be inserted into the DOM. If we don't define this property, nothing happens, and we are responsible for rendering our instance whenever we need to:

```
var panel = Ext.create("Ext.panel.Panel",{
    title: "My First panel",
    width: 400,
    height: 250
});
panel.render(Ext.getBody());
```

If we want to render our component later, we can call the `render` method of our instance and pass the place where we want to add our new component as a parameter. In the previous code, we are rendering our panel on the body of our document, but we can also set the ID of the node where we want to place our component, for example:

```
panel.render("some-div-id");
```

 Note: if the component is inside another component or container then there is no need to call the `panel.render` method as this will be rendered when the container is created / rendered.

The rendering phase

The rendering phase only occurs if the component is not rendered already. In this phase, all the required nodes will be inserted to the DOM, the styles and listeners will be applied, and we will be able to see and interact with our new component. The following diagram shows the steps that are executed during this phase:

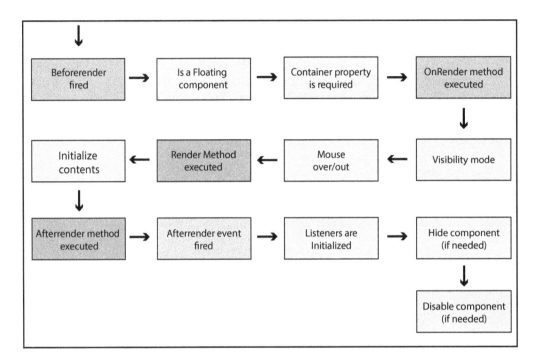

Now, let's understand the preceding diagram in a step-by-step manner:

1. In the first step, the `beforeRender` event is fired. If some of the listeners return `false`, then the rendering phase stops.

2. In the second step, the process checks whether the component that is being rendered is a floating component, such as a menu or a window, to assign the correct `z-index` property. `z-index` is a CSS property that specifies the stack order of an element. The greater number assigned will be always in front of the other elements.

3. The third step is to initialize the container by creating the `container` property, which refers to the DOM element, where the new component will be rendered. The `container` property is an `Ext.dom.Element` instance.

4. In the fourth step, the `onRender` method is executed. The `el` property is created, which contains the main node element of the component. We can define a template for our components; if we do that, then the template will be created and appended to the main node in this step. We can override the `onRender` method in our subclasses to append specific nodes to the DOM.

5. The next step is to set the visibility mode. There are three modes for hiding the component's element (display, visibility, or offset).

6. If the `overCls` property is set, then a listener for the mouse over and mouse out is set to add or remove the `css` class for each state. We can set some CSS rules to these classes to modify the look of our components.

7. In the seventh step, the `render` event is fired. The component's instance is passed as a parameter to the listeners.

8. The eighth step is to initialize the content. There are three ways to set the content of the component:

    1. We can define an `html` property with tags and nodes that will be added to the content of our new component.

    2. We can define the `contentEl` property that should be the ID of an existing DOM element. This element will be placed as the component content.

    3. We can define a `tpl` property with a template to be appended to the content. Also, we should define a `data` property with an object containing the replacements in our template. We will talk about templates in future chapters.

9. The following code shows the three ways to add HTML content to a component. We should use only one way at a time.

```
//Using the HTML property
Ext.create("Ext.Component",{
  width: 300,
  height: 150,
  renderTo: Ext.getBody(),
  html: "<h1>Hello!</h1><p>This is an <strong>example
    </strong> of content</p>"
  });

//Using an existing DOM element with an ID content
Ext.create("Ext.Component",{
  width: 300,
  height: 150,
  renderTo: Ext.getBody(),
```

```
    contentEl: "content"
});

//Using a template with data
Ext.create("Ext.Component",{
  width: 300,
  height: 150,
  renderTo: Ext.getBody(),
  data: {name:"Veronica", lastName:"Sanchez"},
  tpl: ["<h1>Content</h1><p>Hello {name} {lastName}!</p>"]
});
```

10. Returning to the render phase, the next step is to execute the `afterRender` method. If the component contains children, these are rendered in this step too. We're going to talk about containers later.

11. In the tenth step, the `afterRender` event is fired. We can listen to this event in our subclasses to perform some actions when all the required nodes are rendered in the DOM.

12. In the eleventh step, all the listeners that depend on the new nodes are initialized.

13. The last step is to hide the main component node if the `hidden` property is set to `true` in our configurations parameter. And also, if the `disabled` property is set to `true`, then the component executes the `disable` method, which adds some CSS classes to the main node to make the components appearance disabled and mark the `disabled` flag as `true`.

The following code shows an example of how the rendering phase works. We are starting the whole process by calling the `render` method:

```
var mycmp = Ext.create("Ext.Component",{
  width: 300,
  height: 150,
  data: {
    name:"Veronica",
    lastName:"Sanchez"
  },
  tpl:["<h1>Content</h1><p>Hello {name} {lastName}!</p>"]
});

//The rendering phase starts for this component
mycmp.render(Ext.getBody());
```

By knowing the steps that are executed inside of the render phase, we will be able to overwrite the methods such as `onRender`, `render`, or `afterRender` in our own classes. This is very useful when creating new components or widgets.

The destruction phase

The main idea of this phase is to clean the DOM, remove the listeners, and clear the used memory by deleting objects and arrays. It's very important to destroy all of our components when we don't want them anymore. The destroy phase will be executed when the user finishes the task with our component, for example, if we create a window and this window's property `closeAction` is set to `destroy` (this value is set by default), the destroy phase will be invoked when the user closes the window.

The following diagram shows the steps that are executed in this phase:

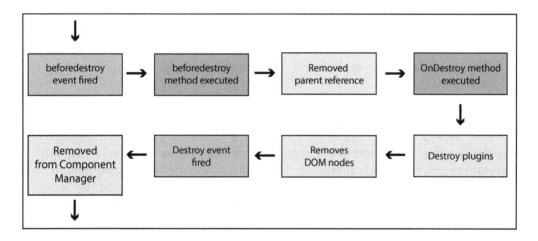

1. The destruction phase starts by firing the `beforeDestroy` event. If any listener returns `false`, then the destruction is stopped; otherwise, if the destruction continues and the component is floating, then this is unregistered from the floating manager.

2. The second step executes the `beforeDestroy` method. Some subclasses use this method to remove their children or to clear memory.

3. In the third step, if the component that is being destroyed is a child of another component, then the parent reference to this component is removed.

4. In the fourth step, the `onDestroy` method is executed. We should extend this method in order to destroy our component properly, and also make sure that child components being added are destroyed and that the custom listeners we create are cleaned up.

5. The fifth step tries to destroy all the plugins, if there are any, and also state that mixins are being destroyed.

6. If the component is rendered, then in the sixth step, all the nodes from the DOM are purged (listeners) and are removed from the document.

7. In the next step, the `destroy` event is fired. We can listen for this event and perform some actions if needed.

8. The last step is to unregister the instance of the component from the component manager and clear all the events.

One important thing to keep in mind is that we should always remove and clear the memory that we're using in our components, as well as the nodes in the DOM that we have added before. We should override the appropriate methods in order to destroy our components correctly.

If we want to eliminate a component, we can execute the `destroy` method of the component. This method will trigger the destroy phase and all the previous steps will be executed:

```
//The destroy phase starts for this component
cmp.destroy();
```

The lifecycle in action

Now that we know the process of the creation of a component, we can create our own component, taking advantage of the lifecycle to customize our component. The following example shows the methods that we can override to add the functionality that we need in any of the available steps of the lifecycle:

```
Ext.define('Myapp.sample.CustomComponent',{
  extend: 'Ext.Component',
  initComponent: function(){
    var me = this;
    me.width = 200;
    me.height = 100;
    me.html = {
    tag: 'div',
    html: 'X',
    style: { // this can be replaced by a CSS rule
      'float': 'right',
      'padding': '10px',
      'background-color': '#e00',
      'color': '#fff',
      'font-weight': 'bold',
```

```
          'cursor': 'pointer'
      }
  };
      me.myOwnProperty = [1,2,3,4];
      me.callParent();
      console.log('Step 1. initComponent');
      },
  beforeRender: function(){
      console.log('Step 2. beforeRender');
      this.callParent(arguments);
      },
  onRender: function(){
      console.log('Step 3. onRender');
      this.callParent(arguments);
      this.el.setStyle('background-color','#ccc');
      },
  afterRender : function(){
      console.log('4. afterRender');
      this.el.down('div').on('click',this.myCallback,this);
      this.callParent(arguments);
      },
  beforeDestroy : function(){
      console.log('5. beforeDestroy');
      this.callParent(arguments);
      },
  onDestroy : function(){
      console.log('6. onDestroy');
      delete this.myOwnProperty;
      this.el.down('div').un('click',this.myCallback);
      this.callParent(arguments);
      },
  myCallback : function(){
      var me = this;
      Ext.Msg.confirm('Confirmation','Are you sure you want to close
        this panel?',function(btn){
          if(btn === 'yes'){
        me.destroy();
              }
          });
      }
});
```

The previous class overrides the **template methods**. This term is used for the methods that are automatically executed during the lifecycle. From the previous code, we can see how to add content using the `html` property, how to add listeners to the elements that we create, and more importantly, how to destroy and clear our events and custom objects.

In order to test our class, we need to create a HTML file called `lifecycle_03.html` file, include the Ext JS library, and our class, and then we need to create the instance of our class as follows:

```
Ext.onReady(function(){
    Ext.create('Myapp.sample.CustomComponent',{
        renderTo : Ext.getBody()
    });
});
```

As a result, we will see something like the following screenshot in our browser:

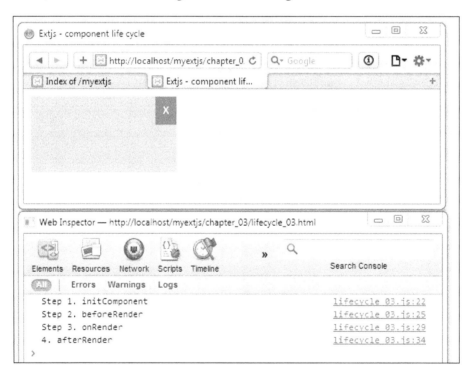

As we can see, there are four messages in the JavaScript console. These messages were sent by each of the methods that we have overridden. We can also see the order of the execution based on the lifecycle. Now, if we want to destroy this component, we need to click the red button at the top-right. This action will call the destroy method that is responsible for clearing the nodes from the DOM, events, and objects from memory.

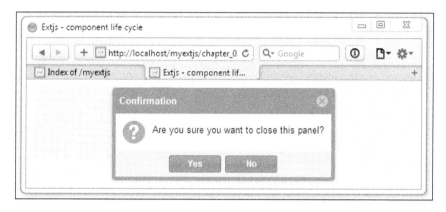

Understanding the lifecycle of the components in Ext JS is essential in order to add custom events/listeners so we can provide proper functionality and custom code in our application.

About containers

At this point, we know all the steps of the lifecycle. If you remember, in the rendering phase there's a step where the children of the components are rendered too. Now we're going to learn about containers and how we can add children to a component.

The Ext.container.Container class is responsible for managing children and to arrange those using layouts. If we want our class to contain other components, we should extend from this class. It's worth saying that this class extends from Ext.Component, so we'll be able to use the component lifecycle in our subclasses too:

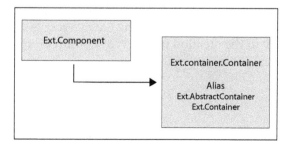

All classes that extend Ext.Container will be able to have children using the items property or use the add method to append a new component as a child. Let's check out the following code snippet:

```
Ext.define("MyApp.sample.MyContainer",{
  extend: "Ext.container.Container",    //Step 1
  border: true,
  padding: 10,
  initComponent: function(){
    var me = this;
    Ext.each(me.items,function(item){  //Step 2
      item.style = {
        backgroundColor:"#f4f4f4",
          border:"1px solid #333"
      };
      item.padding = 10;
      item.height = 100;
    });
    me.callParent();
  },
  onRender: function(){
    var me = this;
    me.callParent(arguments);
    if( me.border ){  //Step 3
      me.el.setStyle( "border" , "1px solid #333" );
    }
  }
});
```

In the code example, we set var me=this;. This is in order to present that me or this is referring to the scope of the current object/class being handled or manipulated.

The previous class extends from the Ext.container.Container class. Now we can use the layout system to arrange the children of the container.

When extending from the Container class, we can use the items property to define the children of the main container. We're looping the items property, which is an array, to add some basic styles. We're using the initComponent method that is executed automatically in the creation phase. We shouldn't forget to call the super class by executing the callParent method.

The last step overrides the onRender method. After executing the callParent method, we can have access to the el property that is a reference to the main node of our component. If the border property is set to true, we will add CSS styles to display a border around the main element's node.

Once we have defined our class, we can create an instance of it. Let's create an HTML page including the Ext library and our class in order to execute the following code:

```
Ext.onReady(function(){
  Ext.create("MyApp.sample.MyContainer",{
    renderTo: Ext.getBody(),
    items: [{
      xtype: "component",
      html: "Child Component one"
    },{
      xtype: "component",
      html: "Child Component two"
    }]
  });
});
```

We're creating the instance of our class as usual. We added the items property as an array of components. We can define as many components as we need because our class is a container.

In this example, we are using the xtype property to define each inner component, but we could also create an instance of the component's child and then pass the reference into the items array.

 Using the xtype property allows us to create components easier than handling the complete class name, and we also use fewer lines of code. When the main container is created, all their children are created as well. We'll find all the available xtype properties in the documentation. Usually xtype is next to the class name. To see all the xtypes available in Ext JS, visit http://docs.sencha.com/extjs/5.1/5.1.1-apidocs/#!/api/Ext.enums.Widget.

The following screenshot shows three components. One is the main component that contains two children. We have achieved this by extending from the `Container` class and using the `items` property.

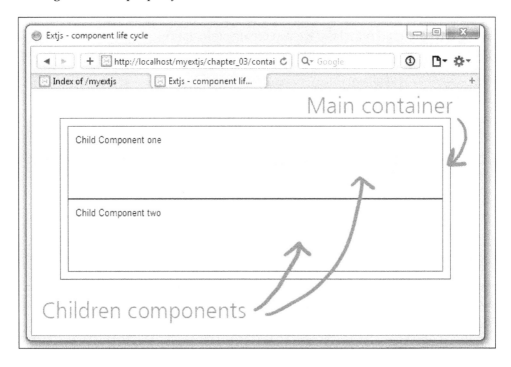

When using containers, we can use a property called `defaults` that allows us to apply the same properties (default values/configurations) to all of the children in the main container. Let's add some default values to our previous example:

```
Ext.onReady(function(){
  Ext.create("MyApp.sample.MyContainer",{
    renderTo: Ext.getBody(),
      defaults: {
       xtype  : "component",
       width  : 100
       },
    items  :[{
      html:"Child Component one" //xtype:"component",
    },{
      html:"Child Component two"  //xtype:"component",
    }]
  });
});
```

The `defaults` property receives an object containing all the configurations that we want to apply to the components inside the `items` array. In this case, we have added the `width` and `xtype` properties. This way, we don't have to repeat the same lines of code for each component:

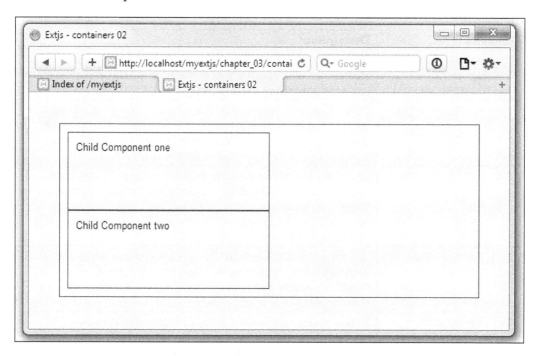

As we can see in the previous screenshot, the sizes of the two children are the same. We can also override a default property by simply adding the property that we want to be different to the specific child.

Every time, we find properties that are repeated in each child component. It's recommended to use the `defaults` property to apply all the properties defined in `defaults` at once. This will reduce the lines of code and will prevent code duplication. If we define the same property in any of the children, the default value will be overridden.

Types of containers

Ext JS uses several components as containers, and each one of them has its own foundation from the `Ext.container.Container` class. Some of the most common containers are as follows:

Container	Description
`Ext.panel.Panel`	This component extends `Ext.container.Container` and is a container with specific functionality. It is also one of the most common containers used in Ext JS.
`Ext.window Window`	This component extends the `Ext.panel.Panel` class and is intended to be used as an application window. Windows are floating components and can be resized and dragged. Also, windows can be maximized to fill the viewport.
`Ext.tab.Panel`	This component also extends the `Ext.panel.Panel` class container and has the ability to contain other `Ext.panel.Panel` components, creating one tab per panel in its header section. Also, the tab panel uses the card layout to manage its child components.
`Ext.form.Panel`	The form panel extends the `Ext.panel.Panel` class and provides a standard container for forms. Essentially, it is a `Panel` container that creates a basic form for managing field components.
`Ext.Viewport`	This container represents the application area (browser viewport). It renders itself to the document body and resizes itself to the size of the browser viewport.

Note that each container has the property layout; this property will give us the ability to present its child components in different ways to arrange them.

The viewport

The viewport, as we mentioned before, represents the viewable application area and the best practice is that *there has to be only one viewport created on the web page*. To create a basic viewport, let's use the following code:

```
Ext.onReady(function(){
  Ext.create('Ext.container.Viewport', {
    padding:'5px',
    layout:'auto',
```

```
    style : {
      'background-color': '#fc9',
      'color': '#000'
    },
  html:'This is application area'
  });
});
```

 It's recommended that no matter what application you build, whether plain code or an application using MVC or MVVM architecture, the use of the viewport component is needed.

The panel

The panel component (Ext.panel.Panel) is one of the most commonly used components in Ext JS. A panel can contain other panels or even other components.

Let's create our first panel by instantiating the Ext.panel.Panel class. We need to create an HTML page, import the Ext JS library, and then execute the following code when the DOM is ready to be used:

```
Ext.onReady(function(){
  var MyPanel = Ext.create("Ext.panel.Panel",{
    renderTo: Ext.getBody(),
    title: 'My first panel...',
    width: 300,
    height: 220,
    html:'<b>Here</b> goes some <i>content</i>..!'
  });
});
```

As you can notice, we have created the instance of the `Panel` class in the same way we created a component in previous examples (the container examples). The only difference is that we have added a new configuration called `title` with the text we want to show as the title of our panel.

Panels versus containers

As we have seen, containers create a basic HTML DOM element containing HTML or child components that we insert into the container. Panels, on the other hand, create extra sections (such as header and tools) and have more functionality (methods and functions) than containers. Some highlights and common parts of the panel are shown in the following screenshot:

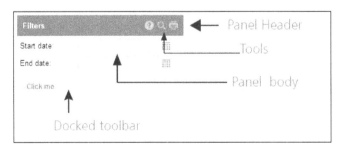

The Window component

A window is basically a floating panel with more features. The `Window` component extends from the `Panel` class. This means that we can use all the methods and properties that the panel has. Also, we can drag a window from the header bar, close it, and maximize it, among other things. Let's create a `.html` file as follows that imports the `Ext` library and runs the code when the DOM is ready:

```
var win = Ext.create("Ext.window.Window",{
  title: 'My first window',
  width: 300,
  height: 200,
  maximizable: true,
  html: 'this is my first window'
});
win.show();
```

Another alternative for this code can be:

```
Ext.create("Ext.window.Window",{
  title: 'My first window',
  width: 300,
  height: 200,
  maximizable: true,
  html: 'this is my first window'
}).show();
```

The only difference in our previous code and the panel's code is the `maximizable` property that allows us to maximize the window. We've removed the `renderTo` property too and used the `show` method to render and display the window.

By default, the window is closable, but we can make it non-closable by setting the `closable` property to `false`. We can move the window across the screen by dragging the header. We can also resize the window with the mouse for each of the four sides.

There are many more options for the window component. You should take a look at the API documentation and play around with this component.

The layout system

One of the greatest features of the Ext JS library is the ability to create layouts in an easy way. We can define fixed layouts or fluid layouts using the right classes.

At this point, you know how a container works. We can arrange the children of a container by setting a layout. If we don't define a layout to our containers, by default the `auto` layout will be used. In our previous examples, we used the `auto` layout and as we could see, the children or HTML are displayed one after another.

There are many available layouts we can use to arrange our components, such as `accordions`, `cards`, `columns`, and so on.

We can find all the available layouts in the `Ext.layout.container` package. Go to the documentation and look into the layouts `enum` class: `http://docs.sencha.com/extjs/5.1/5.1.1-apidocs/#!/api/Ext.enums.Layout`.

Here we will see many classes, each representing a type of layout. Some of the most common layouts are:

- The Border layout
- The Fit layout
- The Card layout
- The Accordion layout
- The Anchor layout

The Border layout

The Border layout divides the container space into five regions (multiple panes): `north`, `south`, `west`, `east`, and `center`. We can place our children in any of the regions, but we are always required to use the center region.

In the following code, we will define the layout as `border`. We will also define the
center, `west`, and `south` regions for the `border` layout:

```
Ext.onReady(function(){
  Ext.create('Ext.panel.Panel', {
    width: 500,  height: 300,
    title:  'Border Layout',
    layout: 'border',
    items: [{
      xtype: 'panel',
      title: 'South Region is resizable',
      region: 'south',      // region
      height: 100,
      split: true            // enable resizing
    },{
      xtype: 'panel',
      title: 'West Region',
      region:'west',    // region
      width: 200,
      collapsible: true,  //make panel/region collapsible
      layout: 'fit',
      split: true     // enable resizing
    },{
      title: 'Center Region',
      region: 'center',
      layout: 'fit',
      margin: '5 5 0 0',
      html:'<b>Main content</b> goes here'
    }],
    renderTo: Ext.getBody()
  });
});
```

We have made the **West** region a collapsible panel. If we click on the small arrow
located in the header or in the division bar, we'll see that the panel will collapse to
the left-hand side. Also, we have defined our **South** panel to be split. This allows
us to resize the **South** panel by dragging the separation bar with our mouse.

 You can directly place another component(s) that supports a
region in order to avoid over-nesting of components.

The Fit layout

This layout is intended to be used for only one child. It allows us to expand the inner component to the size of the container. The child component takes all the available space in the container component. When the parent is resized, the child size is updated too to fit the new dimensions. Let's make the code for this layout:

```
Ext.onReady(function(){
    var win = Ext.create("Ext.window.Window",{
        title: "My first window",
        width: 300,
        height: 200,
        maximizable: true,
        layout: "fit",
        defaults: {
        xtype: "panel",
        height: 60,
        border: false
        },
        items: [
        {title: "Menu", html: "The main menu"},
        {title: "Content", html: "The main content!"}
        ]
    });
    win.show();
});
```

In the previous code, we only added the layout property. In this case, we're setting a string with the name of the layout, but we can also set an object and define some configurations for the selected layout. In fact, every layout is a class that accepts configurations.

The following screenshot shows how the `fit` layout arranges the children of the container component:

As you can see, even though we defined two children components to the window, it only shows one. If we resize the main window, we should see that the **Menu** panel is expanded to fit the new size of the window.

The Card layout

The Card layout can manage multiple child components, so if we need to create a wizard or display only one component at a time, we should use this layout. This layout extends the `fit` layout class, which means that only one component can be visible at any given time and will fill all the available space in the container.

We can also set the initial displayed component by its index using the index from the `items` array. And we can move the components easily by calling the `next` or `prev` method. Let's check out the code for the Card layout:

```
Ext.onReady(function(){
    var win = Ext.create("Ext.window.Window",{
        title: "My first window",
        width: 300,
        height: 200,
        maximizable: true,
```

```
      layout: "card",//Step 1
      defaults:{ xtype: "panel", height: 60, border: false },
      items: [{
        title: "Menu",
        html: "The main menu"
      },{
        title: "Content",
        html: "The main content!"
      }]
    });
    win.show();

    setTimeout(function(){
      win.getLayout().setActiveItem(1);   //Step 2
    },3000);
  });
```

The previous code creates a window component with two panels. We set the layout of the window to card in step one.

In step two, we get the layout instance by calling the getLayout method after 3 seconds and change the initial item using the setActiveItem(1) method to show the **Content** panel. We can also use the prev and next methods from the layout instance to show the next and previous card.

The Accordion layout

Similar to the Card layout, this layout allows us to show one component at a time in an expandable Accordion style. We will see the header of the inner components and we're going to be able to expand and collapse the components by clicking on their title bars. Let's check the following code for the Accordion layout:

```
var win = Ext.create("Ext.window.Window",{
  title: "My first window",
  width: 300,
  height: 200,
  maximizable: true,
  layout: "accordion",
  defaults: { xtype: "panel" },
  items:[
    {title: "Menu", html: "The main menu" },
    {title: "Content", html: "The main content!" },
    {title: "3rd Panel", html: "Content here...!" }
  ]
});
```

Modifying the previous code, we have only changed/defined the Accordion layout and added a new panel to the `items` array. We'll see something like the following screenshot:

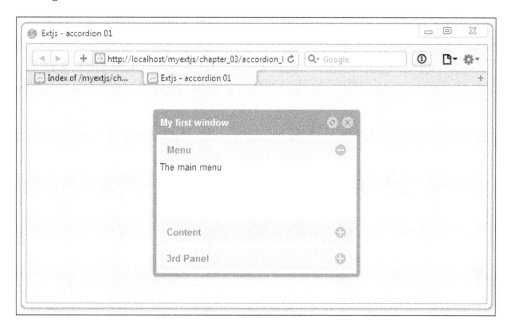

When using the Accordion layout, we'll see only one panel expanded at a time. The expanded panel will take the available height to be displayed. It doesn't matter if we resize the container.

> In the Accordion layout, it is important to point out that we only need to use the `Ext.panel.Panel` class or subclasses of the `Ext.panel.Panel` class.

The Anchor layout

This layout enables the anchoring of contained elements (child elements) relative to the container's dimensions. If the parent container is resized, then the child elements will be resized according to the rules applied to these child elements.

By default, `AnchorLayout` will calculate anchor measurements based on the size of the container itself. But if the container is using the `AnchorLayout` property, it will supply an anchoring-specific `config` property of `anchorSize`. If the `anchorSize` property is specified, the layout will use it as a virtual container for the purposes of calculating the anchor measurements based on it instead the container itself.

Let's make some changes to the previous examples and set the code like this:

```
Ext.onReady(function(){
  var win = Ext.create("Ext.window.Window",{
    title: "My first window",
    width: 300,
    height: 300,
    maximizable : true,
    layout: "anchor",
    defaults: {xtype: "panel", height: 60, border: false},
    items: [
    {
      title: "Menu",  html: "panel at 100% - 10 px",
        anchor:'-10'
    },{
      title: "Content", html: "panel at 70% of anchor",
        anchor:'70%'
    },{
    title: "3rd Panel", html: "panel at 50% width and 40% height
      of anchor", anchor:'50% 40%', bodyStyle:'background-color:
        #fc3;'
    }
    ]
  });
  win.show();
});
```

The screen will look like the following screenshot:

When we use the `anchor` property with only one value, anchoring will be used on the width of the component, for example, `anchor:'70%'` will cover 70% of the parent container's width. Using `anchor:'-10'` will cover 100% minus 10 pixels of the parent container's width. Lastly, when using two values, the anchoring will be applied to the width and height as in the last panel from the code: `anchor:'50% 40%'`.

More layouts

So far we have seen the basic layouts (most frequently used). To see more layouts in action, such as HBox Layout, VBox Layout, Table Layout, and so on, and to also see how they work, please visit `http://dev.sencha.com/ext/5.1.0/examples/kitchensink/#layouts`.

Comments about using layouts

Consider that you can nest layouts using combinations of containers and layouts, and also remember to ensure the right configuration each layout needs. In upcoming chapters, we will use layout nesting and containers-layout combinations so that you can have a more precise idea of how to combine these. Meanwhile, you can try to nest, combine, and play with the layout system.

One of the common mistakes that Ext JS beginners make is with the overnesting components; this can sometimes harm performance. You need to use layouts and set the proper type of container with adequate planning, for example:

```
Ext.onReady(function(){
  Ext.create('Ext.panel.Panel', {
    width: 500,  height: 300,
    title:  'Border Layout',
    layout: 'border',
    items: [
      {// Incorrect Nesting
        xtype: 'panel',
        title: 'West Region',
        region:'west',
        width: 200,
        collapsible: true,
        layout: 'fit'
        items:[{
          xtype: 'form',
          url: 'myForm.php'
          items[
```

```
            // Fields here
        ]
      }]
   },{
      title: 'Center Region',
      region: 'center',
      layout: 'fit',
      margin: '5 5 0 0',
      html:'<b>Main content</b> goes here'
   }],
   renderTo: Ext.getBody()
  });
});
```

As you can see, in the West region we are setting a panel that contains a form (Ext.form.Panel). In this case, we are overnesting, because if you see the documentation, Ext.form.Panel is extending a Panel component and this will cause our browser to make more DOM. This can also reduce memory because we are creating two components instead of one; the right way should be:

```
{
  xtype: 'form',
  title: 'West Region',
  region:'west',
   width: 200,
  collapsible: true,
  url: 'myForm.php'
  items[
    // Fields here
  ]
}
```

This way, the form panel acts the same way as any panel. We reduce one component with many properties, methods, and events that are not necessary and will only consume resources.

Summary

In this chapter, you learned about the component's lifecycle. We don't need to remember every step that is executed in each phase, but we should know the methods that we can override in our subclasses, so that we can add specific functionality in one of the three phases. When creating our custom components, it's very important to remember that we need to destroy all our references and internal components that we have created. This way, we'll free memory.

You also learned about the basic containers and most common used layouts, and how to add other components to a container and arrange them according to our needs.

In the next chapter, we're going to talk about the data package. You'll learn about the models, stores, and associations, and so many more exciting things.

4
It's All about the Data

In this chapter, we're going to learn about the use of the data package in Ext JS. Also, we will talk about Ajax, Data Models, Data Stores, and the available readers and writers that we can use in order to store our data locally.

The data package is what will let us load and save data in our code or application(s). It's important to have a solid understanding of the data package so we can link or bind data into Ext JS components. The data package contains multiple classes to handle data, but there are some main classes which will be used almost always. Take a look at the following figure:

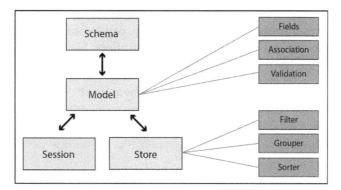

Ext JS creates an abstract layer with a lot of classes and configurations; the idea is to use these classes when dealing with information. All the widgets and components that show information use the data package to manipulate and present the data easily.

 It's important to mention that a web server is required for this chapter and the following chapters. It doesn't matter which one you decide to use because we are not using any specific server-side technology.

Ajax

Before we start learning about the data package it's important to know how we can make an Ajax request to the server. The Ajax request is one of the most useful ways to get data from the server asynchronously. This means that the JavaScript loop is not blocked while the request is being executed and an event will be fired when the server responds; this allows us to do anything else while the request is being performed.

If you are new to Ajax, I recommend you read more about it. There are thousands of tutorials online, but I suggest you read this simple article at `https://developer.` `mozilla.org/en-US/docs/AJAX/Getting_Started`.

Ext JS provides a singleton object (`Ext. Ajax`) that is responsible for dealing with all the required processes to perform a request in any browser. There are a few differences in each browser, but Ext JS handles these differences for us and gives us a cross browser solution to make Ajax requests.

Let's make our first Ajax call to our server. First, we will need to create an HTML file and import the Ext library. Then, we can add the following code inside the `script` tag:

```
Ext.Ajax.request({
  url:"serverside/myfirstdata.json"
});
console.log("Next lines of code...");
```

Using the `request` method, we can make an Ajax call to our server. The `request` method receives an object containing the configurations for the Ajax call. The only configuration that we have defined is the URL where we want to make our request.

It's important to note that Ajax is asynchronous by default. This means that once the `request` method is executed the JavaScript engine will continue executing the lines of code following it, and it doesn't wait until the server responds. You can also run Ajax in a synchronous way, setting the property `Ext.Ajax.async = false`.

For more details, take a look at `http://docs.sencha.com/extjs/5.1/5.1.1-` `apidocs/#!/api/Ext.Ajax-cfg-async`.

In the previous code, we did not do anything when the server responded to our request. In order to get the response date, we need to configure a `callback` function to execute when the server responds, and also, we have functions for `success` or `failure`. Let's modify our previous example to set up those callbacks:

```
Ext.Ajax.request({
  url:"serverside/myfirstdata.json",
  success: function(response,options){
```

```
        console.log('success function executed, here we can do some
          stuff !');
      },
      failure: function(response,options){
        Ext.Msg.alert("Message", 'server-side failure with status code
          ' + response.status);
      },
      callback: function( options, success, response ){
        console.log('Callback executed, we can do some stuff !');
      }
  });
```

The `success` function will be executed only when the server responds with a 200-299 status, which means that the request has been made successfully. If the response status is 403, 404, 500, 503, and any other error status, the `failure` callback will be executed.

Each function (success or failure) receives two parameters. The first parameter is the server response object, where we can find the response text and headers. The second parameter is the configuration option that we used for this Ajax request, in this case the object will contain three properties: the URL and the `success` and `failure` callbacks.

The `callback` function will be executed always, no matter if it's a failure or success. Also, this function receives three parameters: `options` is a parameter to the request call, `success` is a Boolean value according to if the request was successful or not, and the `response` parameter is an `XMLhttpRequest` object that contains the information of the response.

At this point, we have our callbacks set, but we're not doing anything inside yet. Normally, we need to get the data response and do something with it; let's suppose we get the following JSON in our response:

```
{
   "success": true,
   "msg": "This is a success message..!"
}
```

 In the Ext JS community, one of the preferred formats to send and receive data to the server is **JSON**; Ext JS can also handle XML. JSON stands for **JavaScript Object Notation**. If you are not familiar with JSON, you can visit `http://www.json.org/` in order to understand more about JSON.

For the `success` function to take interaction with the data returned, we need to decode the returned JSON data (which comes in text format), and convert the text to an object so we can access its properties in our code. Let's change the following code in the `success` callback:

```
success: function(response,options){
  var data = Ext.decode(response.responseText);
  Ext.Msg.alert("Message", data.msg);
},
```

First we get the server response as a text using the `responseText` property from the `response` object. Then, we use the `Ext.decode` method to convert the JSON text into JavaScript objects and save the result in a `data` variable.

After we have our data object with the server response, we will show an alert message accessing the `msg` property from the data object. Let's keep in mind that if we want to show something using the DOM, we need to put our code inside the `onReady` method that we have learned in the previous chapter.

```
Ext.Ajax.request({
  url: "serverside/myfirstdata.json ",
  success: function(response,options){
    console.log('success function executed, here we can do some
      stuff !');
  },
  failure: function(response,options){
    console.log('server-side failure with status code ' +
      response.status);
  },
  callback: function( options, success, response ){
    if(success){
      var data= Ext.decode(response.responseText);
      Ext.Msg.alert("Message", data.msg);
    }
  }
});
```

It's important for the server-side files to return a proper, error-free response; this means that we need to be sure that the server-side files have the proper syntaxes and no warning or error show (PHP as an example).

Also, it's important to specify, the Header on the server side to ensure proper content. For example, `header('Content-Type: application/json');`.

If we refresh our browser to execute the code we have modified, we should see something like the following screenshot:

Now, let's assume that we want to use XML instead of JSON. We will create the request in a very similar way to our previous code. The following code should be saved in a new file at `serverside/data.xml`:

```
<?xml version="1.0" encoding="UTF-8"?>
<response success="true">
<msg>This is a success message in XML format</msg>
</response>
```

Then, let's proceed to change the URL and the code in the `success` callback, as follows:

```
Ext.Ajax.request({
  url: "serverside/myfirstdata.xml",
  success: function(response,options){
    var data = response.responseXML;
    var node = xml.getElementsByTagName('msg')[0];
    Ext.Msg.alert("Message", node.firstChild.data );
  },
  failure: function(response,options){
    Ext.Msg.alert("Message", 'server-side failure with status code
      ' + response.status);
  }
});
```

We use the `responseXML` property to get the tree of nodes, and then we get the node with a `msg` tag. After that, we can get the actual text using the `firstChild.data` property from the previous node. If we execute the code, we will see something very similar to our previous example with JSON.

As we can notice, it is easier to work with JSON. We just need to decode the text and then we can use the objects. XML is a little bit complicated, but we can also use this format if we feel comfortable with it.

Passing parameters to Ajax request

It's usually in our applications that we need to pass some parameters to the Ajax request in order to get the proper information. To pass parameters we will use the following code:

```
Ext.Ajax.request({
  url: "serverside/myfirstparams.php",
  method: 'POST',
  params: {
    x:200,
    y:300
  },
  success: function(response,options){
    var data = Ext.decode(response.responseText);
    Ext.Msg.alert("Message", data.msg);
  },
  failure: function(response,options){
    Ext.Msg.alert("Message", 'server-side failure with status code'
      + response.status);
    Ext.Msg.alert("Message", 'server-side failure:' +
      response.status);
  }
});
```

Using the `params` property, we can set an object of parameters. In this case, we will send only two parameters: x and y, but we can send as many as we need. Notice that we set the `method` property with the POST value; by default, Ext JS uses the GET value for this property, and if we use GET, the values will be embedded on the URL for request. When we run this code, we'll get the following screenshot:

 Notice that you can return strings in an HTML format (msg value in this case) to give visual enhancements to the response if you are using Ext.Msg.alert

Setting timeout to Ajax request calls

Sometimes, but not all the time, the server may take too long to respond, so, by default, Ext JS has a configured time of 30 seconds to wait for the response. According to our needs, we can decrease or increase this time by setting the timeout property on the Ajax request configuration. The next example shows us how:

```
Ext.Ajax.request({
  url: "serverside/myfirstparams.php",
  method: 'POST',
  params: {x:200, y:300},
  timeout: 50000,
  success: function(response,options){
    var data = Ext.decode(response.responseText);
    Ext.Msg.alert("Message", data.msg);
  },
  failure: function(response,options){
    Ext.Msg.alert("Message", 'server-side failure with status code
      ' + response.status);
    Ext.Msg.alert("Message", 'server-side failure:' +
      response.status);
  }
});
```

We have increased the `timeout` property to 50 seconds (50000 milliseconds); now our request will be dropped after 50 seconds of waiting for the response.

 You can assign a global timeout value for the whole application setting, changing the value in `Ext.Ajax.timeout` (by default it has the value of `30000`). The previous example shows how to set timeouts on independent calls.

If we look into the documentation, we will find some other configurations, such as the scope of the callbacks, headers, cache, and so on. We should read the docs and play with those configurations too, but the ones that we have covered here are the most important ones to learn.

Now we know how to get data using Ajax, but we also need a way to deal with that data. Ext JS provides us with a package of classes to manage our data in an easy way; let's move forward to our next topic.

Models

Models represent objects or entities inside our application, for example, Clients, Users, Invoices, and so on. Those models will be used by the data stores. We can define as many models as we need inside our application.

A model may contain fields, validations, and relationships between other models. We can also set a proxy to persist and pull our data.

 As of version 5.x, field definitions can be optional unless you need conversion, validations, or set an implicit data type. For more information, take a look at `http://docs.sencha.com/extjs/5.1/whats_new/5.0/whats_new.html#Models`.

To create a model, let's write the following code:

```
Ext.define('Myapp.model.Client',{
extend:'Ext.data.Model',  // step 1
idProperty:'clientId ', // step 2
fields:[// step 3
  {name: 'clientId', type: 'int'},
  {name: 'name'    , type: 'string'},
  {name: 'phone'   , type: 'string'},
  {name: 'website' , type: 'string'},
```

```
{name: 'status'   , type: 'string'},
{name: 'clientSince', type: 'date', dateFormat:'Y-m-d H:i'}
]
});
```

As you can notice, we are defining the model in the same way as we defined a class; in step one we extend from the `Ext.data.Model` class, which is the one responsible for adding all the functionality to our models.

In the second step we are defining the property in our JSON response that will contain the ID of each record instance. In this case we are going to use the `clientId` field, but if we don't define the `clientId` configuration, the model will automatically use and generate a property called `id` by default.

In the third step we define the fields for our model. The value of this property is an array; each element in the array is an object containing the configuration for each field. In this case we set the name and type of field, and the last field (date) contains a `dateFormat` property.

 Depending on the type of field, we can add some specific properties. For example, to date type field, we can add a `dateFormat` property. To see more, check documentation on the `Ext.data.field` branch.

The available types of data are as follows:

- `String`
- `Integer`
- `Float` (recommended for use when you are using decimal numbers)
- `Boolean`
- `Date` (remember to set the `dateFormat` property to ensure correct date parse and interpretation of the date value)
- `Auto` (this field implies that no conversion is made to the data received)

Once we have defined our model, we can create an HTML file. Let's import the Ext library and our `Client` class file to test our model as follows:

```
var myclient = Ext.create('Myapp.model.Client',{
  clientId:10001,
  name:'Acme corp',
  phone:'+52-01-55-4444-3210',
  website:'www.acmecorp.com',
  status:'Active',
```

```
    clientSince:'2010-01-01 14:35'
});
console.log(myclient);
console.log("My client's name is = " + myclient.data.name);
console.log("My client's website is = " + myclient.data.name);
```

Using the `create` method we can instantiate our model class, the second parameter is an object with the data that our model (virtual record) will contain. Now, we will be able to use the `get` and `set` methods to read and write any of the defined fields:

```
// GET METHODS
var nameClient = myclient.get('name');
var websiteClient = myclient.get('website');
console.log("My client's info= " + nameClient + " - " +
  websiteClient);

// SET Methods
myclient.set('phone','+52-01-55-0001-8888'); // single value
console.log("My client's new phone is = " +
  myclient.get('phone'));
myclient.set({ //Multiple values
  name: 'Acme Corp of AMERICA LTD.',
  website:'www.acmecorp.net'
});
console.log("My client's name changed to = " +
  myclient.get("name"));
console.log("My client's website changed to = " +
  myclient.get("website") );
```

The previous code shows how to read and write our data. The `set` method allows us to modify one field, or even many fields at the same time, by passing an object containing the new values.

If we inspect the `invoice` instance, we'll find that all the information is held in a property called `data`. We should always use the `get` and `set` methods to read and write our models, but if for some reason we need to have access to all the data in our model, we can use the `data` object as follows:

```
//READ
console.log("My client's name:" + myclient.data.name);
console.log("My client's website:" + myclient.data.website);
// Write
myclient.data.name = "Acme Corp ASIA LTD.";
myclient.data.website = "www.acmecorp.biz";
```

A nice alternative to this code and a better way for `set` and `get` data is:

```
//READ
console.log("My client's name:" + myclient.get("name"));
console.log("My client's website:" + myclient.get("website"));
// Write
myclient.set("name", "Acme Corp ASIA LTD. ");
myclient.set("website", "www.acmecorp.biz");
```

We can read and write any fields in our model. However, setting a new value in this way is not good practice at all. The `set` method performs some important tasks when setting the new value, such as marking our model as dirty, saving the previous value so that we can reject or accept the changes later, and some other important steps.

Mappings

When defining a field inside the model, we can define where the data will be taken for a field with the property mapping. Let's say it's a path, alternate name, which Ext JS will be used in order to populate the field (data) from the data received from the server such as a JSON file or a XML file. Let's have a look at the following JSON example:

```
{
  "success" :"true",
  "id":"id",
  "records":[
    {
      "id": 10001,
      "name": "Acme corp2",
      "phone": "+52-01-55-4444-3210",
      "x0001":"acme_file.pdf"
    }

  ]
}
```

Here we can see on the JSON (or perhaps XML) example that the response comes a field with the name `x0001`. It can happen on some responses that the name of the field has a special code (depending on the database or data design), but in our code, this field is the contract file of the customer. So, using the mapping property, we can populate the field, setting the mapping property for our field, like the following example:

```
Ext.define('Myapp.model.Client',{
extend: 'Ext.data.Model',
```

```
idProperty: 'clientId ',
fields:[
   {name: 'clientId', type: 'int'  },
   {name: 'name'    , type: 'string'},
   {name: 'phone'   , type: 'string'},
   {name: 'contractFileName', type: 'string', mapping:'x0001'}
]
});
```

As you can see, we are defining the `contractFileName` field, which will be using the x0001 data/field from the response; in our code there is no need to make reference for x0001; we will just handle it in our code as `contractFileName`. To see it in action, run the `mapping_01.html` file from the example code. Open your console window and you will see something similar to the following screenshot:

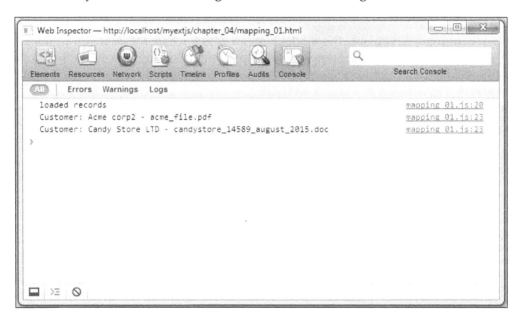

At this moment there is no need to examine all of the code. Advancing in this chapter, you will understand all the code in this example. The purpose is for you to understand the mapping property.

Validators

A nice feature since version 4 of Ext JS is the ability to validate our data directly in the model. We can define rules for each field and run the validations when we need to. In order to define validations into our models we only need to define a property called `validators` that contains an array of rules that will be executed when the validator engine runs. Let's add some validators to our previous model as follows:

```
Ext.define('Myapp.model.Client',{
extend:'Ext.data.Model',
idProperty:'clientId ',
fields:[
  {name: 'clientId', type: 'int'  },
  {name: 'name'    , type: 'string'},
  {name: 'phone'   , type: 'string'},
  {name: 'website' , type: 'string'},
  {name: 'status'  , type: 'string'},
  {name: 'clientSince' , type: 'date', dateFormat: 'Y-m-d H:i'}
],
validators:{
  name:[
    { type:'presence'}
  ],
  website:[
    { type:'presence', allowEmpty:true},
    { type:'length',  min: 5, max:250 }
  ]
}
});
```

When adding validations, we use objects to define each rule. The `type` property defines the type of rule that we want to add. There are a few types built within the library, such as inclusion, exclusion, presence, length, format, and e-mail; these are very common validations. We can also add new types of validations as needed.

When we define a rule, it is required to always use the `type` properties, but some rules require the use of other extra parameters. The `type` property represents a function within the `Ext.data.validator` subclasses. We can read the documentation of this object to see what specific parameters are needed for each rule.

Let's make some new changes to our previous HTML file and save them with a new name:

```
//Step 1
var myclient = Ext.create('Myapp.model.Client',{
    clientId  : '10001',
    name   : 'Acme corp',
    phone: '+52-01-55-4444-3210',
    website: 'www.acmecorp.com',
    status: 'Active',
    clientSince: '2010-01-01 14:35'
});

if  (myclient.isValid()){  //Step 2
  console.log("myclient model is correct");
}

console.log(myclient);
console.log("My client's name is = " + myclient.data.name);
console.log("My client's website is = " + myclient.data.website);
// SET methods   //Step 3
myclient.set('name','');
myclient.set('website','');
if  (myclient.isValid()){//Step 4
  console.log("myclient model is correct");
} else {
//Step 5
  console.log("myclient model has errors");
  var errors = myclient.validate();
  errors.each(function(error){
    console.log(error.field,error.message);
  });
}
```

The steps are explained as follows:

- **Step 1**: We instantiated our `Client` model using some data.
- **Step 2**: We executed the `isValid` method, which in this case returns `true` because all the information is correct.
- **Step 3**: We changed the model's values (name and website).

- **Step 4**: We executed the `isValid` method again to test the validators; in this case the result will be `false`.

- **Step 5**: The `validate` method (`myclient.validate();`) will return a collection with the failed validations. Then, the code will iterate this collection to make the output for the fields and error messages.

 The collection returned by the validate method is an instance of the class `Ext.data.ErrorCollection`, which extends from `Ext.util.MixedCollection`. Therefore, we can use each method to iterate in a simple way.

When we execute the previous example we will see in the console some messages according to the flow of the code. Initially, it will display a message saying that validations were successful. After changing the values, the messages will begin displaying the errors on the name and website fields. Take a look at the following screenshot from the console window/tool:

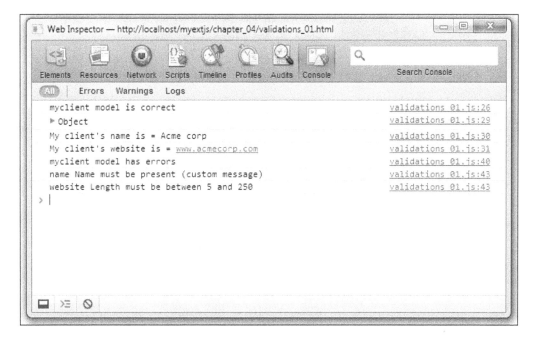

Custom field types

Usually we need to use some types of fields over and over, across different data models, in our application. On Ext 4, there was the practice to create custom validators. On version 5, it's recommended to create custom field types instead of custom validations. Using the following code, we will create a custom field:

```
Ext.define('Myapp.fields.Status',{
    extend: 'Ext.data.field.String',  //Step 1
    alias: 'data.field.status',//Step 2
    validators: {//Step 3
        type: 'inclusion',
        list: [ 'Active', 'Inactive'],
        message: 'Is not a valid status value, please select the
            proper options[Active, Inactive]'
    }
});
```

The steps are explained as follows:

1. We extend the new field based on `Ext.data.field.String`.

2. We define the alias this field will have. It's recommended that the alias does not repeat or override an existent name from the `Ext.data.field` subclasses.

3. We set the validator(s) the field will have.

Let's make some changes to our Client model:

```
Ext.define('Myapp.model.Client',{
extend:'Ext.data.Model',
idProperty:'clientId ',
fields:[
  {name: 'clientId', type: 'int'  },
  {name: 'name'    , type: 'string'},
  {name: 'phone'   , type: 'string'},
  {name: 'website' , type: 'string'},
  {name: 'status'  , type: 'status'}, //Using custom field
  {name: 'clientSince' , type: 'date', dateFormat: 'Y-m-d H:i'}
],
validators:{
  ...
}
});
```

On the model, we made the change {name: 'status', type: 'status'} using the alias we set on the custom field (alias: 'data.field.status'). Now, let's create the code for test:

```
var myclient = Ext.create('Myapp.model.Client',{
  clientId: '10001',
  name: 'Acme corp',
  phone: '+52-01-55-4444-3210',
  website: 'www.acmecorp.com',
  status: 'Active',
  clientSince: '2010-01-01 14:35'
});
if(myclient.isValid()){
  console.log("myclient model is correct");
}
// SET methods
myclient.set('status','No longer client');
if(myclient.isValid()){
  console.log("myclient model is correct");
} else {
  console.log("myclient model has errors");
  var errors = myclient.validate();
  errors.each(function(error){
    console.log(error.field,error.message);
  });
}
```

 If you get confused on how to prepare the code, please check the customfields_01.html and customfields_01.js files in the chapter_04 folder from the source code.

After we run our HTML file, we will get the following output on the console screen:

As you can see, `myclient.set('status','No longer client');` tries to use a value not defined for the acceptable values defined on the custom field `Myapp.fields.Status`, so this will get us a validation error for the model.

Using this technique, we can create and reuse many custom field types across many models in our application. Notice that we can extend from the following classes: `Ext.data.field.Field`, `Ext.data.field.Boolean`, `Ext.data.field.Date`, `Ext.data.field.Integer`, `Ext.data.field.Number`, and `Ext.data.field.String`.

As we talked in *Chapter 2, The Core Concepts*, about extending classes, it's important that you choose which class to extend according to your needs, to avoid using unnecessary extra code if you don't need it.

Relationships

We can create relationships between models to relate our data. For example, a Client has many contact employees, Services, branches, and many more things. Each item is an object with properties. For example:

- Employees for contact (name, title, gender, email, phone, cell phone, and so on)

- Services (service ID, service name, service price, branch where service is provided)

Ext JS 5 extends support to create **one-to-many**, **one-to-one**, and **many-to-many** associations in a very easy way.

One-to-many associations

One-to-many associations are created in the following way:

```
Ext.define('Myapp.model.Client',{
  extend:'Ext.data.Model',  // step 1
  requires: ['Myapp.model.Employee'],
  idProperty:'id ',
  fields:[.... ],
  hasMany:{
    model:'Myapp.model.Employee',
    name:'employees',
    associationKey: 'employees'
  }
});
```

Using the `hasMany` property, we can define the association. In this example, we're assigning an array of objects because we can create as many associations as we need. Each object contains a `model` property, which defines the model with the `Client` class that will be related.

Additionally, we may define the name of the function that will be created in our `Client` class to get the items related. In this case, we used `employees`; if we don't define any name, Ext JS will pluralize (add an "s") the name of the child model.

Now we need to create the `Employee` class. Let's create a new file located at appcode/model/Employee.js:

```
Ext.define('Myapp.model.Employee',{
  extend:'Ext.data.Model',
  idProperty:'id ',
  fields:[
    {name: 'id', type: 'int' },
    {name: 'clientid'  , type: 'int'},
    {name: 'name'      , type: 'string'},
    {name: 'phone'     , type: 'string'},
    {name: 'email'     , type: 'string'},
    {name: 'gender'    , type: 'string'}
  ]
});
```

There's nothing new in the previous code, just a regular model with a few fields describing an item of an employee. In order to test our relationship, we need to create an HTML file importing the Ext JS library and our two models. Then, we can test our models as follows:

```
var myclient = Ext.create('Myapp.model.ClientWithContacts',{
    id: 10001,
    name: 'Acme corp',
    phone: '+52-01-55-4444-3210',
    website: 'www.acmecorp.com',
    status: 'Active',
    clientSince: '2010-01-01 14:35'
});
//Step 2
myclient.employees().add(
{
    id:101, clientId:10001, name:'Juan Perez', phone:'+52-05-2222-333',
        email:'juan@test.com', gender:'male'},
{
    id:102, clientId:10001, name:'Sonia Sanchez', phone:
'+52-05-1111-444', email:'sonia@test.com',gender:'female'}
);
//Step 3
myclient.employees().each(function(record){
    console.log(record.get('name') + ' - ' + record.get('email') );
});
```

The steps are explained as follows:

1. We are creating the `Client` class with some data.

2. We are executing the employee method. When we define our relationship, we set the name of this method using the `name` property in the association configuration. This method returns an `Ext.data.Store` instance; this class is a collection to manage models in an easy way. We also add two objects to the collection using the `add` method; each object contains the data for the `Employee` model

3. We are iterating the items collection from our `Client` model. Using the `get` method, we print the description for each `Employee` model to the console; in this case, we have only two models in our store.

One-to-one associations

To create a one-to-one association, we will create a new class which has a one-to-one relation with a client or customer:

```
Ext.define('Myapp.model.Contract',{
  extend:'Ext.data.Model',
  idProperty:'id ',
  fields:[
    {name: 'id', type: 'int' },
    {name: 'contractId', type: 'string'},
    {name: 'documentType', type: 'string'}
  ]
});
```

As you can see this is a plain model. Now on the Customer class we will define it as follows:

```
Ext.define('Myapp.model.Customer',{
  extend:'Ext.data.Model',
requires: ['Myapp.model.Contract'],
  idProperty:'id ',
fields:[
  {name: 'id', type: 'int'},
  {name: 'name'    , type: 'string'},
  {name: 'phone'   , type: 'string'},
  {name: 'website' , type: 'string'},
  {name: 'status'  , type: 'string'},
  {name: 'clientSince' , type: 'date', dateFormat: 'Y-m-d H:i'},
  {name: 'contractInfo' , reference: 'Contract', unique:true}
  ]
});
```

If you notice, we added a new field called `contractInfo`, but in this case, instead of the property `type` we used the property reference. This property will point to the entity `Contract`. As with the previous example, let's modify the JS code, as shown in the following:

```
var myclient = Ext.create('Myapp.model.Customer',{
  id: 10001,
  name: 'Acme corp',
  phone: '+52-01-55-4444-3210',
  website: 'www.acmecorp.com',
  status: 'Active',
  clientSince: '2010-01-01 14:35',
```

```
contractInfo:{
    id:444,
    contractId:'ct-001-444',
    documentType:'PDF'
  }
});
```

You will notice that this time we set the data directly on the model configuration on the code `contractInfo:{...}`. So, now if you check on the console, it has to appear something like the following screenshot:

As you can see, `contractInfo` is an object inside the data which has the same fields defined on the `Contract` model. Now, if you don't define the `contractInfo` or some other property from the `contractInfo` object, then these properties will not be added to the model (record). As shown in the next example, `contractInfo` was not defined, and you can see the result in the following screenshot (after **Second test**):

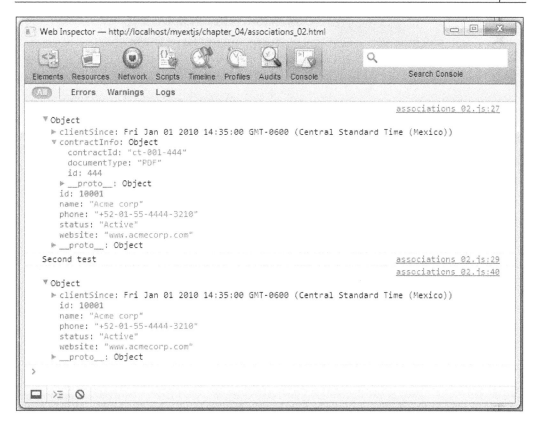

Working with the store

As mentioned before, a store is a collection of models that acts as a client cache to manage our data locally. We can use this collection to perform tasks such as sorting, grouping, and filtering the models in a very easy way. We can also pull data from our server using one of the available proxies and a reader to interpret the server response and fill the collection.

A store is usually added to widgets/components to display data. Components such as the grid, tree, combo box, or data view use a store to manage the data. We will learn about these components in future chapters. If we create a custom widget, we should use a store to manage the data too. This is why this chapter is really important; we use models and stores to deal with the data.

In order to create a store, we need to use the `Ext.data.Store` class. The following example will use the `Customer` model that we already have worked, and will extend the store to create a collection of customers:

```
Ext.define('MyApp.store.Customers',{
   extend : 'Ext.data.Store',        //Step 1
   model  : 'Myapp.model.Customer'   //Step 2
});
```

The steps are explained as follows:

- **Step 1**: To define a store, we need to extend from the `Ext.data.Store` class. This class is responsible for dealing with the models.

- **Step 2**: We associated the model that our store will be using. It is required to specify a valid `model` class; in this case, we're using our `Customer` class that we have been working on in the previous example.

Once we have our store class defined, we are going to create an HTML page to run our test. Let's import the `Ext` library, our `Customer` model, and our `Customers` store:

```
var store = Ext.create("MyApp.store.Customers");
//counting the elements in the store
console.log(store.count());
```

We can use the `create` method to instantiate our `store` class; in this example, we don't need to pass any parameter, but we could do it as any other class.

If we would like to know the number of items that are contained in our store, we can use the `count` method. In this case, we're printing the number returned on the JavaScript console, which is zero, because our store is empty at this moment.

Adding new elements

Adding elements to the collection is very simple. We need to create a `Customer` model with data, and we will use the `add` or `insert` method to add the new item to our store, as shown in the following code:

```
//Step 1 (define /create new model instance)
var mynewcustomer = Ext.create('Myapp.model.Customer',{
   id: 10001,
   name: 'Acme corp',
   phone: '+52-01-55-4444-3210',
   website : 'www.acmecorp.com',
   status: 'Active',
```

```
    clientSince: '2010-01-01 14:35',
    contractInfo:{
        id:444,
        contractId:'ct-001-444',
        documentType:'PDF'
    }
});
store.add(mynewcustomer); //Step 2
console.log("Records in store:" + store.getCount() );
```

The steps are explained as follows:

- **Step 1**: We created the model that we want to add to our store; we also set values to some of the fields.

- **Step 2**: We executed the add method to append our model to the collection. It's important to know that using the add method will always insert the model in the last position of the collection.

Finally, we count our items again and we will see a number **1** in our JavaScript console.

We can also add a new item by just sending an object containing the data, and the add method will create the model instance for us, as shown in the following example:

```
//Method 2 for add Records
    store.add({
        id: 10002,
        name: 'Candy Store LTD',
        phone: '+52-01-66-3333-3895',
        website : 'www.candyworld.com',
        status: 'Active',
        clientSince: '2011-01-01 14:35',
        contractInfo:{
            id:9998,
            contractId:'ct-001-9998',
            documentType:'DOCX'
        }
    });
    console.log("Records in store:" + store.getCount());
```

When running the previous code, we will see a number **2** in the JavaScript console.

We can even add many items at once by passing an array of models to the add method, as shown in the following example:

```
// Method 3 for add multiple records
var mynewcustomer = Ext.create('Myapp.model.Customer', { ...});
var mynewcustomerb = Ext.create('Myapp.model.Customer', {
...});
store.add([mynewcustomer, mynewcustomerb]);
console.log("Records in store:" + store.getCount());
```

We have added two models in the same method call, but we can pass whatever models we need in the array.

If we see the console, there will be a number **4** printed because we have four elements in our collection. As mentioned before, if we use the add method, the new element will be placed in the last position of the collection, but what if we want to add the new element to the first position, or maybe somewhere else? We can use the insert method to add the new element wherever we need.

Looping through the records/models in the store

So far, we know how to retrieve the number of elements in the existing store. Now we can iterate through the elements of the store by using the each method as follows:

```
store.each(function(record, index){
  console.log(index, record.get("name"));
});
```

The each method receives a function as the first parameter. This function will be executed for every record of the store; the anonymous function receives two parameters for our convenience: the record and index parameters for each iteration.

We can also set the scope where the anonymous function will be executed by passing a second parameter to the each method with the object where the anonymous function will be executed.

In our previous example, we only printed the index and name properties in our model, but we can access any property or method defined in our Customer model.

Retrieving the records in the store

Once we have content in our store, we can retrieve objects or perform a search of the collection of models. There are several ways of retrieving models. We are going to look at the most common ways.

By index position

If we only want to get a model at a specific position, we can use the `getAt` method from the store as follows:

```
var modelTest = store.getAt(2);
console.log(modelTest.get("name"));
```

In our previous example, we get the model that is in the third position of the collection. The first position in the store uses the index 0, so if we want to get the third element, we use the index 2. In our example, the name printed should be **Modern Cars of America**.

First and last records

There are also methods to retrieve the first element of the collection and the last element; for this, we can execute the `first` and `last` methods from the store class, as shown in the following code:

```
var first = store.first();
var last = store.last();
console.log(first.get("name"), last.get("name"));
```

Our previous code will print the name of the first and last element in our store; in this case, we will see the name of **Acme Corp** and **Extreme Sports Los Cabos**.

By range

There are times when we need to get many records at once, so there's a method called `getRange` to retrieve a list of records. We may define the limits, or we can even get all the records in the collection, as shown in the following code snippet:

```
var list = store.getRange(1,3);

Ext.each(list,function(record,index){
  console.log(index,record.get("name"));
});
```

In the previous code, we were retrieving records from the index number 1 to the index number 3. We are going to see three elements in our JavaScript console.

By ID

We can retrieve a record directly by its ID, as shown in the following code:

```
var record = store.getById(10001);
console.log(modelTest.get("name"));
```

Removing records

We have been adding and accessing records in our store, but if we would like to remove records from the store, we'd have three ways of doing this task:

```
store.remove(record);
store.each(function(record,index){
  console.log(index,record.get("name"));
});
```

We executed the `remove` method and passed the model from where we wanted to delete the record. In our previous code, we were passing the `model` variable that we created before. If we look at the JavaScript console, we will see that the first record does not exist anymore.

We can also remove many records at once. We only need to pass an array of models to the `remove` method, and those models will be removed from the store, as shown in the following code:

```
store.remove([first,last]);
store.each(function(record,index){
  console.log(record.get("name"));
});
```

When we execute the code, we will see that the two additional records are gone. We should not see those names in the JavaScript console.

There are times when we may not have the reference to the model that we want to delete. In those cases, we can remove a record by its position in the store, as shown in the following code:

```
store.removeAt(2);
store.each(function(record,index){
  console.log(index,record.get("name"));
});
```

The `removeAt` method accepts an index; the record located at this position will be removed. Now we can only see two names in the JavaScript console.

If we want to remove all the records in our store, we only need to call the `removeAll` method and the store will be cleared.

```
store.removeAll();
console.log("Records:",store.count());
```

At this moment, our store is empty. If we execute the `count` method, we will get zero as a result. Now we know how to add, retrieve, and remove records from our store.

Retrieving remote data

So far, we have been working with local data, and hard-coding our information to create a store of records. But in real world applications, we will have our data in a database, or maybe we'll get the information using web services.

Ext JS uses proxies to send and retrieve the data to and from the source. We can use one of the available proxies to configure our store or model.

Proxies in Ext JS are in charge of handling the data/information of a data model; we can say that the proxy is a class that handles and manipulates the data (parsing, organizing, and so on), so the store can read and save or send data to the server.

A proxy uses a reader to decode the received data, and a writer to encode the data to the correct format and send it to the source. We have three available readers to encode and decode our data: the Array, JSON, and XML readers. But we have only two writers available; only for JSON and XML.

There are many types of proxies at our disposal. If we want to change our source of data, we should only change the type of proxy and everything should be fine. For example, we may define an Ajax proxy for our store or model, and then we can change it for a local storage proxy.

Ajax proxy

In order to use this proxy, we need to set up a web server to make the Ajax requests correctly. If we don't have a web server to test our code, we can use the WAMP or XAMPP server (see *Chapter 1, An Introduction to Ext JS 5*). Using a web server is required so that we can make Ajax requests correctly.

When we have everything ready, we can modify our previous example, where we created the `Customers` class to add the required proxy.

```
Ext.define('Myapp.store.customers.Customers',{
    extend:'Ext.data.Store',
```

```
    model: 'Myapp.model.Customer',
    proxy:{
      type:'ajax',
      url: 'serverside/customers.php',
      reader: {
        type:'json',
        rootProperty:'records'
      }
    }
});
```

The previous code adds a new property to the store called `proxy`. We are setting a configuration object containing three properties. The `type` property defines the type of proxy that we're going to use. In this case, we specified `ajax`, but we can use any of the available proxies.

The `url` property defines the resource that we will request using Ajax. It's important to mention that the URL must be in the same domain so that we 'don't get any errors when making the Ajax request. If you plan to use a cross-domain URL then it's recommended that you use the JSONP proxy, or if you have control over the server side, then enable CORS.

To know more about CORS, please take a look at the following URLs:

* http://en.wikipedia.org/wiki/Cross-origin_resource_sharing
* https://developer.mozilla.org/en-US/docs/Web/HTTP/Access_control_CORS

The third property is `reader`; this property is an object containing properties that will specify how the data will be handled (loaded) by Ext JS. It's important that we define a reader, otherwise the store won't be able to load the data properly.

So, at this point, we can load the data from our web server using Ajax. In order to test our code, let's create an HTML file importing the `Ext` library, our model(s), and our store:

```
//Step 1
var store = Ext.create("Myapp.store.customers.Customers");
//Step 2
store.load(function(records, operation, success) {

  console.log('loaded records');//Step 3
  Ext.each(records, function(record, index, records){
    console.log( record.get("name")  + ' - '  +
      record.data.contractInfo.contractId );
  });
});
```

The steps are explained as follows:

- **Step 1**: We create the store as usual and save the reference in a variable.
- **Step 2**: We execute the `load` method. This method internally executes the read operation, makes the Ajax call to the server, and then loads the data into the store. The function that we give to the `load` method as a parameter is a callback that will be executed after the records are loaded into the store. We are doing it in this way because Ajax is asynchronous, and we never know when the server is going to respond.
- **Step 3**: The last step iterates through the records of the store and prints the name for each invoice in the JavaScript console.

Before we execute our example, we should create the `serverside/customers.json` file. We're going to use JSON to encode the data, as follows:

```
{
  "success":true,
  "id":"id",
  "records":[
    {
      "id": 10001,
      "name": "Acme corp2",
      "phone": "+52-01-55-4444-3210",
      "website": "www.acmecorp.com",
      "status": "Active",
      "clientSince": "2010-01-01 14:35",
      "contractInfo":{
        "id":444,
        "contractId":"ct-001-444",
        "documentType":"PDF"
      }
    },{
      "id": 10002,
      "name": "Candy Store LTD",
      "phone": "+52-01-66-3333-3895",
      "website": "www.candyworld.com",
      "status": "Active",
      "clientSince": "2011-01-01 14:35",
      "contractInfo":{
        "id":9998,
        "contractId":"ct-001-9998",
        "documentType":"DOCX"
      }
    }
  ]
}
```

We have an object that contains an array of objects that hold our information; each object contains the same properties as that of our `Customer` model, and also the relation one-to-one from the `Contract` model.

Now, if we execute the test, we will see two records in the console. If we execute the `count` method in our store, we will see that it only contains two elements.

Readers

Readers let Ext JS understand how to handle the response and fill the store with models containing the correct information.

As we saw in the previous example we used:

```
reader: {
  type:'json',
  rootProperty:'records'
}
```

The `type` property defines how our information is decoded. In this case, we are assigning the `json` type to the property, but we can also use the `xml` or `array` type if needed.

The `rootProperty` allows us to define the name of the property in the server response, where all objects containing the information for our models are located. This property should be an array in our JSON response. In this case, we set `records` because our JSON response uses that name, but it could be anything. If we have nested objects, we can use a dot (.) to go as deep as we need. For example, let's suppose we get the following response:

```
{
  "success" :"true",
  "id":"id",
  "output":{
    "appRecords":[{ our data .... }],
    "customerRecords":[{ our data .... }]
  }
}
```

The previous response contains the array of information inside of an object output; we need to configure our reader, so it should be able to read this response correctly. We need to change the `rootProperty` as follows:

```
reader: {
  type:'json',
  rootProperty:'output.customerRecords'
}
```

We have only modified the rootProperty using a dot to get one level deeper. We can go as deep as we need. It doesn't matter how many levels we have to go, but we need to make sure that we are setting this configuration correctly, pointing to the array of data where our models will be filled.

Let's test our code again (proxy_02.js) by refreshing the browser. Now, we'll see the same output as before.

XML reader

The XML reader makes some relative changes to JSON, because in this case, we need to specify some other properties in the reader, to ensure the XML is well interpreted by Ext JS. Take a look at the following code:

```
proxy:{
  type:'ajax',
  url: 'serverside/customers.xml',
  reader: {
    type: 'xml',
    rootProperty: 'data',
    record:'customer',
    totalProperty: 'total',
    successProperty: 'success'
  }
}
```

We have only changed the url property to our reader, so that it points to an XML file that contains our information, instead of the JSON file. The properties we are using are as follows:

- The type property was set to xml. This way, our reader will be able to read the server response correctly.

- The rootProperty defines the Element (node) in XML that Ext JS will check to look for records (sub nodes).

- We also added record. This property allows us to define the tag where the information will be in the XML response; in this case, we used customer.

- Finally, we added totalProperty and successProperty, which are nodes defining some values that the store will read for functionality.

Now, let's create the XML file that holds our information. This file should be called serverside/customers.xml, and will contain the following code:

```
<?xml version="1.0" encoding="UTF-8"?>
<data>
  <success>true</success>
```

```
<total>2</total>
<customer>
  <id>10001</id>
  <name>Acme corp2</name>
  <phone>+52-01-55-4444-3210</phone>
  <website>www.acmecorp.com</website>
  <status>Active</status>
  <clientSince>2010-01-01 14:35</clientSince>
  <contractInfo>
    <id>444</id>
    <contractId>ct-001-444</contractId>
    <documentType>PDF</documentType>
  </contractInfo>
</customer>
<customer>
  <id>10002</id>
  <name>Candy Store LTD</name>
  <phone>+52-01-66-3333-3895</phone>
  <website>www.candyworld.com</website>
  <status>Active</status>
  <clientSince>2011-01-01 14:35</clientSince>
  <contractInfo>
    <id>9998</id>
    <contractId>ct-001-9998</contractId>
    <documentType>DOCX</documentType>
  </contractInfo>
</customer>
</data>
```

First, we have defined the root node that contains the invoices information. This root node is called `data`. If we change the name of this node, then we should also change the `root` property in our reader to match this node.

Each `customer` node contains the data for our models/records. We have defined a new `record` property in our reader configuration to set the name of the node, where the information should be in our XML response.

Now, let's test our changes by refreshing our browser. If everything goes fine, we will see the same response as in the previous examples. Take a look at the next screenshot:

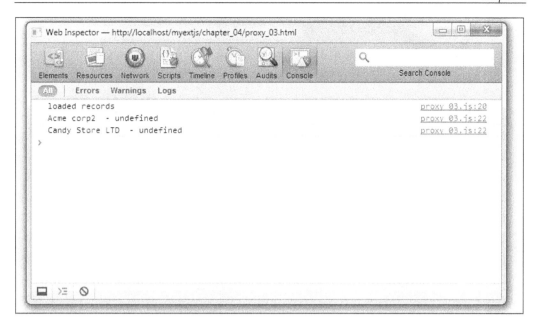

The result is exactly the same as when we used the JSON reader, however, if we go to the **Network** tab in the developers tools, we can see that in this case, the server is responding with XML.

By using readers, we can switch easily from using JSON or XML as our source of data. We don't have to change anything else in our code, but just configure each URL and reader correctly.

Sending data

After adding, editing, or modifying records into the store, we should send the data to our server. Ext JS allows us to do this by the use of a writer property (it has to set in the proxy). This writer will encode the data depending on the type of writer (JSON or XML). In order to archive this, let's create the `CustomersSending.js` file in the path `appcode/store/customers`. We will use the previous models we have created and place the following code:

```
Ext.define('Myapp.store.customers.CustomersSending',{
  extend:'Ext.data.Store',
  model: 'Myapp.model.Customer',
  autoLoad:false,
  autoSync:true,
  proxy:{
    type:'ajax',
```

```
    url: 'serverside/customers.json',
    api: {
      read     : 'serverside/customers.json',
      create   : 'serverside/process.php?action=new',
      update   : 'serverside/process.php?action=update',
      destroy  : 'serverside/process.php?action=destroy'
    },
    reader: {
    ()type:'json',
      rootProperty:'records'
           },
    writer:{
      type:'json',
      encode:true,
      rootProperty:'paramProcess',
      allowSingle:false,
      writeAllFields:true,
      root:'records'
    },
    actionMethods:{
      create: 'POST',
      read: 'GET',
      update: 'POST',
      destroy: 'POST'
    }
  }
});
```

The notable changes made on the code are:

1. **We set the** `api` **property**: On this property, we will set URLs for each CRUD action method (create, read, update, and destroy).

2. **We set the** `writer` **property as a configuration object**: Here, the important properties in the object are:

    ○ `type:'json'`: This property will send the data in JSON format to the server.

    ○ `encode`: This property will make Ext JS encode the information before passing it to the server.

    ○ `rootProperty`: This property will be the name of the parameter containing the information.

    ○ `writeAllFields`: This property will pass all the records to the server. If we set it to `false`, then they will be sent only to the modified fields.

3. **We set the** `ActionMethods` **property**: This property will set how the parameters that are passed by the store will be sent. In the code example, we set POST method for `create`, `update`, and `destroy`, and we set GET for read.

 Do note that `create`, `update`, and `destroy` will be triggered when the proper action takes place with the data. For example, if we add a new model/record in the store, then it will launch the `create` action, encoding and passing the data set in `api` property.

Now, let's create the HTML file `sending_01.html`, as follows:

```
<!doctype html>
<html>
<head>
<meta http-equiv="X-UA-Compatible" content="IE=edge">
<meta charset="utf-8">
<title>Extjs - Sending 01</title>
<link rel="stylesheet" type="text/css" href="../ext-5.1.1/build/
packages/ext-theme-neptune/build/resources/ext-theme-neptune-all.css">
<script src="../ext-5.1.1/build/ext-all.js"></script>
<script src="../ext-5.1.1/build/packages/ext-theme-neptune/build/ext-
theme-neptune.js"></script>
<script type ="text/javascript" src="sending_01.js"></script>
</head>
<body style="padding:10px;"></body>
</html>
```

And finally, the `sending_01.js` file looks as follows:

```
Ext.Loader.setConfig({
    enabled: true,
  paths:{ Myapp:'appcode' }
});
Ext.require([
  'Ext.data.*',
  'Myapp.model.Contract',
  'Myapp.model.Customer',
  'Myapp.store.customers.CustomersSending'
]);
Ext.onReady(function(){

var store = Ext.create("Myapp.store.customers.CustomersSending");
//Step 1
```

```
store.load({ // Step 2 load  Store in order to get all records
  scope: this,
  callback: function(records, operation, success) {
    console.log('loaded records');
    Ext.each(records, function(record, index, records){
      console.log( record.get("name")  + ' - ' +
        record.data.contractInfo.contractId );
    });
    var test=11;
    console.log('Start adding model / record...!');
    // step 3 Add a record
    var mynewCustomer = Ext.create('Myapp.model.Customer',{
      clientId  : '10003',
      name: 'American Notebooks Corp',
      phone: '+52-01-55-3333-2200',
      website   : 'www.notebooksdemo.com',
      status    : 'Active',
      clientSince: '2015-06-01 10:35',
      contractInfo:{
        "id":99990,
        "contractId":"ct-00301-99990",
        "documentType":"DOC"
      }
    });
    store.add(mynewCustomer);

    // step 4 update a record

    console.log('Updating model / record...!');
    var updateCustomerModel = store.getAt(0);
    updateCustomerModel.beginEdit();
    updateCustomerModel.set("website","www.acmecorpusa.com");
    updateCustomerModel.set("phone","+52-01-33-9999-3000");
    updateCustomerModel.endEdit();

    // step 5 delete  a record
    console.log('deleting a model / record ...!');

    var deleteCustomerModel = store.getAt(1);
    store.remove(deleteCustomerModel);

  }
  });
});
```

In **Step 1**, we create the store instance. In **Step 2**, we load the records (load function); after the records are loaded, the callback function will be executed. At this point, the store has two records that come from the JSON file. So, we are ready to begin with the operations create, update, and delete.

In **Step 3**, we create a model/record; we set the data of this model/record, and then we add it to the store. As we set the property `autoSync: true` in the store, Ext JS will send the data to the server.

In **Step 4**, we update a record; in this case, we modified two properties and then called the `endEdit()` method of the model/record. After this method finishes, the store will launch the update URL and pass the data to the server.

And finally in **Step 5**, we select the second model/record of the store with `store.getAt(1)`. Then, we tell the store to remove the record, and the record is deleted from the store. This will make Ext JS launch the `destroy` URL that we set.

Take a look at the following screenshot and notice the network behavior:

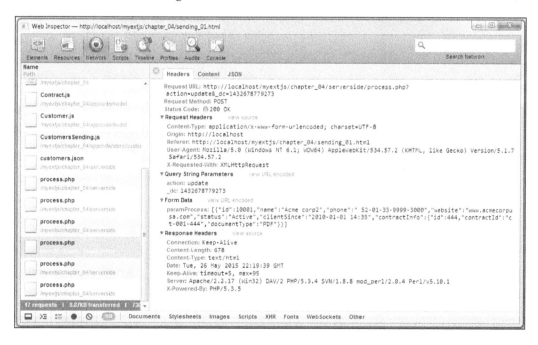

In the screenshot, you will notice the request call for the `update` action. There is also the `paramProcess` variable sent to the server that contains all the data from the updated model/record. Now we need to work on the php (or server page), so that it performs the required actions in the server page.

Summary

In this chapter, we had been working with data; we learned how to create models with fields, mappings, validations, and relationships. We also worked with a collection of models using the `store` class, and learned the basics for retrieving data using proxies, JSON readers, and XML readers. In the upcoming chapters, we will learn how to handle more advanced features available in the stores.

It's important to mention that every widget in Ext JS that displays data uses a store and models (Grids, Combos, Data views, and so on) to manage all the data. When we modify a model in our store, the widget will automatically refresh its view. For example, if we have a grid and we want to delete a record, we only need to use the `remove` method from the store. By doing this, the grid will automatically update the rows and the deleted rows won't appear anymore.

In the next chapter, we are going to learn about events, and how we can respond to the user interaction. So far, we haven't used events, but they are one of the most important parts of the JavaScript development world.

5
Buttons and Toolbars

When working with buttons and toolbars, we will definitely need to arrange them whenever we use window or panel components. Toolbars are a great way of adding buttons and menus, and we can create button groups. However, we also need to understand how to handle events to execute actions. We can add actions to our widgets using callbacks and events to process user interaction.

In this chapter, you are going to learn how to create buttons and toolbars and how to handle an event (or events) in order to begin with user interaction on the Ext JS UI.

Event-driven development

Before we start talking about components, you need to understand how events and listeners work behind the scenes. The first thing you need to learn is the observable pattern.

Basically, the observable pattern is designed to allow entities or objects to communicate with each other using events. When a certain action occurs inside an object or component, this object should broadcast an event to whoever is listening.

For example, when a button is clicked on, it fires the `click` event. When a row of a grid is clicked on, the grid fires the `itemclick` event. All components have defined events and they are fired when an action occurs.

The component that is firing the event doesn't know who will listen to its messages, but its responsibility is to let others know that something has happened. Then, maybe other components will do something about it, or nothing at all.

The `Ext.util.Observable` base class allows us to add, fire, and listen to events from a specific object or component and perform actions when that event is executed.

All widgets included in the Ext JS library have the `Ext.util.Observable` class mixed in, so all widgets fire events that we can listen to perform actions and bring our widgets to life.

As mentioned before, we can define and fire new events on our custom components using the same `Ext.util.Observable` class.

Copy the `singleton_01.js` file (from the code files of `chapter 02`). Then, we have to add the following changes to the `Employee` class:

```
Ext.define('Myapp.sample.Employee',{
mixins: {observable: 'Ext.util.Observable'},
  Code.....
  constructor: function( config ){
    Code.....
    this.mixins.observable.constructor.call( this, config );
  },
  quitJob: function(){
this.fireEvent('quit', this.getName(), new Date(), 2,
 1, 'more params...' );
  }
});
```

As you can notice, the `Employee` class now contains the mixin—the `Ext.util.Observable` class. Also, inside the constructor function, this mixin is initialized by the `this.mixins.observable.constructor.call(this, config);` code. This means that `Ext.util.Observable` will be aware of any event launch inside the employee class, whenever it happens.

 To understand more about mixins, see `http://docs.sencha.com/extjs/5.1/5.1.1-apidocs/#!/api/Ext.Mixin`.

The `quitJob` function, when called, will launch the `quit` event, passing the `this.getName()`, `new Date()`, `2`, `1`, `'more params...'` parameters.

 In previous versions of Ext JS, we had to add the `addEvent(...)` method to create, or define, the proper event (or events) inside the class. If you are upgrading from version 4, be aware of this change. Version 5 is more flexible about it.

Now, we need the code to listen to the `'quit'` event when it's launched. In Ext JS, we have the `listeners` property that is used for such purposes (listen/handle events). Let's modify the code where we instantiate the class:

```
var patricia = Ext.create('Myapp.sample.Employee', {
  name:'Patricia',
  lastName:'Diaz',
  age:21,
  isOld:false,
  listeners:{
    'quit':function(EmployeeName, quitDate, param, paramb, paramc){
      console.log('Event quit launched');
      console.log('Employee:' + EmployeeName);
      console.log('Date:'+ Ext.util.Format.date(
        quitDate,'Y-m-d H:i'));
      console.log('Param :' + param);
      console.log('Param B:' + paramb);
      console.log('Param C:' + paramc);
    }
  }
});
console.log(Myapp.CompanyConstants.welcomeEmployee(patricia));
patricia.quitJob();
```

The listeners property was included in the configuration object (the new Employee class), so in this way, we can intercept and handle the quit event whenever it happens. Let's run the code in our browser and check out the console output, as shown in the following screenshot:

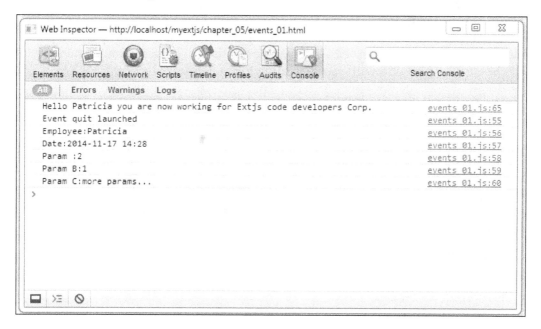

When talking about events and handlers, it's important to mention that we are talking about Ext JS and how it's coded, handled, or used in the framework, and we must make a clarification that this is not pure JavaScript behavior.

At this point, we have defined our event and the listener that will handle it. Another common way of adding the listener is by using the `on` method, which is a shorthand method of `addListener`:

```
patricia.on({
  'quit':function(EmployeeName, quitDate, param, paramb, paramc){
    console.log('Event quit launched');
    console.log('Employee:' + EmployeeName);
    console.log('Date:' + Ext.util.Format.date(quitDate,
      'Y-m-d H:i'));
    console.log('Param :' + param);
    console.log('Param B:' + paramb);
    console.log('Param C:' + paramc);
  }
});
patricia.quitJob();
```

Remember that it's important to add a listener (or listeners) before executing the desired method (or methods). Events are the way we can execute certain sets of actions when events occur. As we can see in the previous example, the `Employee` class is responsible only for broadcasting the event when the `quitJob` method is called. The class itself doesn't care about who may be listening, but on the outside, an object is listening and will react according to the messages received.

The ability to add, fire, and listen to custom events is a very powerful feature in Ext JS.

Creating a simple button

Now that you have a basic understanding of how to handle events, it's time we began working with components and widgets. First of all, we will go for buttons. In order to create buttons, we will need to use the `Ext.button.Button` class. This class will handle all the "ins and outs" of a single button.

Let's create the code for our first button:

```
var myButton = Ext.create('Ext.button.Button', {
  text:'My first button',
  tooltip:'Click me...!',
  renderTo:Ext.getBody()
```

```
});
```

In this code, we create an instance of the `Button` class and passed some configurations. Usually, a button has many more configurations, but for the moment, these are enough.

The `text` property will set the text shown when the button is rendered on the document (using **Document Object Model (DOM)**).

The `renderTo` property will allow us to set the place where the document body is going to be created/inserted (using DOM). Here, the button will be placed in the document's body.

Let's run the sample in the browser. You will see something similar to the following screenshot:

By default, the button has the `scale` property equal to `small`, but we can change the size to `medium` and `large`. The `scale` property lets us define the size of the button. Also related to the `scale` property is the fact that we can set different icon sizes for the buttons depending on the scale. For the moment, let's change the code, and now we are going to create two more buttons:

```
var myButton = Ext.create('Ext.button.Button', {
  text:'My first small button',
  scale:'small',
  renderTo:Ext.getBody()
});

var myButtonB = Ext.create('Ext.button.Button', {
  text:'My first medium button',
  scale:'medium',
  renderTo:Ext.getBody()
});
```

```
var myButtonC = Ext.create('Ext.button.Button', {
  text:'My first large button',
  scale:'large',
  renderTo:Ext.getBody()
});
```

This code will create three buttons using different scales, as shown in this screenshot:

Note that we can also set a custom size using the `width` and `height` properties. This is possible because the `Button` class extends from `Component` class.

Setting icons on buttons

It's frequently seen that on any application, we use icons to differentiate the *action* buttons. In order to set the icons (images) on any button, we will use the `iconCls` property to set a CSS class (rule) that will add the image as the background. Previously, when we talked about the `scale` property, the idea was to use the following sizes:

Scale	Size
Small	16 x 16 pixels
Medium	24 x 24 pixels
Large	32 x 32 pixels

Let's create some new CSS rules inside the last code (HTML file), as follows:

```css
.addicon-16{
  background:transparent url('images/add_16x16.png') center 0
    no-repeat !important;
}
.addicon-24{
  background:transparent url('images/add_24x24.png') center 0
    no-repeat !important;
}
.addicon-32{
  background:transparent url('images/add_32x32.png') center 0
    no-repeat !important;
}
```

We defined three CSS classes (rules), one for each available scale. Note that you can use your very own icons as well. The preceding code assumes that we have a folder called `images` with three different images inside it. In order to make our example work, we need to include those images in that folder. Feel free to use your own images for this example.

Once we have our CSS in place, we need to set one of them for each of our buttons:

```javascript
var myButton = Ext.create('Ext.button.Button', {
  text:'My first small button',
  iconCls:'addicon-16',
  scale:'small',
  renderTo:Ext.getBody()
});

var myButtonB = Ext.create('Ext.button.Button', {
  text:'My first medium button',
  iconCls:'addicon-24',
  scale:'medium',
  renderTo:Ext.getBody()
});

var myButtonC = Ext.create('Ext.button.Button',{
  text:'My first large button',
  iconCls:'addicon-32',
  scale:'large',
  renderTo:Ext.getBody()
});
```

Using the `iconCls` property, we can relate any CSS class to the button. If we refresh our browser, we can see that each button has an icon, as shown here:

Icon alignment on buttons

By default the, icon is aligned to the left-hand side, but we can set the position to the top, bottom, and right-hand side too. We do this using the `iconAlign` property. Let's use the following code:

```
var myButtonA = Ext.create('Ext.button.Button',{
    text:'left icon',
    iconCls:'addicon-16',
    iconAlign:'left',
    renderTo:Ext.getBody()
});

var myButtonB = Ext.create('Ext.button.Button',{
    text:'top icon',
    iconCls:'addicon-16',
    iconAlign:'top',
    renderTo:Ext.getBody()
});

var myButtonC = Ext.create('Ext.button.Button',{
    text:'right icon',
    iconCls:'addicon-16',
    iconAlign:'right',
    renderTo:Ext.getBody()
});

var myButtonD = Ext.create('Ext.button.Button',{
```

```
    text:'bottom icon',
    iconCls:'addicon-16',
    iconAlign:'bottom',
    renderTo:Ext.getBody()
});
```

The use of `iconAlign` sets the alignment of the icon. If we refresh our browser, we can see how every button has the icon in a different position, as shown in the following screenshot:

Handling button events

Once we have our buttons in place, it is very likely that we want to add some actions when they are clicked on. In the coming chapters, we will see how to listen to events using the MVVM pattern. For now, we will listen to events directly on the buttons.

The `Button` class makes use of the `Observable` class (internally) by using it as a mixin; therefore, we can listen to events using the `addListener` method.

Every component has many predefined events that we can use. If we go through the documentation, we can see all the available events, with a description of when the event is fired and what parameters are received by the listeners. In this case, the `Button` class contains the `click` event, which is fired when the button is clicked on by the user. We can listen to this event using the `on` (a shorthand method for the `addListener` method) method:

```
myButtonA.on('click', function(){
    Ext.Msg.alert("Click event", "You clicked left icon button..!");
});
```

In the previous code, we used the `on` method to listen to the `click` event. When this event is fired, it will show a confirmation message.

If we refresh our browser and click on the first button, we should see the following message:

We can do whatever we want inside the callback function. In this case, we are only showing an alert message, but we can also load a store to pull some data from our server. We can show a window component or create a panel with a form inside.

There are many more events that we can listen to, for example, `show`, `hide`, `enable`, `disable`, and so on. For more event names, refer to the Ext JS documentation.

We can define any number of listeners to the same event, and when the event is fired, all the listeners will be executed.

Segmented buttons

A new addition in version 5 is segmented buttons, and they give us the possibility to show buttons as part of a group. In fact, the use of segmented buttons is actually the use of a specific container for a group of buttons. For this, we need to use the `Ext.button.Segmented` class by treating it similar to any container (which was discussed in previous chapters).

Using the previous example files (`button_04.js` and `button_04.html`), let's create a duplicate of these files and save them with the names `button_05.js` and `button_05.html`. Now, let's change the title of the buttons, remove the `iconAlign` property, and add the following after the last line of the code:

```
var mySegmentedbuttons = Ext.create('Ext.button.Segmented', {
    renderTo:'segmentedbuttons',
    vertical:false,
    items:[{
```

```
    xtype: 'button', text:'1st button', iconCls:'addicon-16'
  },{
    text:'2nd button', iconCls:'addicon-16'
  },{
    text:'3th button', iconCls:'addicon-16'
  },{
    text:'4th button', iconCls:'addicon-16'
  }]
});
```

Let's run the example in the browser, and we will get the following result:

As you can notice, the second row of buttons is the segmented button container rendered, and the buttons look nicer than those in the first row (plain buttons on the same row and not grouped). Notice that the first button and the last button in the **segmented button** container have rounded corners, compared to the first row where each button has rounded corners.

Also, we can set the group in a vertical way by setting the `vertical:true` property. Check out the following screenshot to understand this:

By default, the `Ext.button.Segmented` class treats each **item** as a button. In the example code, we set the `xtype` property to the first button. The other three buttons don't have that property and still Ext JS treated each item as a button configuration object.

Segmented buttons, as you can see, are mainly for the purpose of visual aesthetics and give a better look. According to Sencha, this is:

"A very common presentation for multiple selection on mobile."

Adding menus

There are times when we need to create a menu (or menus) to allow the user to choose from the available options. We can achieve this by setting the menu property of the buttons. This will create a floating menu for the selected button, and it will be shown when the user clicks on the button.

Let's create a button that contains a menu with options. For the following example, we need to create an HTML page, import the Ext JS library, and listen for the DOM ready event. Inside the callback, we should modify the code that creates our button, as shown here:

```
var myButton = Ext.create('Ext.button.Button',{
   text:'Add payment method...',
   iconCls:'addicon-32',
   iconAlign:'left',
   scale:'large',
   renderTo:'normalbuttons',
   menu:[
     {text:'Master Card'},
     {text:'Visa'},
     {text:'PayPal'},
     {text:'Other...'}
   ]
});
```

As we can see in the previous code, the menu property receives an array of objects. This array will be used to create an instance of the Ext.menu.Menu class. This class is responsible for managing and displaying the floating menu.

It is also important to say that each object inside the array uses the menu item as the default xtype. As a result, we should see something like what is shown in the following screenshot when we open our HTML file in our browser:

In the previous code, we used object literals to create our menu. If we want to use constructors instead of the literals, we should create an instance of the Ext.menu. Menu and Ext.menu.Item classes, as follows:

```
//Step 1
var menuItemA = Ext.create('Ext.menu.Item',{text:'Master card'});
//Step 2
var menu = Ext.create('Ext.menu.Menu',{
items : [  //Step 3
  menuItemA,    // Variable
  Ext.create('Ext.menu.Item',{text:'Visa'}), // constructor
  {text:'Paypal'} //object config
]
});
var myButton = Ext.create('Ext.button.Button',{
  text:'Add payment method...',
  iconCls:'addicon-32',
  iconAlign:'left',
  scale:'large',
  renderTo:'normalbuttons',
  menu:menu
});
```

In Step 1, we created an instance of the Ext.menu.Item class. In Step 2, we created an instance of the Ext.menu.Menu class, and its items property in Step 3 contains a mixed array. The first element is the menuItemA variable, the second is a constructor for the Ext.menu.Item class, and the third is a configuration object that will become an Ext.menu.Item class:

```
items : [ //Step 3
  menuItemA,   // Variable
  Ext.create( 'Ext.menu.Item' ,{
    text:'American Express'
```

```
    }), // constructor
    {text:'Other'} //object config
]
```

Once we have created our menu, we add our instance to the `menu` property of the button. When the button is created, it detects that the `menu` property is not an array and it's an instance of the `Menu` class.

As a result, we have two buttons with a menu containing the same options, as shown in this screenshot:

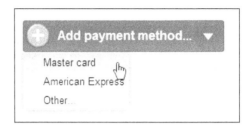

Adding a menu is really easy. Now, if we want to add some functionality to these options, we need to set a listener for each item in the menu. If we go through the documentation, we'll find that the `Ext.menu.Item` class contains a `click` event. This is the event that we need to listen to, to perform some actions when it is fired. However, there are many ways by which we can attach event handlers to a component, or widget. To demonstrate this, let's add a bit more code, as shown in the following example:

```
var myButton = Ext.create('Ext.button.Button',{
  text:'Add payment method...',
  iconCls:'addicon-32',
  iconAlign:'left',
  scale:'large',
  renderTo:'normalbuttons',
  menu:[{
    text:'Master Card',
    listeners:{  // Option 1
      click:function(){
        Ext.Msg.alert("Click event", "You selected Master Card..!");
      }
    }
  },{
    text:'Visa', //Option 2
    handler: onMenuItemClick
  },{
    text:'PayPal',
```

```
    listeners:{ //Option 3
      'click':{fn: onMenuItemClick , single:true}
    }
  },{
    text:'Other...',
    handler: onMenuItemClick
  }]
});
function onMenuItemClick (itemBtn, Event){
  var optionString = itemBtn.text;
  Ext.Msg.alert("Click event","You selected " + optionString +
    " ..!");
}
```

Now, let's check out the options in the code:

1. In `Option 1`, we added a `listeners` property to the configuration object which will raise an alert when clicked.

2. In `Option 2`, we used a property called `handler`. This property will bind the click event to the `onMenuItemClick` function name that is set on the property. Also, the function will receive two parameters (`item` and `event`).

3. In `Option 3`, we again used the `listeners` property, but for the click event. We passed a configuration object with two properties: `fn` and `single`. The `fn` property will specify the function to be executed, and `single` will specify that the execution will be only made once. After the first execution, Ext JS will remove the event handler.

 It's important to read how to add event listeners on components, or widgets, and test the different ways of accomplishing this. Not all the time will we need to use the same ways; it depends on the functionality you need. Knowing the variations of add listeners can save us from writing much extra code for or applications.

You might have noticed that the second and the last menu items have the `handler: onMenuItemClick` property, so both of them are pointing to the same function. This function will recognize which button was pressed/clicked on by accessing them with the `itemBtn` parameter passed to that function. In this case, we need access only to the `text` property:

```
var optionString = itemBtn.text;
```

Refresh the browser, test each option, and see how the listeners work on each button.

It's important to say that we can add as many levels of submenus as we need using the menu property. However, from my personal experience I won't recommend cascading your menus too deeply because the user experience will be affected.

Toolbars

Once we have known the basics about buttons and menus, we can move on to the next component, which is the toolbar. As is very common in applications that have toolbars in order to access our application modules, windows, and so on, the toolbar component acts as a container where we can arrange our buttons the way we need.

Since version Ext JS 4, it has been possible to define a toolbar in any of the four sides of our containers (north, south, east, and west). We can also add more toolbars to each side (more than one). It's important to mention that a toolbar is usually used on containers such as a panel, window, or grid, or on subclasses of containers on which it can be placed.

Let's start creating a basic example of a toolbar at the top of a panel. So, let's create an HTML file, set the reference to the Ext JS library, and write the following code in the DOM ready callback:

```
var myPanel = Ext.create( 'Ext.panel.Panel' ,{
  title: 'My first toolbar...',
  width: 450,
  height: 200,
  dockedItems: [{ //Step 1
    xtype : 'toolbar',
    dock: 'top', //Step 2
    items: [
      {text: 'New record'},
      {text: 'Edit record'},
      {text: 'Remove record'}
    ]
  }],
  renderTo:Ext.getBody()
});
```

Now, let's review the steps in this code:

1. In `Step 1`, we defined the `dockedItems` property. Here we can define an array of components. Any component can be placed, or docked, on any of the four sides (`left`, `top`, `right`, or `bottom`).

2. In `Step 2`, we defined where the toolbar is going to be docked. In this case, the `dock` property is equal to `top`. If the `dock` property is missing or not defined, by default, Ext JS will set it to `top`.

Usually, toolbars are defined as docked items, but we can define other components, such as grids, panels, and forms, among others. One more thing to highlight from the previous code is that, by default, the components in the `items` array of the toolbar are buttons. That's why we didn't set explicitly an xtype.

We can also add any other component to the toolbar, such as `textfield`, `combo box`, and `radiobutton`.

Let's add a few more buttons with icons, as shown in the following code:

```
items:[
  {text:'New', iconCls:'addicon-16'},
  {text:'Edit', iconCls:'editicon-16'},
  {text:'Remove', iconCls:'deleteicon-16'},
  {text:'Export', iconCls:'export-16'},
  {text:'Print', iconCls:'print-16'},
  {text:'Help', iconCls:'help-16'}
]
```

Once we have made the changes, we need to create the CSS classes (rules) that will set the image as the background. Let's add the rules to our HTML file or CSS style file:

```
.addicon-16{ background:transparent url('../images/add_16x16.png')
center 0 no-repeat !important; }
.deleteicon-16{ background:transparent url('../images/delete.png')
center 0 no-repeat !important; }
.editicon-16{ background:transparent url('../images/pencil.png')
center 0 no-repeat !important; }
.help-16{ background:transparent url('../images/help.png') center 0
no-repeat !important; }
.print-16{ background:transparent url('../images/printer.png') center
0 no-repeat !important; }
.export-16{ background:transparent url('../images/page_go.png') center
0 no-repeat !important; }
```

Remember that you can change images or add more images and CSS classes (rules). Let's run the browser. You may see something similar to this:

The screenshot shows the new buttons with an icon. By default, the icons are aligned to the left and the buttons are horizontally aligned.

Toolbar button groups

A nice feature in Ext JS is that we can group toolbar buttons thanks to the `Ext.container.ButtonGroup` class or by using the `xtype:'buttongroup'`. This class is a subclass of `Ext.panel.Panel` that lets us group buttons in a toolbar. Again, let's change the previous code to arrange our buttons in the toolbar, as is done by the following code:

```
var myPanel = Ext.create('Ext.panel.Panel',{
  title:'My first toolbar...',
  width:600,
  height:200,
  dockedItems:[{ //Step 1
    xtype : 'toolbar',
    dock: 'top', //Step 2
    items:[
      { xtype:'buttongroup',
        title:'Actions',
        items:[
        {text: 'New', iconCls: 'addicon-16'},
        {text: 'Edit', iconCls: 'editicon-16'},
        {text: 'Remove', iconCls: 'deleteicon-16'}
```

```
      ]
    },{
      xtype: 'buttongroup',
      title: 'Print / Export & Help',
      items:[
      {text: 'Export', iconCls: 'export-16'},
      {text: 'Print', iconCls: 'print-16'},
      {text: 'Help', iconCls: 'help-16'}
      ]
    }
  ]
}],
renderTo:Ext.getBody()
});
```

We added two button groups to the toolbar and, instead of adding the buttons
directly to the toolbar, we did it on each button group in the items property. Also, we
defined a title for each button group. Now, let's check out the following screenshot,
which shows the output:

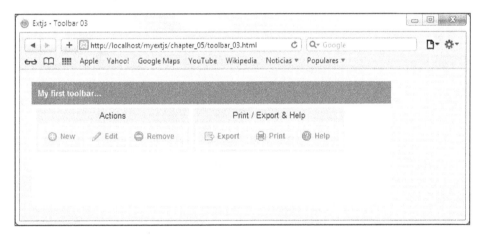

By default, the `buttongroup` xtype created has placed the buttons horizontally (three
columns for each group). We can change this look using the `column` property:

```
var myPanel = Ext.create('Ext.panel.Panel',{
  title:'My first toolbar...',
  width:600,
  height:200,
  dockedItems:[{ //Step 1
    xtype : 'toolbar',
    dock: 'top', //Step 2
```

```
    items:[
      { xtype:'buttongroup',
        title:'Actions',
        columns:2,
        items:[
        {text:'New', iconCls:'addicon-32', scale:'large',
          rowspan:2, iconAlign:'top' },
        {text:'Edit', iconCls:'editicon-16'},
        {text:'Remove', iconCls:'deleteicon-16'}
        ]
      },{
        xtype:'buttongroup', title:'Print / Export & Help',
        defaults:{scale:'large', iconAlign:'top'},
        items:[
        {text:'Export', iconCls:'export-32'},
        {text:'Print', iconCls:'print-32'}
        ]
      },{
        xtype:'buttongroup', title:'Help',
        items:[
        {text:'Help', iconCls:'help-32', scale:'large',
          iconAlign:'bottom' }
        ]
      }
    ]
  }],
  renderTo:Ext.getBody()
});
```

In the previous code, we set the `columns` property to 2 in the first button group. This means that the buttons in that group will be organized in two columns. One important thing to observe closely is the `rowspan` property of the new button. This property is set to 2, which means that the new button will use two rows. We also modified the size of some buttons to `large`, and updated the `iconCls` property to use images of size 32 pixels (width and height).

With these few changes in place, we'll have a better layout and organized buttons, giving the final user interface a very elegant look and feel, as shown in this screenshot:

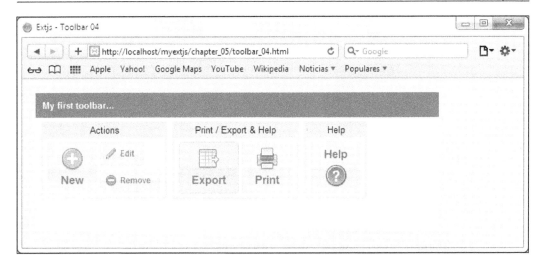

Remember that we can use as many columns as we want, and as we did in our previous example, we can mix button sizes (scales) too.

The breadcrumb bar

A new addition in Ext JS version 5 is the breadcrumb bar. This bar displays hierarchical data from a `TreeStore` as a trail of breadcrumb buttons. In *Chapter 9, The Tree Panel*, we will talk about the tree store in more detail, and also check out more specific information about `TreeStore`.

Let's begin with creating a new HTML file and our JS code. First of all, we need to define our store that contains data for the breadcrumb bar with the following code:

```
Ext.define('Myapp.sample.store.mainMenu', {
  extend: 'Ext.data.TreeStore',
  root: {
    text: 'My app',
    expanded: true,
    children: [{
      text: 'Modules',
      expanded: true,
      children: [
        {leaf: true, text: 'Employees'},
        {leaf: true, text: 'Customers'},
        {leaf: true, text: 'Products'}
      ]
    },{
```

```
          text: 'Market',
          expanded: true,
          children: [
            {leaf: true, text: 'Sales'},
            {leaf: true, text: 'Budgets'},
            {leaf: true, text: 'SEO'},
            {leaf: true, text: 'Statistics'}
          ]
        },{
          text: 'Support',
          iconCls:'help-16',
          children: [
            {leaf: true, text: 'Submit a ticket'},
            {leaf: true, text: 'Forum'},
            {leaf: true, text: 'Visit our web site'}
          ]
        },
        {leaf: true, text: 'Reports'},
        {leaf: true, text: 'Charts'}
        ]
    }
});
```

Let's review what we made in the previous code step by step:

- Our new store/class, Myapp.sample.store.mainMenu, extends the Ext.
  data.TreeStore class.

- The root property inside the store is the initial node / data model that the
  TreeStore will contain, and its child nodes / data models are inside the
  children property, which is an array of nodes, or data models.

As you can notice, the data inside the root property (node) is structured in a tree-like
manner. This will be interpreted by the breadcrumb bar to create the buttons, menus,
and submenus inside its body. Now, let's declare, or create, the breadcrumb bar in
the following way:

```
//step 1
var myMenuStore = Ext.create('Myapp.sample.store.mainMenu',{});
var myPanel = Ext.create('Ext.panel.Panel',{
  title:'My first breadcrumb bar...',
  width:600,
  height:200,
  dockedItems:[{ //Step 2
    xtype : 'breadcrumb',
    dock: 'top',
```

```
        store: myMenuStore,
        showIcons: true,
        selection: myMenuStore.getRoot().childNodes[2].childNodes[0]
    }],
    renderTo:Ext.getBody()
});
```

Step one is the creation of an instance previously defined 'Myapp.sample.store.
mainMenu', then we proceed to create the container myPanel.

Also, just as we declared the toolbar for the panel, we now set the breadcrumb bar by
setting the xtype property to breadcrumb. Also notice that we have other properties,
such as:

- The store: myMenuStore property is indicating to the breadcrumb where it's
  going to retrieve the data to create its proper components (buttons, menus,
  and so on).

- The showIcons:true property will control whether or not to show icons on
  the buttons.

- The selection property will set the initial selected node/data model.
  We can use root for set the first element in the store, or in this case, we
  set myMenuStore.getRoot().childNodes[2].childNodes[0], which is
  selecting the Submit a ticket node, or data model.

Run the file in the browser. We will get something similar to the following screenshot:

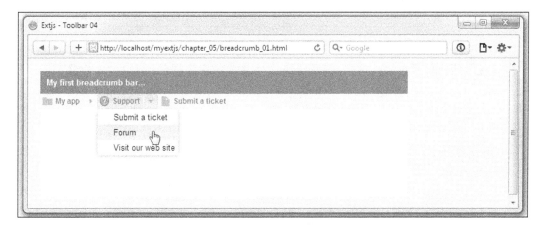

As you can see, at this moment, the breadcrumb is showing three buttons: **My App**,
Support, and **Submit a ticket**. The first two buttons that you see contain a menu
displaying its child elements (the children defined in the store). Also, you can notice
that the first and last button have gray icons. These are, in fact, default icons assigned

by Ext JS. The second button has a help icon that was defined in the store:

```
{
    text: 'Support', iconCls:'help-16',
    children: [
        {leaf: true, text: 'Submit a ticket'},
        {leaf: true, text: 'Forum'},
        {leaf: true, text: 'Visit our web site'}
    ]
}
```

Click on the first button and you will see the second and third disappear, as shown in this screenshot:

Now, let's open the menu from the first button and select **Reports**. A new button will appear on the breadcrumb bar, like this:

Handling selections in the breadcrumb bar

So, we have created the breadcrumb, but we need a way to control it when it changes the selection. The breadcrumb has the event selection change, which will be fired each time we click on a button or a menu item created inside the breadcrumb bar.

Let's change the `dockedItems` property to the following code to control the change of selection:

```
dockedItems:[{
    xtype : 'breadcrumb',
    dock: 'top',
    store: myMenuStore,
    showIcons: true,
    selection: myMenuStore.getRoot().childNodes[2].childNodes[0],
    listeners:{
```

```
    'selectionchange':{
      fn:function(mybreadcrumb, node, eOpts){
        var panel = mybreadcrumb.up('panel');
        panel.update( 'This is the zone for:<b>' + node.data.text +
          '</b>' );
      },
      delay:200
    }
  }
}],
```

We added the `listeners` property and set the handler for `selectionchange`. The function will receive three parameters. The first one is the instance of the breadcrumb bar defined in `mybreadcrumb`, the second parameter is the selected node (data model) defined in `node`, and the third parameter is the options object passed to the `Ext.util.Observable.addListener` listener defined in `eOpts`.

Refresh the browser and change the selections to see the app in action, as follows:

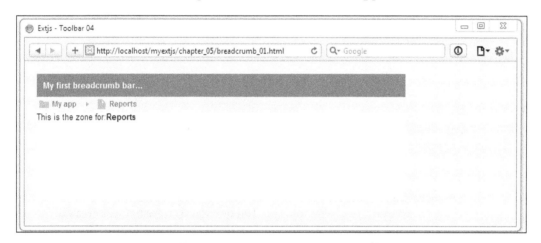

Now, when we change the selection, the panel's contents will be updated with the `'This is the zone for:<b>' + node.data.text + '</b>'` text, where `node.data.text` is the value we set previously on each one of the root's children in the store.

So far, as a new component in version 5, the breadcrumb is a nice addition when we need huge menus, submenus, or many complex ways to access parts of our application. Using it on tablets will be a real space saver.

The main menu for our application

At this point, we are going to go through an exercise to create the main menu for our final application. As of yet, we haven't worked so much on the application itself, mainly because you have been learning the basics about the Ext framework, but from now on, we can focus more on small pieces that will be reused for our final app.

The following screenshot shows how we need to design the main menu for our invoice management application:

 Sencha Architect is very useful for creating prototypes quickly and also for screen examples/wire framing. The previous screenshot was created on Sencha Architect version 3.1.x using the classic theme for a better understanding of how the components are to be placed.

As we can see from the screenshot, we need to create a toolbar docked at the top and another toolbar docked on the bottom. The first toolbar will contain two buttons (each one with its own menu) and one text item, `Ext.toolbar.TextItem`, for displaying the username. The second toolbar, which will be docked at the bottom, will have a text item and a help button at the right side.

Also, for this exercise, we will need a component to take up all of the available space in the browser (document body). So far, we have been using panels as containers, but this time, we are going to use a Viewport.

The Ext.container.Viewport component takes up all of the available space and always listens to the resize event of the window's browser to recalculate the new dimensions every time the user resizes the browser.

 It is good practice to have only one Viewport per application, as this will be our workspace inside the web page (document).

Let's start by creating a class that extends from the Viewport class. As this is only an exercise — and later, we will reuse part of the code — there is not much to worry about file locations and other things. So, to create the Viewport, let's start with this code:

```
Ext.define('MyApp.view.Viewport', {
    extend: 'Ext.container.Viewport',
    layout: 'fit',
    initComponent: function(){
        var me = this;
        me.items = [{
            xtype: 'panel',
        }];
        me.callParent();
    }
});
```

The Viewport class extends from the container component, which means that we can use any of the available layouts. In this case, we are going to use a fit layout, because we want to expand the children of the Viewport.

As mentioned before, if we want to dock a component to any of the four sides, we need to use a panel. The following code adds an empty panel to the Viewport as a child:

```
me.items = [{
    xtype: 'panel',
}];
```

We are using the fit layout to expand the panel to fit all of the Viewport. Now we can set the docked items for this empty panel and dock a toolbar at the top:

```
dockedItems: [{
    xtype: 'toolbar', docked:'top',
    items: [{
        text: 'Home', iconCls: 'home-16',
        menu: [
            {text: 'Categories', iconCls: 'categories-16'},
```

```
      {text: 'Products', iconCls: 'products-16'},
      {text: 'Clients', iconCls: 'clients-16' },
      {text: 'Invoices', iconCls: 'invoices-16'}
    ]
  },{
    text: 'Help', iconCls: 'help-16',
    menu: {
      xtype: 'menu',
      items: [
        {xtype: 'menuitem', text: 'Submit a support ticket'},
        {xtype: 'menuitem', text: 'Forum'},
        {xtype: 'menuitem', text: 'About...'}
      ]
    }
  },
  {xtype: 'tbfill'},
  {xtype: 'tbtext', text: 'User: Brett Fravre'}
  ]
}]
```

As in the previous code samples (toolbar), we have now added two new elements to the toolbar, which are as follows:

- tbfill or Ext.toolbar.Fill: This is an item that will act as a placeholder, forcing the next elements to render in the right-justified way inside the toolbar container

- tbText or Ext.toolbar.TextItem: This is an item that renders text or HTML directly on the toolbar

Before testing, we need to declare the instance of the Viewport class we defined:

```
Ext.onReady(function(){
  Ext.create("MyApp.view.Viewport");
});
```

Indeed, the Viewport doesn't need the renderTo property, because it will automatically get the document body. For the moment, we need to create the HTML file and run the example. We will get something similar to the following screenshot:

Now, let's create the bottom toolbar with this code:

```
dockedItems : [{
  xtype : 'toolbar', docked:'top',
  //your code here…
},
{
  xtype : 'toolbar', dock:'bottom',
  items : [
    {xtype: 'tbtext', text: '<b>Status :</b>Connected'},
    {xtype: 'tbfill' },
    {text:'', iconCls: 'help-16'}
  ]
}]
```

As you can notice, we added another toolbar item with the dock property with a value of bottom. Its children are `tbtext`, `tbfill` and a button configuration object that will be on the right side of the toolbar. Refresh the browser and check the result, as follows:

You'll be able to notice the following:

- The text item has the text property set to `<b>Status :</b>Connected`, which is an HTML text.

- When we use the `tbfill` item, it fills the space between (pushes the next components defined to the right) the previous element defined and the next element defined after the `tbfill` element.

 We can also use an arrow (->) to create an instance of the `tbfill/Ext.toolbar.Fill` class item.

Finally, we need to check out what the menu items look like, as shown in the following screenshot:

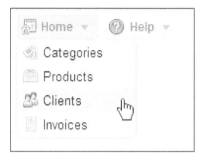

Also see the menu under the Help button, as shown in this screenshot:

Remember that in these examples, we are using the Neptune theme, so changing the themes in Ext JS may vary the visual results of buttons and toolbars.

Also, it's important after this lesson that you test how to declare event handlers and how to set items (as a configuration object, a constructor, and an array) in different ways. This will make you be sure of what type of code you need in some cases and save you coding time in other cases.

Summary

In this chapter, you learned about the basics of how to handle events and how we can add, fire, and listen to events. You also learned about buttons, segmented buttons, menus, toolbars, and the new breadcrumb bar.

At this point, we can use the `addListener` or `on` methods to add some actions when buttons and options are clicked on, but in the next chapters, you are going to learn about how to listen for events in a more convenient way.

Also, we created as an exercise a few toolbars, and we will use them in upcoming chapters for our final application. In the next chapter, you will learn about the basics of forms that use listeners, and different ways to set items and properties inside configuration objects.

6

Doing It with Forms

Ext JS comes with powerful widgets for collecting and editing data. We have the form component and many types of input widgets. These include the textfield, textarea, radio, checkbox, combobox, slider, and many more types.

In this chapter, you are going to learn about the components we can use to collect data in our applications. Also, we will work on some parts to be reused for our final application, as well as create some forms.

The following topics will be covered in this chapter:

- The form component
- The available field types
- The field container
- Submitting data

The form component

Ext JS contains a component called Ext.form.Panel. This component is a subclass of Ext.panel.Panel and uses Ext.form.Basic as a required class. This class is fundamental for handling the form's submission.

When designing applications, it's important to mention that a previous analysis may be clear for us, so we create blocks (code, forms, components, and so on) that can be reused in other modules. The following screenshot represents a part of our application. We can see that the form component will need to have certain functionalities, such as create, edit, delete, and so on.

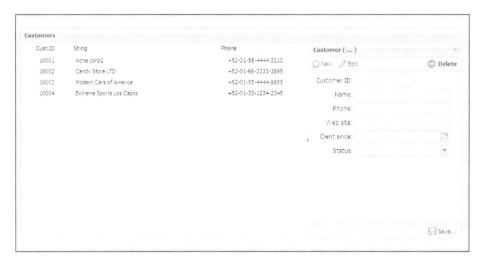

As you can see, the form prototype on the right side contains a title, one toolbar at the top, one toolbar at the bottom, and then six fields. Now we can begin creating the form as a separate component. As in our previous code samples, we extend our new class from the `Ext.form.Panel` class:

```
Ext.define('MyApp.view.CustomerForm01', {
    extend: 'Ext.form.Panel',
    alias: 'widget.customerform01',
    height: 280,
    width: 448,
    bodyPadding: 6,
    title: 'Customer ( .... )',
    items: [ ],
    dockedItems: [ ]
});
```

This code so far does not do very much. We are creating the base code to extend later in the form panel. As you can see, this code sets some default attributes, such as `height`, `width`, `bodyPadding`, and `title`. So far, the items and docked properties are empty.

Keep in mind the conventions defined in *Chapter 2*, *The Core Concepts*, when creating classes. So, we need to create the file and place the previous code in the `appcode/view/CustomerForm01.js` path.

As in the previous code samples, let's create the HTML file and run it to test our basic configuration:

```
<!doctype html>
<html>
<head>
  <meta http-equiv="X-UA-Compatible" content="IE=edge">
  <meta charset="utf-8">
  <title>Extjs - Form 01 </title>
    <link rel="stylesheet" type="text/css" href="../ext-5.1.1/build/
packages/ext-theme-neptune/build/resources/ext-theme-neptune-all.css">
    <script src="../ext-5.1.1/build/ext-all.js"></script>
    <script src="../ext-5.1.1/build/packages/ext-theme-neptune/build/
ext-theme-neptune.js"></script>

<link rel="stylesheet" type="text/css" href="../shared/styles/buttons.
css">
<script type ="text/javascript" src="form_01.js"></script>
</head>
<body style="padding:6px;">
</body>
</html>
```

Now let's create the `form_01.js` file with the following code:

```
Ext.Loader.setConfig({
    enabled: true,
  paths:{Myapp:'appcode'}
});
Ext.require([
  'Ext.form.*',
  'Ext.toolbar.*',
  'Ext.button.*',
  'Myapp.view.CustomerForm01'
]);
Ext.onReady(function(){
  var mypanel = Ext.create('Myapp.view.CustomerForm01',{
    title:'My first customer form...',
    renderTo: Ext.getBody()
  });
  console.log ('Ok');
});
```

Let's run and test the basic code. We will get a result similar to this:

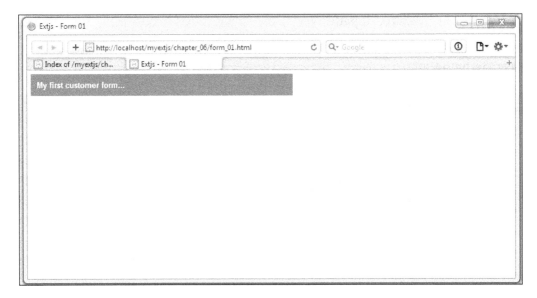

The form panel is created without any content or items. Remember that we can add any available component and widget, so now let's add some fields. Let's change the `items` property as shown in the following code:

```
items: [{
xtype: 'numberfield',
anchor: '60%',
  fieldLabel: 'Customer ID'
},{
xtype: 'textfield',
anchor: '-18',
fieldLabel: 'Name'
},{
xtype: 'textfield',
fieldLabel: 'Phone'
}]
```

The `items` property now has three fields: one number field and two text fields. Also, we set the `anchor` property on two fields, and the third is without it.

 By default, `Ext.form.Panel` uses the anchor layout, which is explained in *Chapter 3, Components and Layouts*.

Let's refresh our browser and see the next result, as follows:

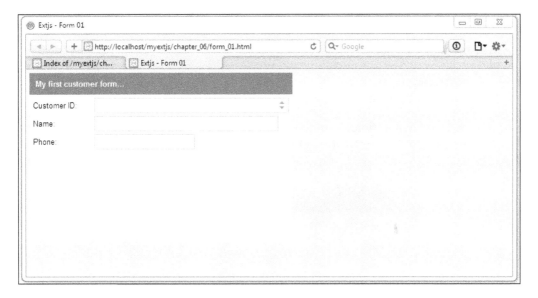

Okay, so now we have three fields in our form, and you can notice that each field has a different width. From Ext JS version 4 onward, we can set them individually for each field, such as `labelWidth`, `labelAlign`, and other properties. We have two useful properties inside the form panel, which are `defaultType` and `defaults`.

The `defaultType` property lets us set the default xtype for each field (where the `xtype` property is not defined), and the `defaults` property lets us define many configurations that will be applied to all child items (if it's possible to apply them). Let's make the following change to the form class:

```
Ext.define('MyApp.view.CustomerForm01', {
    extend: 'Ext.form.Panel',
    alias: 'widget.customerform01',
    height: 280,
    width: 448,
    bodyPadding: 6,
  defaultType:'textfield',
  defaults:{
    anchor:'-18',
    labelWidth:90,
    labelAlign:'right'
  },
    title: 'Customer ( .... )',
    items: [{
```

```
            fieldLabel: 'Customer ID',
                },{
            fieldLabel: 'Name',
                },{
    fieldLabel: 'Phone',
    }],
      dockedItems: [ ]
    });
```

Now all the three items/fields will have `anchor`, `labelWidth`, and `labelAlign` at the same frequency. Let's refresh the browser and see the result, which should be like this:

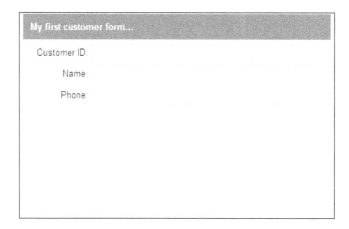

We converted the three fields to `textfield`. Also, the label alignment was set to the `right` and all have the same width. As you can see, the use of `defaultType` and `defaults` is very convenient, so we will have to code only a few lines in our file, and this code will be applied to many fields/components.

Therefore, according to our `Customers` form, let's create the other fields and the toolbars. Let's change the `items` property as follows:

```
    items: [{
    xtype: 'numberfield',fieldLabel: 'Customer ID',
    },{
      fieldLabel: 'Name',
    },{
    fieldLabel: 'Phone',
    },{
    fieldLabel: 'Web site',
    },{
    xtype: 'datefield',fieldLabel: 'Client since',
```

```
}, {
xtype: 'combobox',fieldLabel: 'Status',
}],
```

Now let's create the toolbars (as shown in *Chapter 5, Buttons and Toolbars*):

```
dockedItems: [{
  xtype: 'toolbar',
  dock: 'bottom',
  items: [{
    xtype: 'tbfill'
  }, {
    xtype: 'button',
    iconCls: 'save-16',
    text: 'Save...'
  }]
}, {
  xtype: 'toolbar',
  dock: 'top',
  items: [{
    xtype: 'button',
    iconCls: 'addicon-16',
    text: 'New'
  }, {
    xtype: 'button',
    iconCls: 'editicon-16',
    text: 'Edit'
  }, {
    xtype: 'tbfill'
  }, {
    xtype: 'button',
    iconCls: 'deleteicon-16',
    text: '<b>Delete</b>'
  }]
}]
```

 Notice that we are reusing the same CSS classes as in *Chapter 5, Buttons and Toolbars*. However, you can use new classes and other icons as well.

We have finished our first form, but it is not doing anything yet. We will add the functionality shortly. For now, let's just move forward and check out the other sections in order to understand more about Ext JS's available fields.

The anatomy of the fields

Ext JS provides many components to give the user a great experience when using their applications. The following fields are components we can use in a form or outside of it.

For example, we can add a text field or a combobox inside a toolbar instead of buttons, so in this way, we can place fields inside the toolbar in order to make them act like filters or search options.

Every input field extends the `Ext.Component` class. This means that every field has its own life cycle and events and can also be placed on any container.

There's also a class called `Ext.form.field.Base` that defines common properties, methods, and events across all form fields. This base class also extends from the `Ext.form.Labelable` and `Ext.form.field.Field` classes (by the use of mixins).

The `Labelable` class gives the field the ability to display a label and errors in every subclass, such as textfields, comboboxes, and so on.

The `Field` class gives the fields the ability to manage their value, because it adds a few important methods, such as the `getValue` and `setValue` methods, to set and retrieve the current value of the field. This class also introduces an important concept, the **raw value**.

A great example of the raw value is when we pull data from our server and get a date value in string format. The raw value is in plain text, but the value of the date field should be in a native `Date` object so that we can work easily with dates and times. We can always use the raw value, but it's recommended to use it instead. It is a `Date` object in this example.

The available fields

Ext JS provides many widgets that we can use to collect and edit data in our forms. You are going to learn about the most useful widget and configurations that you can use to create beautiful forms. Some of the fields we are going to see are as follows:

- `text`
- `number`
- `combobox` and `tag`
- `date`
- `checkbox` and `checkboxGroup` fields
- `radio` and `radioGroup` fields

The fields that we are going to cover are the basic ones. Ext JS provides many more fields, which can be seen in the Ext JS examples, and also many of them are based on subclasses from these. For the following examples, we are going to create a class that extends from the Form class and holds the fields that we are going to explain in detail later on:

```
Ext.define('Myapp.view.AvailableFields01', {
    extend: 'Ext.form.Panel',
    alias: 'widget.availablefields01',
    requires: ['Ext.form.*'],
    height: 280,
    width:448,
    bodyPadding: 6,
    title: 'Available Fields',
    defaultType:'textfield',
    defaults:{
        anchor:'-18',
        labelWidth:100,
        labelAlign:'right'
    },
     initComponent: function() {
        var me = this;
        var myItems = me.createFields();
        Ext.applyIf(me,{items: myItems});
        me.callParent(arguments);
     },
    createFields: function (){
        var newItems=[];
        return newItems;
    }
});
```

In this example we set the initComponent function. Here, we can create code for different events: initialization, field validation, and so on. In this case, we are calling the createFields function in order to get the fields we need to set on the property Items.

Also, we defined the createFields function. This is where we are going to set the other fields while we are advancing in this chapter.

 Using a function to define the items array is a great way of writing our code for readability. Also, if you wish to extend this class, we can override this method and add more components to your form in the subclass.

The TextField class

We have already used the TextField class to create our Customer form panel, and we used the xtype property to create it. We can always create the instance using the Ext.create method, and the class that we should instantiate is Ext.form.field. Text.

This class extends from the Ext.form.field.base class and is intended to manage text as a string value. It defines some important events, such as keydown, keypress, and keyup. These events are very useful for catching the keys that the user enters in a textfield component.

It's important to keep in mind that if we want to use these events, we need to set the enableKeyEvents property to true. Therefore, let's change our createFields function to the following code:

```
createFields: function (){
var newItems=[];
// Step 1
var myTextField = Ext.create('Ext.form.field.Text',{
    fieldLabel:'Name',
    name:'firstname',
    enableKeyEvents : true
});
// Step 2 (assign listener to the text field)
myTextField.on({
  keyup:{
    fn:function( thisField, evt, eOpts ){
      if(evt.getCharCode() === evt.ENTER){
      if (thisField.getValue()!=''){
        Ext.Msg.alert('Alert','Welcome: '+
thisField.getValue() );
        }
        }
      }
    }
  });
  newItems.push( myTextField );
  return newItems;
}
```

In Step 1, we created a new instance of the Ext.form.field.Text class and set the fieldLabel, name, and enableKeyEvents properties.

In the second step, we attached an event listener to the field. In this case, the field will react to the `keyup` event. So, every time the user releases a key on the keyboard, the callback function will be executed. In the code, we wait for the user to press the **Enter** key, and when that happens, the code shows an alert message with the value entered on the text, if there is any value for the field.

 Ext JS provides a wrapper for the native event object. This wrapper defines many constants, such as the Enter key. We can see all the available constants in the Ext JS documentation, in the `Ext.event.Event` class.

Okay, now let's run the code or refresh the browser to see how the text field works. You may see something like this:

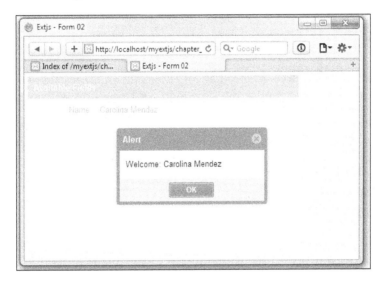

As we can see in the previous example, all the fields extend from the `Observable` class. Therefore, we are able to add events and listeners to all form fields. We should take a look at the documentation to see all the available events that we can use to our advantage.

Other common properties frequently used on text field are `minLength` and `maxLength`. These two properties allow on field restrictions and possesses a range of a minimum number and a maximum number of input characters that the field can accept. Let's change the text field properties to implement these features:

```
var myTextField = Ext.create('Ext.form.field.Text',{
    fieldLabel:'Name',
    name:'firstname',
```

```
    enableKeyEvents : true,
    minLength : 4,
     minLengthText: 'Name is too short, at least {0} chars..!',
    maxLength : 25,
    maxLengthText: 'Name is too long, max length is {0} chars..!'
});
```

The `minLength` property is set to `4`, so Ext JS will handle/ensure that the minimum length is met, otherwise the field will be marked as invalid and with an error. See the following screenshot to understand this:

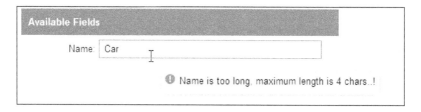

As you can notice, this field is marked as invalid (with an error), thanks to the red border. Now let's place the mouse over the field, and a tool tip will appear.

By default, fields in Ext JS have a property called `msgTarget`. This property will set how the error message should be displayed on the field. The most common values for this property are `qtip`, `under`, and `side`. Also, Ext JS allows us to customize the error message with the help of the `minLengthText` and `maxLengthText` properties. Consider the following line of code:

```
    minLengthText: 'Name is too short, at least {0} chars..!',
```

In the preceding line of code, the `{0}` part will be like a variable/placeholder to be replaced automatically by Ext JS, using the `minLength` value if the min length is not fulfilled.

 You can define the `msgTarget` property in all the field components that Ext JS handles, and you can also assign customized messages for errors according to your needs.

It's important to mention that we should take a look at the documentation to see all the available configuration options, properties, and events that we can use to our advantage, and use them according to our needs.

The number field

When dealing with numbers, Ext JS has a number field that only accepts numbers as values. In this way, we can ensure that the user will not be able to introduce any invalid characters. We can also customize the value range to be accepted (minimum and maximum values), decimal places, and much more. This field comes with integrated spinners/triggers to let us increase or decrease the value in it.

Let's add the following code to our `createFields` function:

```
createFields: function (){
  var newItems=[];
  ...
  newItems.push( myTextField );
  var myAgeField = Ext.create('Ext.form.field.Number',{
    fieldLabel:'Age',
    name:'age',
    minValue: 18,
    maxValue: 70,
    allowDecimals : false
  });
  var myIncomeField = Ext.create('Ext.form.field.Number',{
    fieldLabel:'Income',
    name:'income',
    minValue: 0,
    allowDecimals : true,
    decimalPrecision : 2,
    negativeText : 'The income cannot be negative..!',
    msgTarget:'side'
  });
  newItems.push( myAgeField );
  newItems.push( myIncomeField );
  return newItems;
}
```

We are adding two fields, one for age and the other for income. The **age** field has a validation value range from 18 to 70; other values will make this field invalid. The **income** field, on the other hand, allows decimals (`allowDecimals: true,` `decimalPrecision: 2,`), but does not allow negative values. Otherwise, we will get the **The income cannot be negative..!** message error. Now refresh the browser and test the new fields; you should see something like the following screenshot:

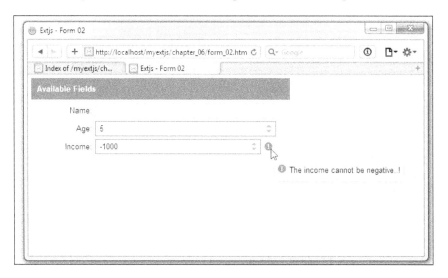

Check out the **Income** field; we set the `msgTarget` property to `side`. This creates an alert icon next to the field (to the right side), and when we place the mouse arrow over the icon, the tooltip appears showing the error message set in the `negativeText` property. Also notice that the age field is marked as invalid because the value is **5**.

Notice that on the right side of the field, there is the spinner/trigger (up arrow and down arrow). This lets us increase the value according to the `step` property. By default, it is set to `1`, but we can change it. Let's make a small change to the income field; we add the step property and set its value to 500. Refresh browser and check the increment when pressing the up button from the spinner, as shown here:

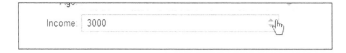

Finally, we need to make a change to the age field. This field doesn't require the spinner to be there, so it's fine for us to hide the spinner from the numeric field with the `hideTrigger` property:

```
var myAgeField = Ext.create('Ext.form.field.Number',{
    fieldLabel:'Age',
    name:'age',
    minValue: 18,
    maxValue: 70,
    allowDecimals: false,
    hideTrigger:true
});
```

In this way, the spinners will not be shown and we will have something similar to a text field, with the ability to accept only numbers.

 If you set more triggers to this field, the `hideTrigger` property will also consider them to be hidden (we will talk about triggers later).

There are many more configurations for this field, such as the ability to change the decimal separator so that only numbers without decimals will be allowed, and many more options that we can use to our advantage.

 Even if we accept numbers (a text field or number field), it's important to set validations on the server side and never rely on the client side. Not using server-side validation may be subject to code injections.

The ComboBox field

The ComboBox field is one of the most widely used widgets in Ext JS. This type of field lets us display a list of options (select input). It is a very flexible component that we can customize to our needs.

Also, these types of fields rely on the data package (store), which you have learned earlier in this book (*Chapter 4, It's All about the Data*). We are going to use the `Store` class with a local data to fill our combobox. So let's create the code for our combobox in our `createFields` function:

```
//Combobox Step 1 (store)
var occupationStore = Ext.create('Ext.data.Store',{
    fields: ['id', 'name'],
    data  : [
        {id: 1 ,name: 'CEO' },
        {id: 2 ,name: 'Vicepresident' },
        {id: 3 ,name: 'Marketing manager' },
```

```
        {id: 4 ,name: 'Development manager' },
        {id: 5 ,name: 'Sales manager' }
    ]
});
//Combobox Step 2 (create field)
    var myFirstCombo  = Ext.create('Ext.form.ComboBox', {
    fieldLabel: 'Occupation',
    name:'employeeoccupation',
    store: occupationStore,
    queryMode: 'local',
    displayField: 'name',
    valueField: 'id'
});
    newItems.push( myFirstCombo);
```

Step 1 is the definition of the store with static (local) data that the combobox will use. Also note that this store is not using an existing model (as seen in *Chapter 4, It's All about the Data*); Ext JS internally creates the model, thanks to the field's property that we set on the store.

In Step 2, we create Ext.form.ComboBox, defining the name for the fieldLabel property as the previous fields. But there are some new configurations set in order to make the combobox work properly.

First, we set the store property. The combobox will use it to display the data (options). The queryMode property set to local indicates to the combobox not to load data of the store in a remote way (when the list of options is displayed). Finally, we set how the combobox field will display and handle the selected option with the displayField and valueField properties.

Let's save the changes and refresh our browser to see the following result:

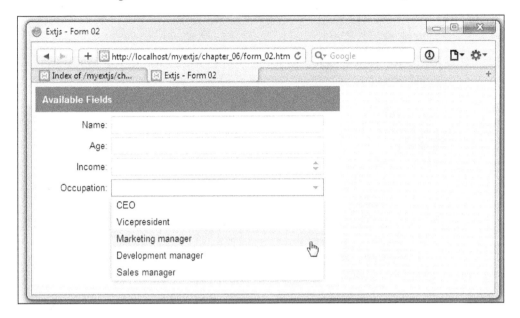

We are watching the combobox we created. Now set the focus on the combobox field and type **de**. You can see that the combobox will automatically reduce the list, as shown in this screenshot:

Internally, the combobox will try to filter its store's data according to what the user is typing to reduce the range of selection and make a quick selection process (for better user experience).

Now, since we are using a store to hold the displayed data, we can use an AJAX proxy to get the content of the store from our server. Try changing the code in the store like this:

```
var occupationStore = Ext.create('Ext.data.Store',{
  fields  : ['id','name'],
  autoLoad:true,
  proxy:{
  type:'ajax' ,
  url :'serverside/occupations.json',
  reader:{
    type:'json',
    root:'records'
  }
  }
});
```

Now we need to create the occupations.json file. Create and save it inside the / serverside folder and place the following code in it:

```
{
  "success":true,
  "id":"id",
  "records":[
    {"id": 1 ,"name": 'CEO' },
    {"id": 2 ,"name": 'Vicepresident' },
    {"id": 3 ,"name": 'Marketing manager' },
    {"id": 4 ,"name": 'Development manager' },
    {"id": 5 ,"name": 'Sales manager' }
  ]
}
```

As you can see, we only changed the proxy of the store. We also defined an AJAX proxy and a JSON reader. Now, if we refresh our browser, we can see that the data loads remotely.

This is one of the greatest advantages of Ext JS. We can change things very easily because Ext is built with small classes that can be switched at any time. It's very common that we need to do something when an option from the list is selected; for example, loading another combobox or hiding or showing some other fields. We can listen to the select event and perform the required actions:

```
myFirstCombo.on('select',function(combo,records){
    Ext.Msg.alert('Alert',records[0].get('name'));
  });
```

The previous code listens to the `select` event and only shows an alert message with the name of the selected record. Here, we can do whatever we need, such as loading the data of another combobox depending on the selection of the first. The callback receives the array of records selected; it's an array because we can also configure our combobox to allow the user to select more than one option.

We can use any of the available events to perform some actions, but one of the most important events for this widget is the select event.

The Tag field

In version 5, the tag field was introduced. It is a subclass of the combobox. Its creation is similar, but it allows us to make multiple selections. Let's add this code to our `createFields` function:

```
var zonesStore = Ext.create('Ext.data.Store',{
  fields  : ['id','name'],
  data   : [
     {id: 1 ,name: 'Zone A' },
     {id: 2 ,name: 'Zone B' },
     {id: 3 ,name: 'Zone C' },
     {id: 4 ,name: 'Zone D' },
     {id: 5 ,name: 'Zone E' }
  ]
});
  var myFirstTag  =Ext.create('Ext.form.field.Tag', {
    fieldLabel: 'Select zone',
    store: zonesStore,
    displayField: 'name',
    valueField: 'id',
    filterPickList: true,
    queryMode: 'local'
  });
  newItems.push( myFirstTag );
```

As you can see, the process is similar to that of the combobox. In this case, we have a new property called `filterPickList`. This property will make sure that the selected options aren't displayed again when expanding the options list.

Upon refreshing the browser, we see the following result:

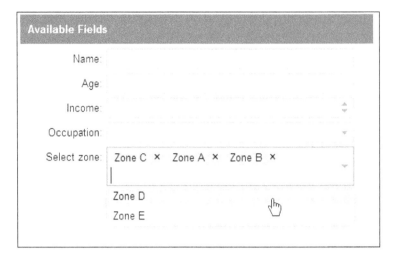

You can erase a selected item by clicking on the **X** sign on the right side of each selected option. Also, you can see that the selected options are not repeated in the list. One of the disadvantages of this field is that depending on the number of selections you have made, the size (height) of the field will grow.

The Date field

Ext JS provides an easy way to collect dates; we have at our disposal a date picker that will handle the selection of a date using a fancy calendar, or by allowing the user to type the date in the format we define. The most basic usage is by setting only the name and the label of the field, as shown in this code:

```
var datefield = Ext.create('Ext.form.field.Date',{
  fieldLabel: 'Birthday',
  name: 'birthday'
});
```

This will give us the following output:

We defined our date field in a very simple way, but there are many more configurations we can use. Let's dig a bit more to customize these fields to meet our requirements.

By default, the format used to display the date is m/d/Y (05/22/2012). This is a common format used in the U.S., but not in other countries. To define a custom format for a different region or country, we need to use the format property, as follows:

```
var datefield = Ext.create('Ext.form.field.Date',{
  fieldLabel: 'Birthday',
  name: 'birthday',
  format: 'd/m/Y',
  submitFormat: 'Y-m-d'
});
newItems.push( datefield );
```

We can use any format to display the date, and also set the format that we want the field to be in when we submit the form or retrieve it and when we get the values. Defining the submitFormat property is very important because it is this format that we will be using under the hood; in this example, we use a format common in databases.

The m/d/Y format refers to the commonly used mm/dd/yyyy format. This may be confusing, but we should take a look at the Ext.Date object documentation to see all the supported formats that we can use.

Right now, the user is able to type in the field to enter the date in the correct format. However, using slashes may slow down the user's typing. We can allow alternative formats to make things easier for them; for example, we can define d-m-Y as a valid format and as many other formats as needed:

```
var datefield = Ext.create('Ext.form.field.Date',{
  fieldLabel: 'Birthday',
  name: 'birthday',
  format:'d/m/Y',
  submitFormat:'Y-m-d',
  altFormats: 'd-m-Y|d m Y|d.m.Y'
});
```

Using the altFormats property, we can define all the formats we want. We only need to separate each format by a pipe character (|), and those formats will be used to parse the text to a date object. We should not use the pipe inside any of the formats because there is no way to escape this character. A format like m|d|Y will not work.

We have many more properties available, such as minValue and maxValue, and the ability to disable some specific dates, such as weekends and holidays:

```
var datefield = Ext.create('Ext.form.field.Date',{
fieldLabel: 'Deliver Date',
  name: 'deliverdate',
  format:'d/m/Y',
  submitFormat:'Y-m-d',
  altFormats: 'd-m-Y|d m Y|d.m.Y',
  disabledDates: ['31/12/2014','01/01/2015']
});
```

If we want to disable a range of days, we can use regular expressions to match the dates that we want to disable. Some examples are as follows:

```
//disable everyday in march 2012
disabledDates: ['../03/2012']

//disable everyday in march for every year
disabledDates: ['../03/..']
```

```
//disable the 05 and 21 of march for every year
disabledDates: ['05/03','21/03']
```

We can also use the `select` event which is fired when the user selects a date. We can do whatever we need inside the callback function, just as we did in the combobox.

The Checkbox and the CheckboxGroup fields

We have the option of using a single checkbox to set a single record as active or inactive. Or maybe, we can have a group of options that we need to display and allow the user to select a few of them. Let's add a single checkbox to our form:

```
var mysinglecheckbox = Ext.create('Ext.form.field.Checkbox',{
  fieldLabel:' ',
  labelSeparator:' ',
  boxLabel: 'employee has hobbies ? ',
  name: 'hobbies'
});
newItems.push( mysinglecheckbox );
```

Here, we have created our checkbox. We are using the `boxLabel` property to set the label of our checkbox. It's important to know that we are setting the `fieldLabel` and `labelSeparator` properties as empty space. Therefore, the checkbox will be aligned correctly. If we set `fieldLabel` as an empty string, then Ext JS will assume that no field label has been created, and this may cause something like what is shown in the following screenshot:

Now we have our checkbox in place. Having a single checkbox is great, but there are times when we need to define a few more options. We can use a group of checkboxes to arrange the components horizontally, vertically, or in columns:

```
//Step 1
var groupCheckboxes = Ext.create('Ext.form.CheckboxGroup',{
  fieldLabel: 'Hobbies',
  columns: 2,
  items: [
  {name: 'hobby',boxLabel: 'Videogames',inputValue: 'vg'},
  {name: 'hobby',boxLabel: 'Sports',inputValue: 'sp'},
```

```
    {name: 'hobby',boxLabel: 'Card games',inputValue: 'cg'},
    {name: 'hobby', boxLabel:'Movies',inputValue: 'mv'},
    {name: 'hobby', boxLabel:'Collecting toys',inputValue: 'ct'},
    {name: 'hobby', boxLabel:'Music',inputValue: 'ms'},
    {name: 'hobby', boxLabel:'Others...',inputValue: 'ot'}
    ]
});
newItems.push( groupCheckboxes );//Step 2
```

In the first step, we created an instance of the `CheckboxGroup` class. We defined the label of the group and gave each item a checkbox, with its label and value. We arranged the items in two columns. In the last step, we added the group to the returning array so that it appears in our form, like this:

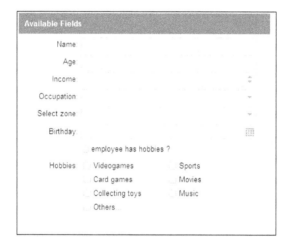

The Radio and RadioGroup buttons

Radio buttons are useful when we want to force the user to select only one item from a small group of choices. If we want to present more choices, a combobox is an easier widget to code and use.

A radio button is very similar to a checkbox. In fact, the radio button extends from the `Checkbox` class. This means that radio buttons also have the same properties and methods as the checkbox. Now let's proceed to add two radio fields to our form:

```
var radioYes = Ext.create('Ext.form.field.Radio',{
  name: 'option',
  fieldLabel: 'Employee has a car?',
    labelSeparator : '',
    boxLabel: 'Yes',
    inputValue : true
```

```
    });
    var radioNo = Ext.create('Ext.form.field.Radio',{
      name: 'option',
      hideLabel:true,
      boxLabel: 'No',
      inputValue: false
    });
    newItems.push( radioYes, radioNo  );
```

We are creating two instances of the `Radio` class in exactly the same manner as we created the `Checkbox` class. During the creation of the `Checkbox` class, we added two radio buttons to the returning array. The following screenshot shows what the two radio buttons that were created look like:

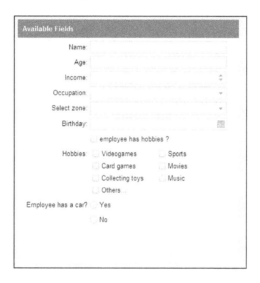

It is important to assign the same name to the radio buttons so that only one option can be selected among the available options.

As we can see in the previous screenshot, the radios are arranged one on top of the other because they were declared as separate instances. But what if we want to align them horizontally? We can use a `radiogroup` component, which is the most common practice for radio buttons, and set the number of columns as two. In this way, we will have our two radio buttons in the same line:

```
    var radioGroup  = {
      xtype: 'radiogroup',
      fieldLabel: 'Employee level',
      columns: 2,
      vertical:true,
```

```
items: [
  { boxLabel: 'Beginner', name: 'rb', inputValue: '1' },
  { boxLabel: 'Intermediate', name: 'rb', inputValue: '2'},
  { boxLabel: 'Advanced', name: 'rb', inputValue: '3',
  checked: true
  },
  { boxLabel: 'Ninja', name: 'rb', inputValue: '4' }
]};
newItems.push( radioGroup );
```

This is very similar to what we did with the checkbox group. We can define as many radio buttons as we need, and all of them will be arranged in two columns, as shown in the following screenshot:

Note that in the radio with `boxLabel: 'Advanced'`, we set a property called `checked`. This will allow us to set the initially selected radio button.

The field container

There are times when we need to group more fields or components other than checkboxes and radio buttons. Ext JS provides a field container for grouping of any type of field.

One of the advantages of using a field container is the ability to use a layout; we can use any of the available layouts in the framework. You learned about layouts in previous chapters.

The following code shows how we can group a textfield and a combobox to show these fields in the same line. Now we have to add two new fields and the field container:

```
var myFieldContainer = {
   xtype: 'fieldcontainer', //step 1
   height: '',
   fieldLabel: 'Shoes / Dress size',
   layout: { type: 'hbox', align: 'stretch' }, //step 2
   items: [{
        xtype: 'numberfield',
        flex: 1,
        hideLabel:true
},{
             xtype: 'splitter' //Step 3
      },{
        xtype: 'combobox',
        flex: 1,
        hideLabel:true,
        labelWidth: 10,
        store:Ext.create('Ext.data.Store',{
        fields   : ['id','name'],
        data: [
          {id:1 ,name:'small'},
          {id:2 ,name:'medium'},
          {id:3 ,name:'large'},
          {id:4 ,name:'Xl'},
          {id:5 ,name:'XXL'}
          ]
        }),
        queryMode: 'local',
        displayField: 'name',
        valueField: 'id'
    }
  ]
};
newItems.push( myFieldContainer );
```

First, we defined a config object and set the xtype property to 'fieldcontainer'. In step 2, we defined the layout property that fieldcontainer will use for the items contained in it. The layout used was flex in order to make it flexible.

In the third step, we created a splitter object (Ext.resizer.Splitter). In this way, we can *create a small gap* between the two fields. Finally, we set invisible labels using hideLabel:true on the combobox and numberfield properties respectively.

This was done because fieldcontainer will handle the fieldLabel property shown in the form. The form shown in this screenshot reflects the changes in our code:

This is how we can arrange the fields—in any way we want. Using the field container is a great way to accomplish this task. We can add as many components as we need, and also use any available layout for the field container component.

Triggers

In Ext JS version 5, the Trigger field was deprecated, and now triggers are set inside text fields. So now, we can add one or many triggers to a single field.

In order to work with triggers, let's write the following code:

```
var myTriggers = Ext.create( 'Ext.form.field.Text' , {
  fieldLabel: 'My Field with triggers',
  triggers: {
    searchtext: {
      cls: 'x-form-search-trigger',
```

```
    handler: function() {
      Ext.Msg.alert('Alert', 'Trigger search was clicked');
      this.setValue('searching text...');
    }
  },
  cleartext: {
    cls: 'x-form-clear-trigger',
    handler: function() {
      Ext.Msg.alert('Alert', 'Trigger clear was clicked');
      this.setValue('');
    }
  }
}
});
newItems.push( myTriggers );
```

First, we created an instance of the Ext.form.field.Text class, and set the triggers property, which will be a configuration object defining one or more triggers. In this case, we defined two: searchtext and cleartext. Each trigger has two properties:

- cls: This is used to define the icon that the trigger will use

- handler: This is the function that will be executed when the trigger is clicked on

Now let's check the handler of one trigger:

```
cleartext: {
  cls: 'x-form-clear-trigger',
  handler: function() {
    Ext.Msg.alert('Alert', 'Trigger clear was clicked');
    this.setValue('');
  }
}
```

When the `cleartext` handler is executed, an alert message will be displayed and then the `this.setValue('');` code will be executed. It's important to mention that the scope of the trigger's handler will be the component, which in this case is the instance of `Ext.form.field.Text` that we created. So, when `this.setValue('');` is executed, it will clear the value/text in the component itself. Refresh the browser and test the handlers of each trigger. You will see something similar to the following screenshot:

Submitting the data

So far, we have seen how to create and configure the components to collect data using the available widgets, but we need to do something with it. Ext JS provides different ways to submit the captured data to our server.

The `Ext.form.Panel` class contains an instance of the `Ext.form.Basic` class. This class is used to manage the data within the form, such as validations, settings, retrieving data from the fields, submitting and loading data from the server, and so on.

Let's make some slight changes to our first form:

```
Ext.define('Myapp.view.CustomerForm02', {
  ...
  initComponent: function() {
    var me = this;
    me.dockedItems= [{
      xtype: 'toolbar',
```

```
          dock: 'bottom',
          items: [
            {
              xtype: 'tbfill'
            },{
              xtype: 'button',
              iconCls: 'save-16',
              text: 'Save...',
              handler:function(){   //step one
                this.submitMyForm();
              },
              scope:this
            }
          ]
      }];
      Ext.applyIf(me,{});
      me.callParent(arguments);
    },
    submitMyForm:function (){ step 2
      var me = this;
      me.getForm().submit({
        url:'serverside/submitaction.php',
        success: function(form, action){
          Ext.Msg.alert('Success', 'Successfully saved');
        },
        failure: function(form,action){
          Ext.Msg.alert('Failure', 'Something is wrong');
        }
      });
    }
  });
```

We defined a handler on the **Save** button and executed the submitMyForm function
defined in the form panel. So, when the button is clicked on, the submitMyForm
function is executed.

In the second step, we defined the submitMyForm function. In this function, we get
what is in the basic form and then execute the submit method. This method receives
an object with the URL where the AJAX request will be made and the success/failure
callback.

The submit method executes an AJAX request using the POST method and sends
all of the data inside the form (either the input by the user or the hidden fields).
The way we get these parameters on the server side depends on the technology
we are using.

For example, if we are using PHP, we can use something like the following code:

```php
<?php
  $name   = $_POST['cust_name'];
  $phone  = $_POST['cust_phone'];
....
```

 When you handle values in the server-side files (PHP, ASP, and so on) you need to be careful to treat and validate POST values in order to avoid injections or hacking attempts.

You can check out how parameters are passed, as shown in the windows in the following screenshot:

The server code provided here is just an example and is not complete. The implementation of that is beyond the scope of this book. However, based on the received data, you can take that information and do whatever you need to do with it.

Summary

In this chapter, you learned about forms and the basic fields that you can use to collect and edit data. We have many options and configurations available, and we can use them to customize our forms. The field container is one of the new components added since version 4 of the Ext JS framework, and it allows us to arrange fields using any of the available layouts in the framework, giving us a powerful layout system.

You also learned about the new trigger configuration on text fields and how to submit data.

In the following chapter, you will learn about the grid component. This is one of the most powerful widgets in the framework because it's very flexible, with lots of plugins and configurations.

7
Give Me the Grid

The grid component is one of the most popular and widely used components of the Ext JS library. It allows us to display, sort, group, and perform many more operations in easy ways, thanks to the use of plugins and features. We can show grids with a large amount of data and get a nice performance from our application.

In this chapter, we are going to see how the Grid panel works and look at the basic configurations that we need. We will cover the following topics in this chapter:

- The basic Grid panel
- Columns
- Renderers
- Widgets and the widget column
- Selection models
- Grid listeners
- The Grid's features
- The Grid's Plugins — `CellEditing` and `RowEditing`
- Grid paging
- Infinite scrolling

The data connection (models and stores)

The main function of the Grid panel is to display data, so this means that we always need to use a store. In *Chapter 4, It's All about the Data*, we talked about the use of data packages (models and stores). Like other components, the grid uses the data in the store in order to display it. It's usually seen that Ext JS has classes that have their own responsibilities. On one hand, the grid is responsible for displaying data, while on the other hand, the responsibility of the store is to fetch, update, erase, and manipulate data.

At this moment, in order to advance further, we need to use the Customer data model used in the *One-to-one association* section of *Chapter 4, It's All about the Data*. The code is as follows:

```
Ext.define('Myapp.model.Customer'{
    extend:'Ext.data.Model',   // step 1
    requires: ['Myapp.model.Contract'],
    idProperty:'id',   // step 2
    fields:[ // step 3
      {name: 'id'    , type: 'int'},
      {name: 'name'    , type: 'string'},
      {name: 'phone'    , type: 'string'},
      {name: 'website' , type: 'string'},
      {name: 'status'  , type: 'string'},
      {name: 'country' , type: 'string'},
      {name: 'sendnews', type: 'boolean'},
      {name: 'clientSince', type: 'date', dateFormat: 'Y-m-d H:i'},
      {name: 'contractInfo', reference: 'Contract', unique:true }
    ]
});
```

As you may remember, we created a customer model that extends from Ext.data.model and has all the properties (fields) of the data that we need for each client. Now it's time to create the store that our first grid will use to display the data:

```
Ext.define('Myapp.store.customers.Customers', {
    extend: 'Ext.data.Store',
    model: 'Myapp.model.Customer',
    autoLoad: true,
    proxy:{
      type: 'ajax',
      url: 'serverside/customers.json',
      reader: {type:'json', rootProperty:'records'}
    }
});
```

Finally, we need the `customers.json` file, which may contain the response data that our store will retrieve:

```json
{
  "success" :"true",
  "id":"id",
  "records":[
    {
      "id": 10001,
      "name": "Acme corp2",
      "phone": "+52-01-55-4444-3210",
      "website": "www.acmecorp.com",
      "status": "Active",
      "clientSince": "2010-01-01 14:35",
      "sendNews": true,
      "contractInfo":{
        "id":444,
        "contractId":"ct-001-444",
        "documentType":"PDF"
      }
    },{
      "id": 10002,
      "name": "Candy Store LTD",
      "phone": "+52-01-66-3333-3895",
      "website": "www.candyworld.com",
      "status": "Active",
      "clientSince": "2011-01-01 14:35",
      "sendNews": false,
      "contractInfo":{
        "id":9998,
        "contractId":"ct-001-9998",
        "documentType":"DOCX"
      }
    }
  ]
}
```

Okay, so far we have defined the data connection for our first example. In a real-world application, we may need to get information from the server with the help of the store's proxies, such as XML, JSON, and so on.

A basic grid

Once we have defined our data package (model and store), we are ready to create our first grid. In this example, we are going to create the customers grid, as shown in the following code:

```
Ext.onReady(function(){
  var myStore = Ext.create("Myapp.store.customers.Customers");
  var myGrid = Ext.create('Ext.grid.Panel',{
    height: 250,
    width:  800,
    title: 'My customers',
    columns: [{
      width: 70,
      dataIndex: 'id',// *** model field name
      text: 'Id'
    },{
      width: 160,
      dataIndex: 'name', //***
      text: 'Customer name'
    },{
      width: 110,
      dataIndex: 'phone',//***
      text: 'Phone'
    },{
      width: 160,
      dataIndex: 'website',//***
      text: 'Website'
    },{
      width: 80,
      dataIndex: 'status',//***
      text: 'Status'
    },{
      width: 160,
      dataIndex: 'clientSince',//***
      text: 'Client Since'
    }],
    store: myStore,
    renderTo: Ext.getBody()
  });
});
```

In this code, we created a grid that renders itself in the document body of our web page. We assigned the `store` property to `myStore`, which is an instance of the `customers` store, so the grid will get the data from this store in order to display information.

An array was defined in the `columns` property. This array contains object configurations for each column that the grid's view will have.

In this case, each object (column configuration object) contains three properties: `width`, `dataIndex`, and `text`. The `dataIndex` property is responsible for assigning, which data field will be linked to the column.

 The model fields' names have to match the column's data index so that the grid renders the data properly.

Let's run this page in our browser. You may get something similar to the following screenshot:

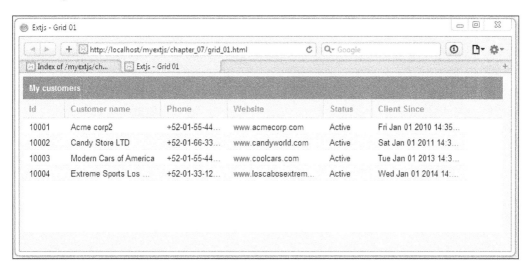

Now that you have your first Grid panel, note that the **Client since** and **Phone** columns in some cases show some dots (**...**). This is because the content in the cell exceeds the width of the column. In the next part, we will cover more details about columns and see how to fix the display and other things related to columns.

Columns

The Columns property in the Grid panel is for defining which columns the grid will have, show, hide, and so on. The Columns property can be an array of configuration objects or just a configuration object.

By default, each column is sortable, and also each column header has a menu that shows up when we click on the right-hand side of the column header. The column's menu lets us sort data and show or hide columns on the grid. Now take a look at the following screenshot:

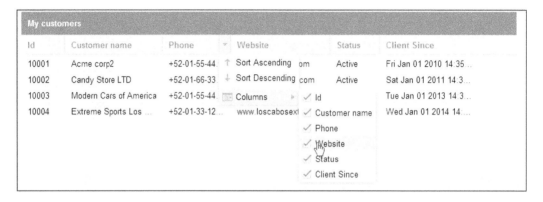

Ext JS offers many types of columns, and all are located under the Ext.grid.column namespace. In the next code, we are going to explain how the basic types of column work by modifying the code, as shown here:

```
columns: [{
  xtype: 'rownumberer'
},{
  xtype: 'numbercolumn',
  width: 70,
  dataIndex: 'id',
  text: 'Id',
  format: '0' //0,000.00
},{
  xtype: 'templatecolumn',
  text: 'Country',
  tpl: '<div><div class="flag_{[values.country.toLowerCase()]}">'
    + ' </div>  {country}</div>'
},{
  xtype: 'gridcolumn',
  width: 150,
```

```
    dataIndex: 'name',
    text: 'Customer name'
}, {
    xtype: 'datecolumn',
    dataIndex: 'clientSince',
    width: 110,
    text: 'Client Since',
    format: 'M-d-Y'
}, {
    xtype: 'booleancolumn',
    dataIndex:'sendnews',
    width: 120,
    text: 'Send News?',
    falseText: 'No',
    trueText: 'Yes'
}, {
    xtype: 'checkcolumn',
    dataIndex:'sendnews',
    width: 120,
    text: 'Send News ?'
}, {
    xtype: 'actioncolumn',
    width: 90,
    text: 'Actions',
    items: [{
        iconCls: 'editicon-16',
        tooltip: 'Edit customer',
        handler: function(grid, rowIndex, colIndex){
            var rec = grid.getStore().getAt(rowIndex);
            alert("Edit customer:" + rec.get('name'));
        }
    }, {
        iconCls: 'sendmail-16',
        tooltip: 'Send email to customer',
        handler: function(grid, rowIndex, colIndex){
            var rec = grid.getStore().getAt(rowIndex);
            alert("Send email to :" + rec.get('name'));
        }
    }]
}],
```

Let's refresh our browser or file. We will see something like what is shown in the following screenshot:

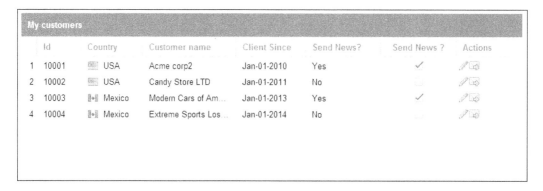

Now let's begin checking each column in detail.

The column row number

This column provides automatic row numbering. Usually, it does not need other settings, unless you want to customize width or alignment (by default, it is `right`), as seen in these examples:

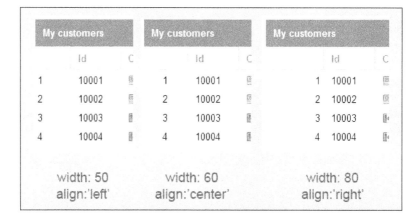

The number column

The number column is intended for use when we need to render numeric values and we can specify the proper numeric format using the `format` property:

```
{
    xtype: 'numbercolumn',
    dataIndex: 'id',
    text: 'Id',
    format: '0' //default value 0,000.00
}
```

You can see some format variations in the following screenshot:

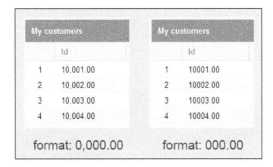

We can have multilanguage/localization support in our applications. To learn more, see `http://docs.sencha.com/extjs/5.1/core_concepts/localization.html`.

The template column

The template column renders the value by the use of a template configuration object for an `Ext.XTemplate` class, so we define the `Xtemplate` in the `tpl` property:

```
{
    xtype: 'templatecolumn',
    text: 'Country',
    dataIndex: 'country',
    tpl: '<div><div class="flag_{[values.country.toLowerCase()]}">' +
        ' </div>  {country}</div>'
}
```

In this case, when using a template column, it's recommended to use simple templates, otherwise it may compromise the performance of our app (because of the large amount of data).

The date column

This type of column renders a passed date according to our locale settings or a defined format set in the configuration settings:

```
{
  xtype: 'datecolumn',
  dataIndex: 'clientSince',
  text: 'Client Since',
  format: 'M-d-Y'
}
```

The output should look like the following screenshot:

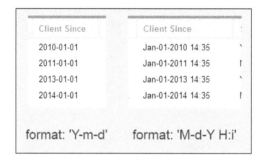

 To understand more about date formats, check out `Ext.Date` and `Ext.util.format` in the Ext JS documentation.

The Boolean column

This column helps us render Boolean values in our grids in an easy way. With the `trueText` and `falseText` properties, we can define the text to display in each case. In our example, we are setting the `Yes` and `No` values respectively on each property:

```
{
  xtype: 'booleancolumn', // important to define the boolean column
  dataIndex:'sendnews',
  text: 'Send News?',
  falseText: 'No',
  trueText: 'Yes'
}
```

The check column

This type of column renders a checkbox on each column cell and type of column, and this lets us toggle with a checkbox the value of the related field for each row. This type of column is recommended for use on grids that are intended to have an editing functionality:

```
{
    xtype: 'checkcolumn',
    dataIndex:'sendnews',
    text: 'Send News ?'
}
```

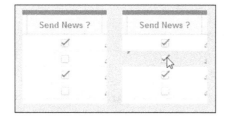

As you can see in the preceding image, the screenshot on the left side has data as shown in the original data. In the screenshot on the right side, we checked the box in the second row and a red triangle appeared in the top-left corner. This indicates to us that the record has had a change, but it has not yet been confirmed to be updated in the store/model.

The action column

This type of column lets us render one or many icons that will have a handler for each icon, letting us perform individual code for each desired action:

```
{
    xtype: 'actioncolumn',
    text: 'Actions',
    items: [{
        iconCls: 'editicon-16',
        tooltip: 'Edit customer',
        handler: function(grid, rowIndex, colIndex){
            var rec = grid.getStore().getAt(rowIndex);
            alert("Edit customer:" + rec.get('name'));
        }
    }]
}
```

One nice feature of this column is that we can set one `action icon` based on some conditions, like this:

```
items: [{
  getClass: function(v, meta, rec) {
    if (rec.get('sendnews')==0) {
      return 'sendmailblock-16';
    } else {
      return 'sendmail-16';
    }
  },
  getTip: function(v, meta, rec) {
    if (rec.get(' ')==0) {
      return 'Do not Send';
    } else {
      return 'Send Email for news...!';
    }
  },
  handler: function(grid, rowIndex, colIndex) {
    var rec= grid.getStore().getAt(rowIndex),
    action = (rec.get('sendnews')==0 ?'' : 'Send');
    if (action==''){
      Ext.Msg.alert('Alert..!', "you can't send news...!");
    } else {
      Ext.Msg.alert(action, action +' news to '+ rec.get('name'));
    }
  }
}]
```

This new configuration object will produce an output as follows:

Now that we have described the basic column types, you are ready to learn how column renderers work. Do not forget to take a look at the Ext JS documentation so that you can learn more about individual columns and their properties; then you can combine them according to your needs.

Column renderers

Column renderers give us the ability to customize the behavior and rendering of the cells inside a grid's panel. A renderer is tied to a particular column, and will run for each cell that it has to display/create in that column.

In the Ext JS library, many renderers are already set inside the `Ext.util.Format` class, such as `Ext.util.Format.dateRenderer`, `Ext.util.Format.uppercase`, and many more functions. To define a renderer in a column, we must add the `renderer` property, as shown in the following code:

```
{
  xtype: 'datecolumn',
  dataIndex: 'clientSince',
  text: 'Client Since',
  format: 'M-d-Y H:i',
  renderer: function(value, metaData, record, rowIndex, colIndex,
    store, view ){
    // Our code here....
  }
}
```

As we see, the function has some parameters, which are as follows:

*   `value`: This is the data value for the current cell.
*   `metaData`: This is a collection of metadata related to the current cell, such as `tdCls`, `tdAttr`, and `tdStyle`. This parameter is useful for changing or overriding the style (or styles) set by default by Ext JS.
*   `record`: This is the data model for the current row.
*   `rowIndex`: This is the current index of the row being worked on.
*   `colIndex`: This parameter is the current index of the column.
*   `store`: This is the current data store (the grid's store).
*   `view`: This is the grid's view.

When using a renderer, we need to return a string that will be the final output for the function (the cell display value). So now, let's add some renderers to our customer's grid, as follows:

```
columns: [{
  xtype: 'rownumberer',
  align:'center'
},{
```

```
  xtype: 'numbercolumn',
  dataIndex: 'id',
  text: 'Id',
  format: '0' //0,000.00
},{
  xtype: 'templatecolumn',
  text: 'Country',
  dataIndex: 'country',
  tpl: '<div><div class ="flag_{[values.country.toLowerCase()]}">'
     + ' </div>  {country}</div>'
},{
  width: 190,
  dataIndex: 'name',
  text: 'Customer name',
  // Renderer # 1
  renderer: function(value, metaData, record, rowIndex, colIndex,
    store, view ){
    if (record.get('country')!="USA"){
      metaData.tdCls = 'customer_foregin';
    }
    return value;
  }
},{
  xtype: 'datecolumn',
  dataIndex: 'clientSince',
  align: 'center',
  width: 150,
  text: 'Client Since',
  format: 'M-d-Y H:i',
  // Renderer # 2
  renderer: function(value, metaData, record, rowIndex, colIndex,
    store, view ){
  if (value.getFullYear() < 2014 ){
    metaData.tdStyle = " font-size:0.9em; color:#666; ";
  }
  return Ext.util.Format.date(value, 'Y-M-d');
}
},{
  width: 150,
  dataIndex: 'status',
```

```
    align: 'center',
     text: 'Status',
    // Renderer # 3
    renderer: function(value, metaData, record, rowIndex, colIndex,
      store, view ){
      var myclass= 'cust_' + value.toLowerCase();
      metaData.tdCls = myclass;
      if (value.toLowerCase()=='inactive'){
        metaData.tdStyle = " font-size:0.9em; ";
      } else if (value.toLowerCase()=='suspended'){
        metaData.tdStyle = " font-size:0.9em; ";
        metaData.tdAttr = 'bgcolor="ffc6c6"';
      }
      return value;
    }
  }],
```

In the previous code, we assigned renderers to three columns of the grid. Here is their explanation:

- `Renderer #1`: This is assigned to the **Customer name** column, and the function checks whether the customer is from USA or a foreign country. If it's a foreign country, then will apply the `customer_foregin` class to the cell by changing the value of `metaData.tdCls`. As you can see, we are using values from other fields to set a style for the customer name value.

- `Renderer #2`: In this one assigned to the **Client since** column, we check the year in which the customer began with us, and also check whether the year is earlier than 2014. Then we will change the style (color and font size). Also if you notice, this is a date column, but as soon as we set `renderer`, the `format` property will no longer be of any use because the renderer is the one responsible for the output.

- `Renderer #3`: Here, we assign a class upon the `var myclass= 'cust_' + value.toLowerCase();` to the **Status** value. Also, depending on the value, the class name will change the style and attributes of the Grid's cell when those conditions are met; for example, `cust_active`, `cust_prospect`, and so on.

It's important that renderers should not be too complicated or large in code, because this may compromise the performance and rendering time of the loaded records.

Let's see how the grid may look after these changes, as shown here:

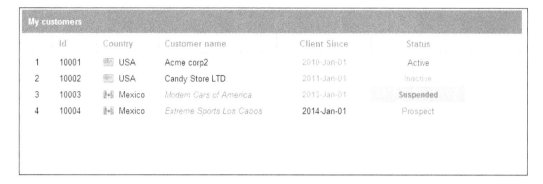

The Widget column

Ext JS 5 introduced in the last version a lightweight class called **widget** and a new type of grid column called **widget column**. Widgets are similar to components. They mainly consist of an `Ext.dom.Element` and associated listeners. Also, they are not derived from `Ext.Component`. Components have a more complex life cycle.

 For some review, check out the explanation of a component's life cycle in *Chapter 3, Components and Layouts*.

As a tradition, the flexibility and power that Ext JS offers let us create our custom widgets, and also, the library comes with some basic widgets, such as these:

- Progress Bar (`Ext.ProgressBarWidget` or `progressbarwidget`)
- Slider (`Ext.slider.Widget` or `sliderwidget`)
- Sparklines (`Ext.sparkline.*`):
    - Line (`sparklineline`)
    - Bar (`sparklinebar`)
    - Discrete (`sparklinediscrete`)
    - Bullet (`sparklinebullet`)
    - Pie (`sparklinepie`)
    - Box (`sparklinebox`)
    - TriState (`sparklinetristate`)

As we can't cover all of these in this chapter, we will check out only three of them. You can refer to the documentation to learn how to enhance or play with the properties of these widgets.

For our new example of widget columns, we will first create our model and store:

```
Ext.define('Myapp.model.CustomerWidgets',{
  extend: 'Ext.data.Model',  // step 1
  idProperty: 'id',   // step 2
  fields: [ // step 3
    {name: 'id', type: 'int'},
    {name: 'name', type: 'string'},
    {name: 'progress', type: 'float'},
    {name: 'piesequence'}
  ]
});
```

Our store will be the following:

```
var myStore = Ext.create('Ext.data.ArrayStore',{
  model: 'Myapp.model.CustomerWidgets',
  data:[
    [10001,"Acme corp2", 0.75, [30,14,20,36]],
    [10002,"Candy Store LTD", 0.9, [50,14,20,16]],
    [10003,"Modern Cars of America", 0.35, [15,10,39,36]],
    [10004,"Extreme Sports Los Cabos", 0.174, [30,29,5,18]
  ]
});
```

So now, let's create our grid in the same way as before, and we will focus on the column model, as shown in this code:

```
var myGrid = Ext.create('Ext.grid.Panel',{
  height: 250,
  width:  800,
  title: 'My customers',
  columns: [{
    xtype: 'rownumberer',
    align:'center'
  },{
    xtype: 'numbercolumn',
    dataIndex: 'id',
    text: 'Id',
```

```
      format: '0'
  },{
      width: 200,
      dataIndex: 'name',
      text: 'Customer name'
  },{
      xtype: 'widgetcolumn',
      text: 'Project Advances',
      dataIndex: 'progress',
      widget: {
        xtype: 'progressbarwidget',
        textTpl: [' <div style="font-size:0.9em;">{
          percent:number("0")}% done.</div> ']
      }
  },{
      xtype: 'widgetcolumn',
      text: 'Slider',
      width: 100,
      dataIndex: 'progress',
      widget: {
        xtype: 'sliderwidget',
        minValue: 0,
        maxValue: 1,
        decimalPrecision: 2,
        listeners: {
          change: function(slider, value) {
            if (slider.getWidgetRecord) {
              var rec = slider.getWidgetRecord();
              if (rec) { rec.set('progress', value); }
            }
          }
        }
      }
  },{
      xtype: 'widgetcolumn',
      width: 100,
      align:'center',
      dataIndex:'piesequence',
      text: 'Pie chart',
      widget: { xtype: 'sparklinepie' }
  }],
  store: myStore,
  renderTo: Ext.getBody()
});
```

We added three columns with `xtype` equal to `widgetcolumn`. On the first widget column, we set `dataIndex` and `text` as normal, and we added the `widget` property. This property is a configuration object, like creating any other new component.

The `xtype` was set to `progressbarwidget`, and we set the `textTpl` property. This will work in the same way as an `Ext.XTemplate` object.

In the second widget column, we set `dataIndex` the same as in the first widget column in order to make/update and interact with the values in the grid. In this case, the widget `xtype` was set to `sliderwidget`, and we added some specific properties of this widget, such as `minValue`, `maxValue`, and `decimalPrecision`.

We added a listener for the event change. It will be triggered when we move the slider, so it will update the progress field's value.

The third widget column is set with `xtype` as `sparklinepie`. This means that it will render a pie chart in the grid's cell. The `dataIndex` property for this column is `piesequence`, and you may notice that this value is an array that contains the values for each piece of the pie chart.

- Let's run the example code. We may see this result:

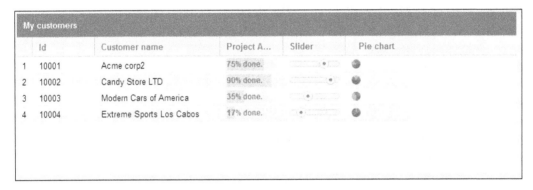

Now for the test, let's move the slider in row number 3 and see how the value in the third column changes as we move it, as shown in these two screenshots:

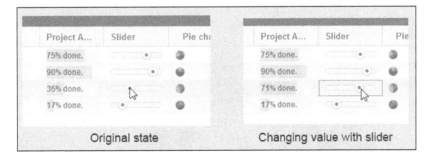

Having widgets in a grid's columns can be very useful for integrating more user interaction and functionality. Keep in mind, however, that as long as the data grows, or on larger datasets, it may slow down the performance of the grid.

Selection models

So far, we have seen how to create a basic grid and set the columns for displaying data. Selection models are an important part of the Grid panel, because they will let us set the manner in which we can interact in terms of selections (data selection) in the grid's view.

The two main selection models on the framework are `Ext.selection.RowModel`, where single or multiple rows are selected, and `Ext.selection.CellModel`, where individual grid cells are selected.

By default, the Grid panel uses `rowmodel` when it's not defined (as in our previous examples).

In the next example code, we need to use the code in which we set the action column icons, and make some changes (first of all, make a duplicate of the code). In the grid configuration, let's add the `selModel` property:

```
selModel:{
  selType:'rowmodel',
  mode:'SINGLE'
}
```

The `mode` property can have one of these three values:

- `SINGLE`: This allows selection of one item at a time
- `SIMPLE`: This allows us to make a simple selection of multiple items one by one
- `MULTI`: This allows us to select multiple items using the *Ctrl* and *Shift* keys

Now let's change the action column, as shown in the following code:

```
{
  xtype: 'actioncolumn',
  width: 90,
  text: 'Actions',
  items: [{
    iconCls: 'editicon-16',
    tooltip: 'Edit customer',
```

```
        handler: function(grid, rowIndex, colIndex){
          var mysm = grid.getSelectionModel();
          var selection = mysm.getSelection();
          var record = selection[0];
          alert('You are going to edit ' + record.get('name'));
        }
      }]
    }
```

Here is the explanation: when the user clicks on the pencil icon first, we set var mysm with the grid.getSelectionModel() method. This method will return us the current instance of the grid's selectionModel object. Then we set the selection variable with the mysm.getSelection() method. This method will return an array of the currently selected record/model (only one item), because we set the selection model mode to SINGLE.

The record variable will be the first element in the array (the selection variable), so we set the record equal to selection[0].

Let's run our example. We may get this result:

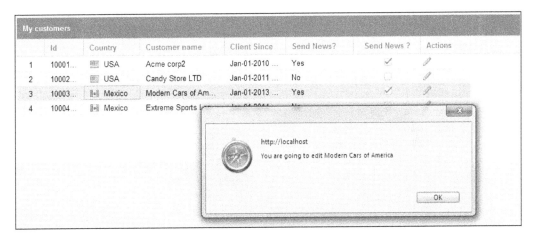

In this example, you can notice that only one row can be selected at a time (**click on the row or use the keyboard navigation keys**), so we won't be able to select multiple rows unless we change the mode property in the selModel property configuration.

Now the cell model behaves differently. Let's change the `selModel` property to `cellmodel` and refresh the browser. You will notice that only one cell has been selected, as follows:

Notice the blue border around the country cell on row 2. This means that only the cell with row 2 and column 1 is selected. Let's change the action columns to the following code:

```
{
  xtype: 'actioncolumn',
  width: 90,
  text: 'Actions',
  items: [{
    iconCls: 'editicon-16',
    tooltip: 'Edit customer',
    handler: function(view, rowIndex, colIndex){
      var model = view.getNavigationModel();
      var columnName = model.column.text;
      var columnDataIndex = model.column.dataIndex;
      var myData = model.record.get(columnDataIndex);
      alert('You are going to edit column: '+ columnName + ' with
        the value: ' + myData);
    }
  }]
}
```

In this code, what we did was this: first, we retrieved the column object configuration from the grid view with the `view.getNavigationModel()` code. Then we retrieved the value for the `columnName` and `columnDataIndex` variables. After these variables were set, we got the data value of the selected cell with the `model.record.get(columnDataIndex)` code, because in the model object the related selected record and cell are also included. Let's look at the following screenshot, where we can see our code in action:

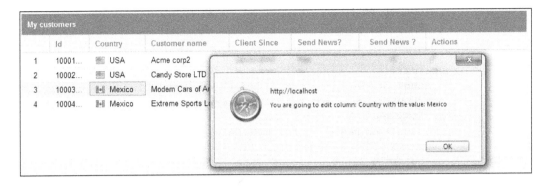

Grid listeners

The event listener is a core feature in the components of the Ext JS library. The Grid panel is not an exception. Because of its nature, this panel has a very well designed set of listeners that allow us to process all kinds of events.

Taking our last example (the `rowmodel` selection), let's write some code to add event listeners to our grid. The code will look similar to this:

```
Ext.onReady(function(){
  Ext.tip.QuickTipManager.init();
  //Step 1
  var myEventsArea = Ext.create('Ext.form.field.TextArea',{
    itemId:'myResultArea',
    width : 400,
    height : 200,
    renderTo:'myResults'
  });
  var myStore = Ext.create("Myapp.store.customers.Customers");
  var myGrid = Ext.create('Ext.grid.Panel',{
    // Grid config
    listeners:{ //Step 2
      render:{
        fn:function(grid, eOpts){
          var myResult= Ext.ComponentQuery.query('#myResultArea')[0];
          var currentText= '\n' + myResult.getValue();
          myResult.setValue('Grid has render' + currentText);
        }
      },
      select:{
        fn:function(grid, record, index, eOpts){
          var myResult = Ext.ComponentQuery.query(
            '#myResultArea')[0];
          var currentText= '\n' + myResult.getValue();
```

```
            myResult.setValue('Record #(' + (index + 1)  + ')
               selected' + currentText);
          }
        },
        itemclick:{
          fn:function(grid, record, item, index, ev, Opts){
            var myResult = Ext.ComponentQuery.query(
               '#myResultArea')[0];
            var currentText= '\n' + myResult.getValue();
            var myNewMsg = 'Item #' + (index+1) + " was clicked (
               customer id=" + record.data.id + ")";
            myresult.setValue(myNewMsg + currentText);
          }
        },
        itemkeydown:{
          fn:function(grid, record, item, index, ev, eOpts){
            var myResult = Ext.ComponentQuery.query(
               '#myResultArea')[0];
            var currentText= '\n' + myResult.getValue();
            var myNewMsg = '';
            var myKey = ev.getKey();
            if (myKey === ev.DELETE ){
              myNewMsg = "Delete Record";
            } else if (myKey == ev.RETURN ){
              myNewMsg = "Edit customer #" + record.data.id + "";
            } else if ((myKey === ev.N && ev.shiftKey)||
               myKey=== ev.F8 ){
              myNewMsg = "Add new record";
            } else if ((myKey === ev.D && ev.shiftKey)){
              myNewMsg = "view detail of customer #"  +
                 record.data.id + "";
            } else if (myKey ===ev.F9 ){
              myNewMsg = "Other action...";
            } else {
              return;
            }
            myResult.setValue(myNewMsg + currentText);
          }
        }
      }
    });
  });
```

The steps of this code are explained as follows:

- `Step 1`: We created a Text Area field to show the event results (the grid's event listeners).

- Step 2: We added the `listeners` property (as a configuration object) to the grid's configuration in the `listeners:{...}` code.

- Step 3: Inside the `listeners` property, we added four listeners. Each one, when triggered, will display new text in the text area field. The listeners are as follows:

  - `render`: This one will be triggered when the grid has been rendered (finish render).

  - `select`: This event is triggered when a record is selected.

  - `Itemclick`: This is triggered when an item (inside the grid view) is clicked.

  - `Itemkeydown`: This is triggered when a key is pressed down while an item is currently selected. On this last listener, we set to show a message only if the following combinations are pressed: *Delete*, *Enter*, *N + Shift*, *D + Shift*, *F8*, and *F9*. You can make any combination you want as long as you don't make a combination used by the browser.

As you can notice, each listener has different parameters. To find out exactly how many and what each parameter does, check out the Ext JS documentation at `http://docs.sencha.com/extjs/5.1/5.1.1-apidocs/#!/api/Ext.grid.Panel`, and go to the events section/menu.

Now let's refresh our browser and view the output, like this:

My customers							
	Id	Country	Customer name	Client Since	Send News?	Send News ?	Actions
1	10001...	USA	Acme corp2	Jan-01-2010 ...	Yes	✓	🖊
2	10002...	USA	Candy Store LTD	Jan-01-2011 ...	No	☐	🖊
3	10003...	Mexico	Modern Cars of Am ..	Jan-01-2013 ...	Yes	✓	🖊
4	10004...	Mexico	Extreme Sports Los...	Jan-01-2014 ...	No	☐	🖊

```
Item #1 was clicked (curtomer id=10001)
Record #(1) selected
Item #4 was clicked (curtomer id=10004)
Record #(4) selected
Item #3 was clicked (curtomer id=10003)
Record #(3) selected
Item #2 was clicked (curtomer id=10002)
Record #(2) selected
Item #3 was clicked (curtomer id=10003)
Record #(3) selected
Grid has render
```

Test the example and the key combinations to see the output in the text area. You will also notice how the events we set behave. Moreover, remember that it is not always required to add listeners, or even add all listeners, but it's very useful to perform certain actions on real-world applications according to your needs.

Features

The `Ext.grid.feature.Feature` class is a new class included since Ext JS 4, and designed for being a type of plugin specific for the Grid panel. In older versions of the framework, plugins were the way of adding custom functionality to grids, but the Sencha team has created a more organized way of doing this.

With this class, we can inject additional functionality into certain points of the grid's creation cycle. Since Ext JS 4, we have four main classes that extend from the `Ext.grid.feature.Feature` class, as covered in the following sections.

Ext.grid.feature.Grouping

This feature displays the grid rows in groups. The configuration has to be done in the grid with the feature property, and has to be done on the grid store as well.

First, we have to change our store a little, as shown in the following code:

```
Ext.define('Myapp.store.customers.Customers',{
    extend:'Ext.data.Store',
    model: 'Myapp.model.Customer',
    groupField: 'country',
    autoLoad:true,
    proxy:{
        type:'ajax',
        url: 'serverside/customers.json',
        reader: {
            type:'json',
            rootProperty:'records'
        }
    }
});
```

Here in the store, we added a new property, `groupField`. This property will tell the store and grid which field to group by. Now we will add the following code for the grid in our example:

```
var myGroupingFeature = Ext.create('Ext.grid.feature.Grouping',{
    groupHeaderTpl: '{columnName}: {name} ({rows.length} Customer{
      [values.rows.length > 1 ? "s" : ""]})',
    hideGroupedHeader: false,
    startCollapsed: false
});
var myGrid = Ext.create('Ext.grid.Panel',{
    height: 250,
    width:  900,
    title: 'My customers',
    columns: [ /* columns here....*/],
    features: [myGroupingFeature],
    store: myStore,
    selModel:{
      selType:'rowmodel',
      mode:'SINGLE'
    },
    renderTo: 'myGrid'
});
```

In the `myGroupingFeature` variable, we created an instance of the grouping feature class, and so we assigned three properties:

- `groupHeaderTpl`: This is a string template that decides how we are going to show the group title (in the next chapter, you will learn about templates in more detail)

- `hideGroupedHeader`: This property specifies whether we are going to show the column specified for the grouping or not (in this case, the country column)

- `startCollapsed`: This is used to specify whether to show all groups collapsed or expanded

Inside the grid's configuration, we set the `features` property as an array with an element called `myGroupingFeature`. Keep in mind that we can add more than one feature to the grid. Let's run our code, and we will see something similar to this screenshot:

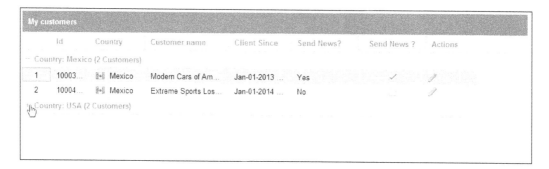

Ext.grid.feature.GroupingSummary

This feature adds an aggregate summary row at the bottom of each group that is defined by the `Ext.grid.feature.Grouping` feature. This feature has several built-in summary types, such as count, sum, min, max, and average.

Let's add a grouping summary feature to our grid, as shown in the following code. Use the previous example's code as a base:

```
var myGroupingSummaryFeature = Ext.create(
  'Ext.grid.feature.GroupingSummary',{
  groupHeaderTpl: '{columnName}: {name}',
  hideGroupedHeader: true,
  startCollapsed: false
});
```

Now we will change the column (ID) configuration, as follows:

```
{
  xtype: 'numbercolumn',
  width: 100,
  dataIndex: 'id',
  text: 'Id',
  format: '000.00',
  summaryType: 'count',
  summaryRenderer: function(value){
    return Ext.String.format('{0} student{1}',
    value, value !== 1 ? 's': '');
  }
}
```

Then let's add another column to the grid:

```
{
    xtype: 'numbercolumn',
    dataIndex:'employees',
    width: 160,
    format: '0',
    text: 'Customer Employees',
    summaryType: 'sum'
}
```

In this type of feature (groupingSummary), we need to set the summaryType property on the desired columns and specify which type of summary will perform. In the case of the column ID, we set the summaryRenderer property, which is a function. This function will be called before displaying a value; it's optional, and if it's not defined, the default calculated value will be shown:

```
summaryRenderer: function(value){
    return Ext.String.format('{0} student{1}',
value, value !== 1 ? 's': '');
```

Let's run our example, and we may get the following result:

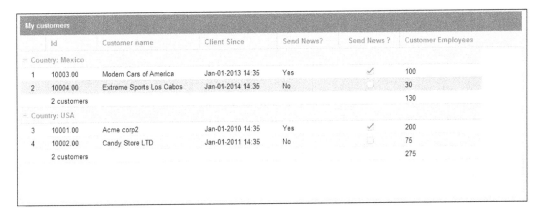

At the bottom of each group, we will see in the columns (**Id** and **Customer Employees**) the summary result we defined for each column (count and sum).

Ext.grid.feature.RowBody

This feature adds an extra TR->TD->DIV for each grid row that contains any markup. This `grid` feature is useful for associating additional data of a particular record. It also exposes additional events to the grid view, such as `rowbodyclick`, `rowbodydbclick`, and `rowbodycontextmenu`.

Now let's add the row body feature to our grid, as shown in the following code:

```
// Step 1
var myRowBodyFeature = Ext.create('Ext.grid.feature.RowBody',{
  getAdditionalData:function (data, index, record, orig){ //Step 2
    return {
      rowBody:'<span style="padding-left: 10px"><b>Website : </b>
        <a href="http://' + record.data.website + '" target=
          "_blank">' + record.data.website + '</a></span>'
    };
  }
});
```

In the Grid `features` property, set it to this:

```
features:[myRowBodyFeature], // Step 2
```

The steps are explained as follows:

- `Step 1`: We defined the `rowbody` feature
- `Step 2`: In the `getAdditionalData` method, we rendered the total data of our client in the `rowBody` property

With this configuration, we will have the output as shown in the following screenshot:

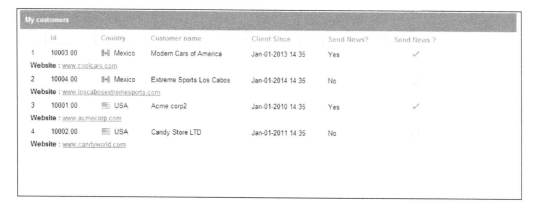

Ext.grid.feature.Summary

This is the last grid feature we are going to explain. This feature adds a summary row at the bottom of *all the grid rows* with aggregate totals for a column. The configuration for the columns that you want to set the summary type for is exactly the same as we saw in the `groupingsummary` feature. Let's create the feature, as follows:

```
var mySummaryFeature = Ext.create('Ext.grid.feature.Summary',{
  dock:'bottom'
});
```

Indeed, this feature does not have many properties. The most commonly used is the `dock` property, and its valid values are top and bottom. Let's set the `features` property to this:

```
features:[mySummaryFeature],
```

Now let's run the example. We may see this output:

	Id	Country	Customer name	Client Since	Send News ?	Customer Employees
1	10001.00	USA	Acme corp2	Jan-01-2010 14:35	✓	200
2	10002.00	USA	Candy Store LTD	Jan-01-2011 14:35		75
3	10003.00	Mexico	Modern Cars of America	Jan-01-2013 14:35	✓	100
4	10004.00	Mexico	Extreme Sports Los Cabos	Jan-01-2014 14:35		30
	4 Total customers					405 Total employees

Let's change the property `dock` to `top` and refresh our browser to see this:

	Id	Country	Customer name	Client Since	Send News ?	Customer Employees
	4 Total customers					405 Total employees
1	10001.00	USA	Acme corp2	Jan-01-2010 14:35	✓	200
2	10002.00	USA	Candy Store LTD	Jan-01-2011 14:35		75
3	10003.00	Mexico	Modern Cars of America	Jan-01-2013 14:35	✓	100
4	10004.00	Mexico	Extreme Sports Los Cabos	Jan-01-2014 14:35		30

Without setting any configuration property for the feature (the `dock` property), the result is the following:

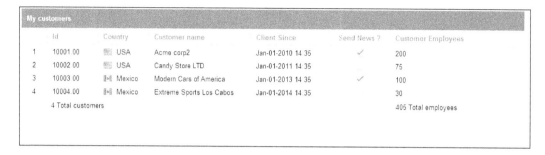

Plugins

The Grid's plugins provide custom/extra functionality for the component.

Overall, plugins in Ext JS don't need to extend another class, but the idea/purpose is to give extra functionality and behavior to existing components.

For the Grid panel, we have some plugins already implemented in the Ext JS library. The most commonly used are `Ext.grid.plugin.CellEditing` and `Ext.grid.plugin.RowEditing`.

These two extend `Ext.grid.plugin.Editing`, and their primary function is to provide the grid with the ability to make cells and rows editable.

 `Ext.grid.plugin.Editing` should never be used directly because it is the base class for `Ext.grid.plugin.CellEditing` and `Ext.grid.plugin.RowEditing`.

Also, to make the columns editable, it is recommended to set the `editor` property in the column configuration.

Ext.grid.plugin.CellEditing

This plugin makes a single cell in our grid editable. We can edit only a single cell at a time. The editor is defined in the `editor` property on each of the column's configurations. If we don't define an editor in a column, it will be skipped by the `editor` plugin.

It's recommended that we always choose an appropriate field type to match our data, so if we were using a date type, it would be useful to use an `Ext.form.field.Date` class.

Let's start configuring our grid and columns:

```
var myGrid = Ext.create('Ext.grid.Panel',{
  height: 250, width:  980, title: 'My customers',
  columns: [{
    xtype: 'rownumberer',
    width: 50,
    align:'center'
  },{
    xtype: 'numbercolumn',
    width: 100, dataIndex: 'id', text: 'Id',
    format: '000.00'
  },{
    width: 200,
    dataIndex: 'name',
    text: 'Customer name',
    editor:{ //Step 1
      xtype:'textfield',
      allowBlank:false,
      minLength:4,
      maxLength:70
    }
  },{
    xtype: 'datecolumn',
    dataIndex: 'clientSince', width: 150,
    text: 'Client Since',
    format: 'M-d-Y H:i',
    editor:{ //Step 1
      xtype: 'datefield',
      maxValue: new Date()
    }
  },{
    xtype: 'checkcolumn', //Step 2
    dataIndex:'sendnews',
    width: 120,
    text: 'Send News ?'
  },{
    xtype: 'numbercolumn',
    dataIndex:'employees',
    width: 160,
    format: '0',
    text: 'Customer Employees'
  }],
```

```
    store: myStore,
    selModel:{selType:'cellmodel'}, //Step 3
    plugins:{ptype:'cellediting',clicksToEdit:2}, //Step 4
    renderTo: 'myGrid'
});
```

In our previous code, we added the `cellediting` plug in. The steps are explained as follows:

- `Step 1`: We defined the editor property on some columns (**Customer name** and **Client since**). The `editor` property was defined as any Ext JS field ("We talked about fields in *Chapter 6, Doing It with Forms*).

- `Step 2`: The **Send News ?** column, which we defined as `checkcolumn`, automatically creates the editor (checkbox) for this cell.

- `Step 3`: We defined the grid's selection model as `cellmodel`.

- `Step 4`: We set the `plugins` property with a config object, set the `ptype` (plugin type) property to `cellediting`, and added the `clicksToEdit:2` property. This means when we double-click, we can begin editing the cell.

So let's run the example in our browser. We double-click on the **Client Since** cell, as shown in the following screenshot, and we can begin to edit:

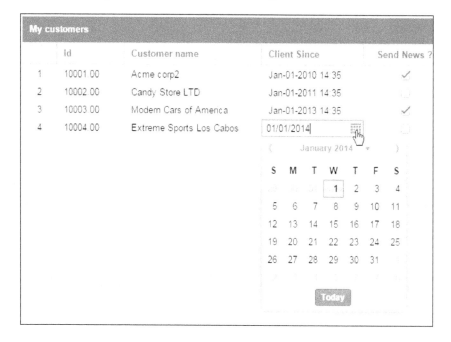

Change the value and press *Enter*. This will confirm the edit action for the cell. If you press *Esc*, then the edit action will be canceled. Now, after editing the cell, we will see that *a red triangle* has appeared in the top-left corner. This means that the record has changed and the new value is not yet committed as changed in the record (model) in our store.

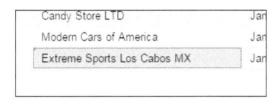

Ext.grid.plugin.RowEditing

This plugin adds full row editing capabilities to the Grid panel. When editing begins, each editable column will show the field for editing, a **Save** button, and a **Cancel** button, which will be displayed in the dialog for editing. Let's configure our grid for the RowEditing plugin:

```
var rowEditing = Ext.create('Ext.grid.plugin.RowEditing', {
  clicksToMoveEditor: 1,
  autoCancel: false
});   //Step 1

var myGrid = Ext.create('Ext.grid.Panel',{
  height: 250, width:  980, title: 'My customers',
  columns: [{
    xtype: 'rownumberer',
    width: 50,
    align:'center'
  },{
    xtype: 'numbercolumn',
    width: 100,
    dataIndex: 'id',
    text: 'Id',
    format: '000.00'
  },{
    width: 200,
    dataIndex: 'name',
    text: 'Customer name',
    editor:{
      xtype:'textfield',
```

```
            allowBlank:false,
            minLength:4,
        }   //Step 4
    },{
        xtype: 'datecolumn',
        dataIndex: 'clientSince',
        width: 150,
        text: 'Client Since',
        format: 'M-d-Y H:i',
        editor:{
            xtype: 'datefield',
            maxValue: new Date()
        }
    },{
        xtype: 'checkcolumn',
        dataIndex:'sendnews',
        width: 120,
        text: 'Send News ?'
    },{
        xtype: 'numbercolumn',
        dataIndex: 'employees',
        width: 160,
        format: '0',
        text: 'Customer Employees'
    }],
    store: myStore,
    selModel: {selType:'rowmodel'},   //Step 3
    plugins: [rowEditing],   //Step 4
    renderTo: 'myGrid'
});
```

The preceding code creates a Grid panel with a row editing plugin. The steps are explained as follows:

1. Step 1: We defined our row editing plugin in **var rowEditing**

2. Step 2: we defined the editors on the columns in the grid

3. Step 3: We set the selModel property to rowmodel, which in fact is not so indispensable

4. Step 4: Then we set the plugins property to [rowEditing]

Now, when we begin to edit the row, we can navigate through the row with the *Tab* key. To cancel the edit action, we can use the *Esc* key, and confirm the edit action with *Enter*.

Let's run the example. This last configuration outputs the grid shown in the following screenshot:

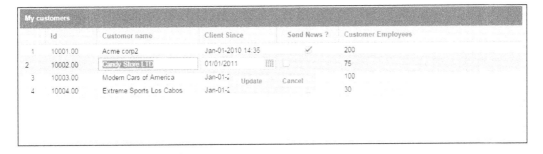

You can notice in the output that **Id** and **Customer Employees** have no field. This means that those columns are *read-only*, because we did not define an editor in their configurations. Also, you might have noticed the **Update** and **Cancel** buttons in the middle part below the row. These buttons can be clicked on to confirm each action.

When a column has no editor set, it is recommended that you use the `editRenderer` property. This renderer works as the normal column renderer property, but this property works when the row is edited:

```
{
    xtype: 'numbercolumn',
    dataIndex:'employees',
    width: 160,
    format: '0',
    text: 'Customer Employees',
    editRenderer: function(value){
        return 'can\'t edit'
    }
}
```

This will give us the following output:

Grid paging

The Grid panel supports paging through a large set of data with the help of a
`PagingToolbar` item. To accomplish this we have to make some modifications to
our store and add a `PagingToolbar` item to our grid. For this, we need to create our
store, as shown in the following code:

```
Ext.define('Myapp.store.customers.CustomersC',{
    extend:'Ext.data.Store',
    model: 'Myapp.model.Customer',
    pageSize: 3,
    autoLoad:true,
    proxy:{
        type:'ajax',
        url: 'serverside/customersc.php',
        reader: {
            type:'json',
            rootProperty:'records',
            totalProperty:'total'
        },
        actionMethods :{read:'POST'}
    }
});
```

In the definition of our store, we declared a `pageSize` property of 3 and defined a
proxy so that we can get the data from the server. Thus, we will be able to paginate
our data.

Then we define our grid and the `PagingToolbar` item that this grid will have:

```
var myStore = Ext.create("Myapp.store.customers.CustomersC");
var myGrid = Ext.create('Ext.grid.Panel',{
    height: 250,
    width:  980,
    title: 'My customers',
    columns: [{
        xtype: 'numbercolumn',
        width: 100,
        dataIndex: 'id',
        text: 'Id',
        format: '000.00'
    },{
        width: 200,
        dataIndex: 'name',
```

```
        text: 'Customer name'
    },{
      xtype: 'datecolumn',
      dataIndex: 'clientSince',
      width: 150,
      text: 'Client Since',
      format: 'M-d-Y H:i'
    },{
      xtype: 'checkcolumn',
      dataIndex: 'sendnews',
      width: 120,
      text: 'Send News ?'
    },{
      xtype: 'numbercolumn',
      dataIndex:'employees',
      width: 160,
      format: '0',
      text: 'Customer Employees'
    }],
    store: myStore,
    selModel:{selType:'rowmodel'},
    bbar: [{
      xtype: 'pagingtoolbar',
      store: myStore,
      displayInfo: true,
      displayMsg: 'Displaying customers {0} - {1} of {2}'
    }],
    renderTo: 'myGrid'
});
```

In the previous code, we declared a `PagingToolbar` item on the `bbar` property of our grid. Here, we assigned the same store of our grid so that the `PagingToolbar` item references the same store. The previous code generates the output shown in the following screenshot:

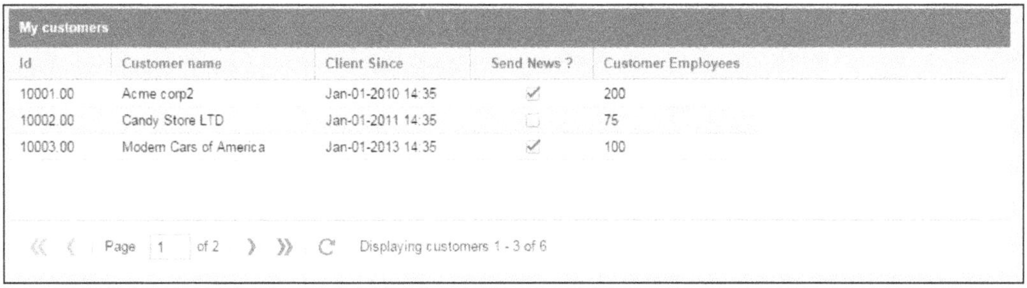

My customers				
Id	Customer name	Client Since	Send News ?	Customer Employees
10001.00	Acme corp2	Jan-01-2010 14:35	✓	200
10002.00	Candy Store LTD	Jan-01-2011 14:35	☐	75
10003.00	Modern Cars of America	Jan-01-2013 14:35	✓	100

《 〈 Page 1 of 2 〉 》 C Displaying customers 1 - 3 of 6

Notice that at the bottom of the grid, there is a toolbar with many parts (buttons, text, and so on). Also, it's indicating the number of pages (2) and the **Displaying customers 1-3 of 6** information text.

Infinite scrolling

Ext JS offers us an alternative to the `PagingToolbar` item. In Ext JS 4, a new type of grid, called the **infinite scrolling** grid, was introduced. In Ext JS 5, that grid is deprecated, and now it depends on `Ext.data.BufferedStore`. To understand more about the buffered store, see `http://docs.sencha.com/extjs/5.1/5.1.1-apidocs/#!/api/Ext.data.BufferedStore`.

So, `Ext.data.BufferedStore` gives the grid the ability to render thousands of records without needing the `PagingToolbar` item. The grid should be bound to a store with a `pageSize` property that will load data dynamically according to the `pageSize` property.

Let's see an example. First, we need to add some configuration to our store:

```
Ext.define('Myapp.store.clients',{
  extend:'Ext.data.BufferedStore',
  model: 'Myapp.model.Customer',
  autoLoad: true,
  leadingBufferZone: 150,
  pageSize: 100,
  proxy:{
    type:'ajax',
    url: 'serverside/clients.php',
    reader: {
      type:'json',
      rootProperty:'records',
      totalProperty:'total'
    }
  }
});
```

In our previous store configuration, we declared a `pageSize` property of `100` and set the `leadingBufferZone` property to `150`. Setting the `leadingBufferZone` property indicates the number of extra rows to keep cached on the leading side of the scrolling buffer as the scrolling proceeds.

Now let's see the definition of our grid, as shown in the following code:

```
var myGrid = Ext.create('Ext.grid.Panel',{
  height: 250,
  width:  550,
  title: 'My clients (buffered)',
  columns: [{
    xtype: 'rownumberer', width: 50
  },{
    xtype: 'numbercolumn',
    width: 100, dataIndex: 'id', text: 'Id',
    format: '0'
  },{
    width: 200, dataIndex: 'name',
    text: 'name'
  },{
    width: 200, dataIndex: 'lastname',
    text: 'lastname'
  }],
  store: myStore,
  loadMask: true,
  selModel:{
    pruneRemoved: false
  },
  renderTo: 'myGrid'
});
```

In the Grid configuration, we set `selModel` with the `pruneRemoved:false` property. According to the Sencha documentation:

> *"When using paging or a Ext.data.BufferedStore, records which are cached in the Store's data collection may be removed from the Store when pages change, or when rows are scrolled out of view. For this reason pruneRemoved should be set to false when using a buffered Store."*

With these configurations made, we will get the output shown in the following screenshot:

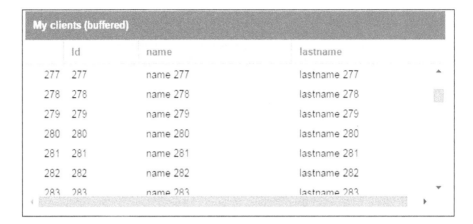

If we check out the Developer tools (Safari or Chrome), we will see this:

As we keep scrolling, the AJAX requests that the store will be setting different parameters (page number and start) and will be changing in order to get the proper data for the grid.

Now let's see how clients.php is composed:

```php
<?php
  $success= true;
  $total   = 2000;
  $page    = $_GET['page'];
  $start   = $_GET['start'];
  $limit   = $_GET['limit'];
  $datause = array();
  for ( $i= ($start +1); $i<= ( $start + $limit ); $i++ ){
    $datause[] = array(
      'id'=> $i,
      'name'=> 'name ' . $i,
```

```
      'lastname'=> 'lastname ' . $i
    );
  }
  echo json_encode(
    array(
      'success'=>$success,
      'total'=>$total,
      'records'=>$datause
    )
  );
?>
```

This code will create dummy data for the request made by the store as we scroll.

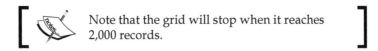

Note that the grid will stop when it reaches 2,000 records.

Summary

In this chapter, you learned how to configure the basics for our Grid panels so that we can get the best out of them when developing our applications. It is important to know what a Grid panel's capabilities are and how can we add custom functionality using column renderers, grid features, and grid plugins.

It's also important that you perform tests and play with different combinations (configurations and event listeners) so that you can recognize which ones you find more comfortable to use, depending on the different scenarios you may need for your applications. Most of the time, it's impossible to learn 100 percent all the Grid configurations or event listeners, but remember that you can always take a look at the Ext JS documentation.

In the next chapter, we will take a look at and learn about data views and templates in Ext JS. This chapter may help you enhance more things (visual appearance) in your grids (renderers and presentations using templates).

8
DataViews and Templates

The DataView component has a function similar to the grid—showing data in a formatted way—but it can be lighter or heavier, depending on how it's handled. When we say "formatted way", we mean that we use a template to render an HTML output for each record in the store.

For the rendering process, the DataView uses an `Ext.XTemplate` class, so we can give the proper output (HTML) and style to each record in the store. This component is very useful when you want to render data in a customized way and also don't require the functionality of the grid.

In this chapter, you'll learn how the `Ext.view.View` class (DataView) and the `Ext.XTemplate` class work together.

The topics we are going to cover in this chapter are as follows:

- The data connection (models and stores)
- A basic DataView
- Handling events in DataView
- Templates
- A more complex DataView component

In all the examples in this chapter's code, we will be using many CSS codes that will give our examples/DataView items some nice formatting and visual appearance. The full CSS code is given at the end of this chapter.

The data connection (model and store)

As we saw in *Chapter 7, Give Me the Grid*, the grid needs the use of a data store in order to display contents. The DataView component works the same way. In *Chapter 4, It's All about the Data*, we talked about the use of data packages (models and stores). So, let's begin using the following model:

```
Ext.define('Myapp.model.Users',{
    extend:'Ext.data.Model', // step 1 (extend datamodel)
    idProperty:'id',
    fields:[ // step 2 (field definition)
      {name: 'id', type: 'int'},
      {name: 'firstName', type: 'string'},
      {name: 'lastName', type: 'string'},
      {name: 'twitter_account', type: 'string'},
      {name: 'active', type: 'boolean'},
      {name: 'avatar', type: 'string'}
    ]
});
```

In the previous code, we have our user model definition. This code goes into the model's definition folder of our application. This model will get the data through the ajax calls that are defined in the type property of the store's proxy.

The url property will be serverside/users.json, and the way the readers will fetch the data will be in a json format. They will get the data from the records node of our data response. Now let's define our store in the following way:

```
Ext.define('Myapp.store.users',{
    extend:'Ext.data.Store',
    model: 'Myapp.model.Users',
    autoLoad:true,
    proxy:{
      type:'ajax',
      url: 'serverside/users.json',
      reader: {
        type:'json',
        totalProperty:'total',
        rootProperty:'records'
      }
    }
});
```

A basic DataView

Now, that we have our data connection set, we are going to define the view of our application:

```
//Step 1
var myTpl = [
'<tplfor=".">',
'<div class="user">{firstName} {lastName}</div>',
'</tpl>'
].join('');
//Step 2
var myDataview = Ext.create('Ext.view.View', {
  store: myStore, //step 3
  tpl: myTpl,      //step 4
  padding:6,
  emptyText: '<b>No users available</b>'
});
```

In the previous code, we defined our user's DataView. So, let's see the code step by step:

1. We created the template configuration in `var myTpl` so that the DataView can use it.

2. We created an instance of the `Ext.view.View` class in the `myDataview` variable.

3. Then we added the data source of our view in `step 3`.

4. We set the template in the DataView by setting the `tpl:myTpl` property.

5. Finally, we have the `emptyText` property, which is text to be displayed when our view has nothing to show (no records).

Once we have our data connection and view defined, we are ready to write the code for the output:

```
Ext.onReady(function(){
  Ext.tip.QuickTipManager.init();
   var myStore = Ext.create('Myapp.store.users');
  var mytpl = [
    '<tplfor=".">',
    '<div class="user">{firstName} {lastName}</div>',
    '</tpl>'
  ].join('');
  var myDataview = Ext.create('Ext.view.View', {
    store: myStore,
```

```
      tpl: myTpl,
      padding: 6,
      itemSelector: 'div.user',
      emptyText: '<b>No users available</b>'
   });
   var MyPanel = Ext.create('Ext.panel.Panel',{
      title: 'My Dataview',
      height: 295,
      width: 450,
      items: [myDataview],
      renderTo: 'myPanel'
   });
});
```

This code defines a panel that will contain our DataView and give us the following output:

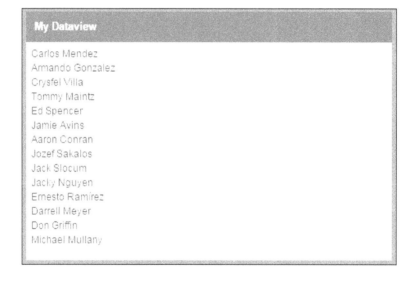

Handling events in DataView

Once we have our DataView defined, we are going to see some basic event handling for it. To do this, we need to add some new properties to our view definition so that we can assign events:

```
var myDataview = Ext.create('Ext.view.View', {
  store: myStore,
  tpl: myTpl,
  padding: 6,
  itemSelector: 'div.user', //Step 1
  emptyText: '<b>No users available</b>'
});
```

We added the `itemSelector` property (`Step 1`). It defines which DOM node item will be used to select each item (data model) with which the DataView will be working.

You can use CSS selectors to define the `itemSelector` property.

And now, let's add the event listener:

```
var myDataview = Ext.create('Ext.view.View', {
store: myStore,
  tpl: myTpl,
  padding: 6,
  itemSelector: 'div.user',
  emptyText: '<b>No users available</b>',
  listeners: {
    itemclick: {
      fn:function( view, record, item, index, evt, eOpts ){
        Ext.Msg.alert(
          "Dataview record selected", record.get('firstName') +
              " " + record.get('lastName') + " has been selected"
        );
      }
    }
  }
});
```

In the previous code, we added an event listener to our DataView, which is executed when we click on one of our DataView's items. The following screenshot shows us the result:

So far, this is the basic way to add event listeners to the DataView. You may check out the Ext JS documentation to see other available events, and play with this application to check out the most appropriate listeners for your application.

Templates

In the Ext JS library, we have two types of templates: Ext.Template and Ext. XTemplate. Let's see what the main differences between these two classes are:

- Ext.Template represents an HTML fragment. This one, in my personal opinion, can be used in small things or simple representations.

- Ext.XTemplate extends the Ext.Template class and provides advanced functionality.

Ext.Template

Let's look an example of Ext.Template:

```
Ext.onReady(function(){
  Ext.tip.QuickTipManager.init();
  var myTemplate = new Ext.Template([ //Step 1
    '<div class="container">','<div class="header">',
    '<img src="images/{logo}"width="88" height="53" alt=""/>',
```

```
            '<span>{titlecontents}</span><br>','</div>',
            '<div class="bookscontainer">','<span class="book">',
            '<img src="images/{book_a}"
                width="112"
              height="138"
                  alt=""
        data-qtitle="Hot book"
          data-qtip="This is another great book for EXT JS!" />',
            '</span>','<span class="book">',
            '<img src="images/{book_b}"
                width="112"
              height="138"
                  alt=""
        data-qtitle="Trend book"
          data-qtip="This is another great book for EXT JS!" />',
            '</span>','</div>','<div class="footer">',
            '<a href="{url}"
            target="_blank">Click here to see more</a>',
            '</div>', '</div>'
        ]);
    myTemplate.compile(); //Step 2
        myTemplate.append('myPanel', { //Step 3
            logo: 'Packt.png',
            titlecontents: 'Visit PACK PUB for great deals...!',
            book_a: '40050Scov.jpg.png',
            book_b: '68460S.jpg.png',
            url: 'https://www.packtpub.com/'
        });
    });
```

Let's review the previous code step by step:

1. We define our template Ext.Template, which will show a nice format, with some images, some description, and a link to https://www.packtpub.com.

2. We compile our template (Ext JS creates the template as an internal function) in order to render faster.

3. We append our template to the HTML `<div>` element with the myPanel ID in our page, and also pass some data (as an object) as the second parameter in the myTemplate.append function of our template.

The following screenshot shows the result of the previous code:

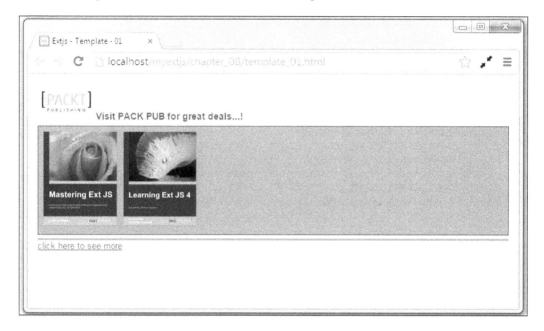

Ext.XTemplate

Now, let's talk about the Ext.XTemplate class. This class is more complex than the Ext.Template class because it supports advanced functionality, such as these:

- Auto-filling arrays using templates and subtemplates
- Conditional processing with basic comparison operators
- Basic math function support
- Executing arbitrary inline code with special built-in template variables
- Custom member functions

Ext.XTemplate provides the template mechanism for Ext.view.View, so when we use the DataView, we will have all the Ext.XTemplate capabilities available. Let's see a basic example of an Ext.XTemplate implementation:

```
Ext.onReady(function(){
  var myStore = Ext.create('Myapp.store.users');
  var myXTemplate = new Ext.XTemplate( //Step 1
    '<tpl for=".">', //Step 2
    '<div class="user">',
    'Record number {[xindex]} - {firstName} {lastName} - ',
```

```
//Step 3
   '<tpl if="active ==0">', //Step 4
 '<span class="inactiveuser">user is Inactive (need
   activation)</span>',
   '<tpl else>',
   '<span class="activeuser">user is active</span>',
   '</tpl>',
   '- Reference number for user :',
   '{id+1000}', //Step 5
   '</div>',
   '</tpl>'
);
myStore.on({ //Step 6
  'load':{
    fn:function(store, records, success, eOpts){
      var data = [];
      Ext.each(records, function(record, index, records){
        data.push(record.data);
      },this);
      var myEl = Ext.get('myPanel');
      myXTemplate.overwrite(myEl, data); //Step 7
    },
    scope:this
  }
});
myStore.load();
});
```

In Step 1, we created the instance of a new Ext.XTemplate class and define the overall HTML structure.

In Step 2, we set in the template (HTML) structure the <tplfor="."> text. This means that a loop will be made, repeating the template for each item in the data array.

Then in Step 3, we defined 'Record number {[xindex]} - {firstName} {lastName} - ',. This means that {firstName} and {lastName} will be populated/replaced with the specific value from the data object. The {[xindex]} variable is contained in the scope of the template, and this will return us the index of the loop we are in (1-based).

In Step 4, we set an `if` condition inside the template, and perform the evaluation according to the condition we have set:

```
'<tpl if="active ==0">',
'<span class="inactiveuser">user is Inactive....</span>',
'<tpl else>',
'<span class="activeuser">user is active</span>',
'</tpl>',
```

Notice that the condition has to start with `<tpl...>` and end with `</tpl>`. This is an important thing to remember when setting conditionals inside the `XTemplate` content.

In Step 5, we used an `'{id+1000}'` math condition. `XTemplate` lets us perform mathematical operations, and these can be applied directly to numeric data values.

In Step 6, we added the listener to the store's load event. This event will handle and pass the data of each model/record as an array so that we can populate the `XTemplate` content.

Finally, in Step 7, we called the `myXTemplate.overwrite` method to overwrite the inner HTML of the element with the data applied to the template. Let's run the example in our browser. We will get something like this:

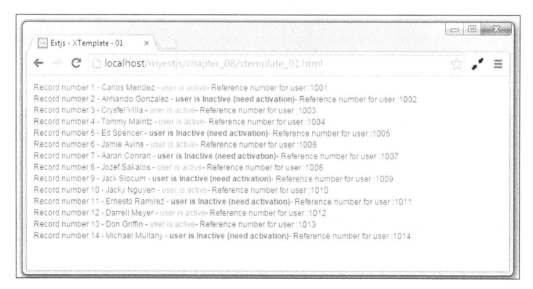

It's important that you do more exercises, checking out the documentation of `Ext.XTemplate` in order to know how to add functions, subtemplates, and so on. Now that you have learned the basics of how templates work, we are ready to perform a more complex example.

A more complex DataView component

A DataView component is a great component in the Ext JS library. In the next example, we are going to list the users in the application and activate or deactivate them with a double click on the user record. Let's add some new lines to our previous DataView code:

```
var myXTemplate = new Ext.XTemplate( //step 1
'<tplfor=".">',
'<div class="user {[this.getActiveclass(values.active)]}">',
'<div class="user_row">',
'<div class="user_img">',
'<img src="images/{twitter_account}.jpg" width="37"
  height="37">',
'</div>',
'<div class="usr_name">{firstName} {lastName}<br>',
'<span class="usr_account">{twitter_account}</span>',
'</div>',
'</div>',
'</div>',
'</tpl>',
{
  getActiveclass:function(value){
    return (value!=0)?"active":"inactive";
  }
});
```

Here, we are creating an instance of the Ext.XTemplate class. In this code, we added a function inside the template called getActiveclass. This class will return the value depending on the value of active in the data, and it is called by the {[this.getActiveclass(values.active)]} code.

Now let's change the DataView:

```
var myDataview = Ext.create('Ext.view.View', {
  store: myStore,
  tpl:myXTemplate,
  padding:6,
  itemSelector: 'div.user',
  emptyText: '<b>No users available</b>',
  listeners:{
    itemdblclick':{
    fn:function( view, record, item, index, event, eOpts){
      var item = Ext.fly(item);
      if(record.get('active')){
                Ext.fly(item).removeCls('active');
```

```
          Ext.fly(item).addCls('inactive');
        }else{
          Ext.fly(item).removeCls('inactive');
          Ext.fly(item).addCls('active');
        }
        record.data.active = !record.data.active;
        }
      }
  }
});
```

Here, we changed the `tpl` property to `tpl:myXTemplate`, assigning the `XTemplate` variable to the property. Also, we added the listener with the `itemdblclick` event. This function will change the value of `active` in our model/record.

Now that we have our code complete, we can see the final result, as shown in the following screenshot:

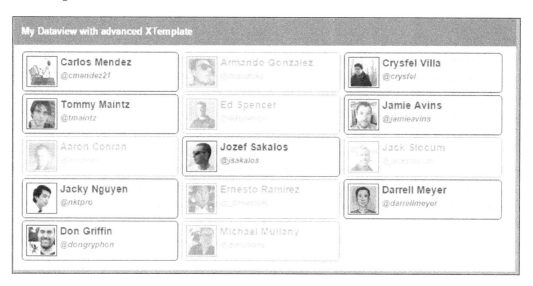

Here is the complete CSS code for the example:

```
/* Dataview examples */
.user{cursor:pointer;}
.user{
    margin-left: 5px;
    margin-top: 3px;
    padding: 5px;
    background-color: #CCC;
    display: block;
```

```css
    border: 1px solid #333;
    border-radius: 5px;
    overflow:hidden;
    width:220px;
    float:left;}
.user_row{
    position:relative;
    display:block;
    overflow:visible;}
.usr_titles{
    float: left;
    padding-top:6px;}
.user_img{
    padding:2px;
    border: 1px solid #036;
    margin-right:4px;
    width:43px;
    height:42px;
    float: left;
    background-color:#FFF;}
.active{
    opacity:1;
    background: #E6FFE6;}
.inactive{
    opacity:.5;
    background: #F5F5F0;}
.usr_name{
    color:#036;
    font-size:14px;
    font-weight:bold; }
.usr_account{
    color:#666;
    font-size:11px;
    font-style:italic;}

/* template example */
.container{ padding:4px; }
.container .header{
    font-size:14px;
    font-weight:bold;
    color:#333; }
.container .bookscontainer{
    margin-top:5px;
    padding:5px;
```

```
        border:#333 solid 1px;
        overflow:auto;
        display:block;
        background-color:#999;}
    .book{
        padding:3px;
        float:left;
        width:auto;
        margin-right:4px;
        display:block;}
    .container .footer{
        clear:both;
        border-top:medium #F60 solid;
        margin-top: 5px; }

    /* Xtemplate example */
    .user{
        font-size:12px;
        color:#333;
        cursor:pointer; }
    .activeuser{color:#096; }
    .inactiveuser{
        color:#900;
        font-weight:bold;}
```

Summary

The DataView is a very flexible component, and it is useful when we want to render data in customized ways. It is easy to use and has a powerful API. Because of the flexibility of the Ext.XTemplate class, we can do a variety of things using these two components.

In this chapter, you learned how the DataView class works. We saw how to use stores, models, and views to format the data we want to render. In Ext JS, a DataView is used commonly with templates, and the Ext.XTemplate class offers a lot of useful configurations to validate and format our data. It is very important to know the capabilities of Ext.view.View compared to the features of Ext.grid.Panel because in terms of performance, it is sometimes much better to use a DataView.

In the next chapter, we will see another awesome component, which is Ext.tree.Panel. This component is one of the well-designed and powerful components in the Ext JS library, so keep reading.

The Tree Panel

The `Ext.tree.Panel` class is a component in Ext JS, and also a great tool that allows us to display and use hierarchical data. A good example of this is a file directory application.

`Ext.tree.Panel` extends from `Ext.panel.Table`, which is the same class that the `Ext.grid.Panel` extends from. Features such as columns, sorting, filtering, renderers, dragging and dropping, plugins, and extensions are expected to work in `Ext.tree.Panel` as well. The main difference between the `Ext.grid.Panel` and `Ext.tree.Panel` classes is in the way they render data.

It's important to mention that this component is also data aware, so for it, we must use `Ext.data.TreeStore`, which is a data store specially designed to work with the tree panel. In this chapter, you'll learn how `Ext.tree.Panel` works, its versatility, and ease of use.

The topics we are going to cover in this chapter are as follows:

- A basic tree panel
- `Ext.data.TreeStore`
- Tree nodes
- Adding and removing nodes
- The check tree
- The grid tree

A basic tree panel

In this example, we are going to display a simulation of a file directory using the `Ext.tree.Panel` component. So, our first step for creating a tree panel is to define our data using the `Ext.data.TreeStore` class. After this example, we will explore the `Ext.data.TreeStore` class deeper. Let's start with the following code:

```
var MyTreeStore = Ext.create('Ext.data.TreeStore',{
  storeId: 'myTreeStoreDS',
  root: {
    text: 'My Application',
    expanded: true,
    children: [{
      text: 'app',
        children:[
          { leaf:true, text: 'Application.js' }
        ]
    },{
      text: 'controller',
      expanded: true,
      children: []
    },{
      text: 'model', expanded:true,
      children: [
        { leaf:true, text: 'clients.js' },
        { leaf:true, text: 'providers.js'},
        { leaf:true, text: 'users.js' }
      ]
    },{
      text: 'store',
      children: [
        { leaf:true, text: 'clients.js' },
        { leaf:true, text: 'providers.js' },
        { leaf:true, text: 'users.js' }
      ]
    },{
      text: 'view',
      children: [
        { leaf:true, text: 'BasicTreePanel.js' },
        { leaf:true, text: 'TreeStorePanel.js' }
      ]
    },{
      text: 'resources',
      children: [
```

```
            { text: 'images' },
            { text: 'css',
            children: [
              { leaf:true, text: 'main.css' },
              { leaf:true, text: 'clients.css' }
            ]
          }
        ]
      }]
    }
  });
```

In the preceding code, we have the data (store) definition for our tree panel. First, we have to understand our tree data source format. This data format is different from the store data source format we have used in previous chapters. In this component, the store needs to have a root node, which will be containing the data for our tree. This node will be the main (first) node of our tree, from which the rest of the nodes will be drawn.

When we talk about a tree store's records, usually the common term is *node*. This node has some specific properties (fields) that make it possible for the component to handle and draw data. As an example, properties such as expanded, text, and leaf are some common properties each node has to have. Now let's create our panel:

```
Ext.onReady(function(){
  Ext.tip.QuickTipManager.init();
  var MyTreeStore = // [ previous code ];
  var MyTreePanel = Ext.create('Ext.tree.Panel',{
    title: 'My tree panel',
    width: 250,
    height: 350,
    frame: true,
    store: MyTreeStore,
    renderTo: 'myPanel'
  });
});
```

The `Ext.tree.Panel` class extends from `Ext.Panel.Table` and `Ext.Panel.Panel`, so we can use it in a similar way as the grid and panel components. This also means that the behavior will be very similar. So, let's run the code in our browser and check the result, as follows:

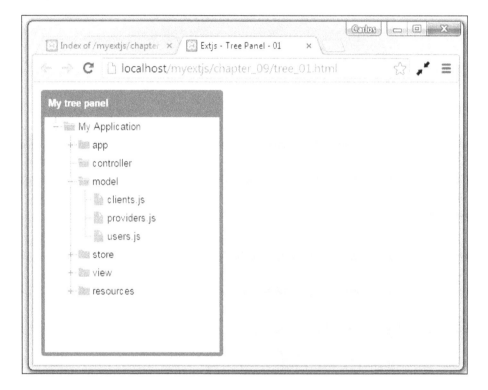

In the example, we are using the **Neptune** theme. You can see that Ext JS, by default, automatically sets the icons on each **node** in the tree according to the nature of the node (whether it has children or not). The following image shows theme comparisons:

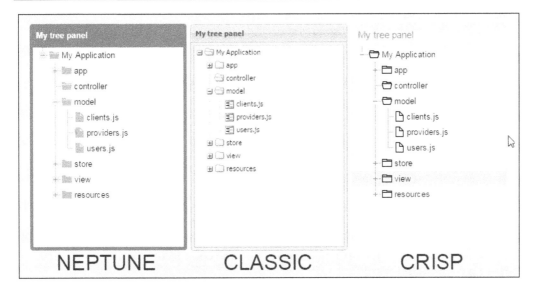

As we have seen in this example, the configuration and use of an `Ext.tree.Panel` component is very simple, but there are some properties that we need to know so we can understand this component better.

The TreeStore

The TreeStore (`Ext.data.TreeStore`) is a special store in the Ext JS library. It is designed especially for working with the tree structure, which is `Ext.tree.Panel` in this case. As this class extends `Ext.data.Store` which in turn sequentially extends `Ext.data.AbstractStore`, you will notice that the behavior is similar to `Ext.data.Store`.

When we define our stores, we need to specify a data model. In this case (TreeStore), if we don't specify a model, then Ext JS will create an implicit data model using the `Ext.data.NodeInterface` class, which will lead to creating a model for our store.

Let's see an example of loading data from the server into our `Ext.data.TreeStore` class:

```
Ext.onReady(function(){
  Ext.tip.QuickTipManager.init();
  //Store Definition
  var MyTreeStore = Ext.create('Ext.data.TreeStore',{
    autoLoad: true,
    storeId:'myTreeStoreDS',
    proxy:{
```

```
        type: 'ajax',
        url: 'serverside/menu.json'
      }
    });
    var MyTreePanel = Ext.create('Ext.tree.Panel',{
      title: 'My app menu',
      width: 270,
      height: 370,
      frame: true,
      store: MyTreeStore,
      renderTo: 'myPanel'
    });
  });
```

As you can notice, the tree class configuration becomes very simple. We have just added a store, and now we only need to specify the code to render the panel. So, we will get the following result:

 Take some time to review and see how the `serverside/menu.json` file is created. Also examine its structure, in order to make similar JSON structures.

Take note, if you are using PHP, ASP, or other server-side technologies, it's advisable that you check and ensure that you create a correct JSON/XML output in order to make the tree panel work properly.

Tree nodes

The `Ext.data.NodeInterface` class is a set of methods that are applied to the model to decorate it with a node API. This means that when we use a model with a tree, the model will have all the tree-related methods. This class also creates extra fields on the model to help maintain the tree state and the UI.

The most common field configurations are the following:

- `text`: This property configures the text to show up on the node label.
- `root`: This property is `true` if this is the root node.
- `leaf`: If this property is set to `true`, it indicates that this child can have no children. The expand icon/arrow will not be rendered for this node.
- `expanded`: This is `true` if the node is expanded.
- `iconCls`: This property configures the CSS class to apply for this node's icon.
- `children`: This configures an array of child nodes.
- `checked`: This property is set to `true` or `false` to show a checkbox alongside this node.

For better understanding, take a look at the following diagram:

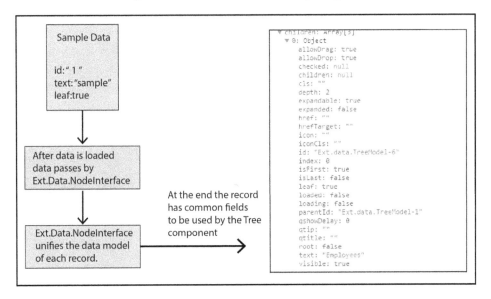

Remember that you don't always need to define all the fields (common in the node) in the output—just all of the most relevant. Also, you can add custom fields, for example, the country, document ID, tax ID, and so on. The fields will also be unified in the store model.

Adding and removing nodes

We can even add nodes dynamically to our tree panel. This is very handy because when we use the tree panel, in most cases, we will end up facing this requirement. Here, we will see how we can solve this problem.

In the following example, we are going to add nodes dynamically to our tree panel. In order to familiarize you with the upcoming chapters that cover this example, we will use MCV architecture. Let's start creating a file to be saved in chapter_09/ appcode/view/ as nodeForm.js, and place the following code:

```javascript
// JavaScript Document
Ext.define('Myapp.view.nodeForm', {
  extend:'Ext.form.Panel',
  alias: 'widget.mynodeForm',
  requires: [
    'Ext.toolbar.Toolbar', 'Ext.toolbar.Fill',
    'Ext.button.Button', 'Ext.form.field.Text',
    'Ext.form.RadioGroup', 'Ext.form.field.Radio'
  ],
  border: false,
  frame: true,
  height: 137,
  width: 323,
  bodyPadding: 10,
  header: false,
  title: '',
  dockedItems: [{
    xtype: 'toolbar',
    dock: 'bottom',
    items: [
      {xtype: 'tbfill'},
      {xtype: 'button', text: 'Save node', action: 'savenode'}
    ]
  }],
  items: [{
    xtype: 'textfield',
    fieldLabel:'Name',
    name:'nodetext',
```

```
        anchor: '100%',
        allowBlank: false,
        enableKeyEvents: true,
        listeners:{
          keyup:function(o, e){
            if(e.button==31){
              this.setValue(this.getValue() + " ");
            }
          }
        }
      },{
        xtype: 'radiogroup', fieldLabel: 'is leaf ?',
        items: [
          {xtype: 'radiofield',
            name:'usenodetype',
            boxLabel: 'No',
            inputValue:0},
          {xtype: 'radiofield',
            name:'usenodetype',
            boxLabel: 'yes',
            inputValue:1,
            checked: true}
        ]
      }],
    initComponent: function(){
      this.callParent();
    }
});
```

In this file, we are extending `Ext.form.Panel` as in the previous. This form will be used to create new nodes in our tree panel. Now let's create a new file in chapter_09/appcode/controller/, named nodeForm.js, and add the following code:

```
Ext.define('Myapp.controller.nodeForm', {
  extend:'Ext.app.Controller',
  refs: [{
    ref: 'myform',
    selector: 'mynodeForm',
    xtype: 'mynodeForm'
    autoCreate: false,
  }],
  init: function() {
    this.control({
      'button[action=savenode]': {
        click: this.savenewNode
```

```
      }
    });
  },
  savenewNode: function() {
    var myTree = Ext.ComponentQuery.query('#menuTreePanel')[0];
    var myTreesm = myTree.getSelectionModel();
    if (myTreesm.hasSelection()){ //check if has selection
      var mynode = myTreesm.getSelection()[0];
      //get first selection item
    } else {
      var mynode = myTree.getRootNode();
    }
    var values = this.getMyform().getValues();
    var newNode = {
      text: values.nodetext,
      leaf: (values.usenodetype==1)?true:false
    };
    mynode.insertChild(0, newNode);
    var mybtn = Ext.ComponentQuery.query('#addnodebutton')[0];
    mybtn.menu.close();
  }
});
```

This file (controller) will be in charge of controlling actions (the **Save** button) launched in the form. This is possible thanks to the `refs` property in the controller. Now, in the `savenewNode` function, what we do is as follows:

1. We query for the tree panel component with the `Ext.ComponentQuery.query('#menuTreePanel')[0]` code (this is not always recommended to use in real-world apps), and get the selection model from the tree component.

> To query a component by ID is not considered best practice. This is because the ID may be repeated and you can lose control. You can use the `refs` property to control component behavior, or you can rely on component queries at the component level, using the `up` and `down` methods to retrieve the specific component you want. For more information see http://www.sencha.com/blog/top-10-ext-js-development-practices-to-avoid-2/ and also http://docs.sencha.com/extjs/5.1/5.1.1-apidocs/#!/api/Ext.ComponentQuery.

2. We check whether there is any selection existing inside our tree component. If so, then we get the selected node, otherwise we will select the root node.

3. We create a data object with the values we need for our new node (remember how things work with the Ext.data.NodeInterface class), and insert the new node into the selected node. When you run the example, you will notice the type of node (the leaf value equals to yes or no) by watching the icon that is assigned to the node.

4. Finally, we close the menu from the button (the form will be placed and used as a menu item later in this example).

Now let's write our main code:

```
Ext.Loader.setConfig({ //Step 1
  enabled: true,
 paths:{ Myapp: 'appcode'}
});
Ext.require([//Step 2
  'Ext.*',
  'Myapp.view.nodeForm',
  'Myapp.controller.nodeForm'
]);
var myForm = Ext.create('widget.mynodeForm'); //Step 3
Ext.application({ //Step 4
  name: 'Myapp',
  controllers: ['nodeForm'],
  launch: function() {
    Ext.tip.QuickTipManager.init();
    //Step 5
    var MyTreeStore = Ext.create('Ext.data.TreeStore',{
      autoLoad: true,
      storeId: 'myTreeStoreDS',
      proxy:{ type:'ajax', url:'serverside/menu.json'}
    });
    var MyTreePanel = Ext.create('Ext.tree.Panel',{
      itemId: 'menuTreePanel',
      title: 'My app menu',
      width: 270,
      height :370,
      frame: true,
      store: MyTreeStore,
      tbar:[{
        text: 'Add',
        itemId: 'addnodebutton',
        iconCls: 'addicon-16',
        menu:{
          enableKeyNav: false,
```

```
                  items: myForm
               }
            },{
               text: 'Delete',
               iconCls: 'deleteicon-16',
               handler:function(){   //Step 5
                  var myTree = Ext.ComponentQuery.query('#menuTreePanel')[0];
                  var myTreesm = myTree.getSelectionModel();
                  if (myTreesm.hasSelection()){
                     //check if has selection
                     var mynode = myTreesm.getSelection()[0];
                     //get first selection item

                     mynode.remove(true);
                     // True (for destroy the node)
                  } else {
                     Ext.Msg.alert('Alert..!', "please select a node in the
                        tree...!");
                  }
               }
            }],
            renderTo: 'myPanel'
         });
      }
   });
```

Here's what this code does:

1. In Step 1, we define the Ext loader and set the path for the Myapp workspace as appcode.

2. In Step 2, we tell Ext JS what we require. In this case, we tell it to load Ext.*, which means that the Ext JS loader will load all classes. If you don't want to do this, then you can use Ext.tip.*, Ext.data.*, Ext.tree.*, and Ext.form.*. So, in this way, we are only loading the most necessary classes to make our code work.

 In real-world applications, it is advised that you never use Ext.* for the Ext JS loader. You should specify only the classes used, and this will avoid loading classes that you will not be using in the application. In this way, the code will be lighter than when loading the entire Ext JS framework for your application.

3. Then in `Step 3`, create an instance of the `Myapp.view.nodeForm` class using the `myForm` variable.

4. In `Step 4`, instead of using `Ext.onReady`, as in previous examples, we use `Ext.application`. This will be a similar function, waiting for all the necessary classes to load, and then beginning (executing the launch function) with this code. We define the name of the application as `Myapp`, and also define which controllers the application will use.

5. In `Step 5`, we create the data store for the Tree panel loading JSON data remotely, and define our tree panel. This new tree panel has a toolbar (defined in the `tbar` property) with two buttons. The first one contains a menu that has our form (`myForm`) as a menu item. The second button will be a button for deleting the selected node, and we have defined in this case the handler directly on the button and not on the controller.

For people who have little experience with MVC or MVVM architecture, all of this can be quite complex or a hard experience. So, in this example, we are trying to mix traditional code with MVC. Thus, you (if you do not have experience) will be able to get more familiar with it at a slower pace, instead of a barrage of information and terms that you may not understand.

The function (handler) set in the button for the delete action will do the following:

1. We query for the tree panel component and get the selection model from the tree component.

2. We check whether there is any selection existing inside our tree component, and if so, then we get the selected node. Otherwise, we alert the user that they have to select a tree node in order to complete the action.

3. If a node is selected, then we call the `mynode.remove(true)` action. The `true` parameter will tell Ext JS to destroy the node completely from the Tree. Otherwise, Ext JS will hide the node for future reuse, if needed.

The `getSelectionModel()` function was first used in *Chapter 7, Give Me the Grid*. The behavior of this function is quite similar to the `Grid` component.

Now let's run our example. We may get results similar to what is shown in the following screenshots. They show examples of adding and removing nodes.

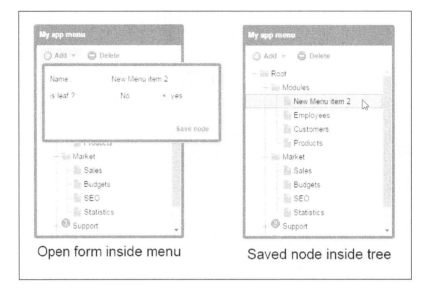

Open form inside menu | Saved node inside tree

The check tree

The tree panel also has the ability to add checkboxes to its nodes. To do this, we need to add one more property to each node in the data source that we are applying to the tree panel.

Let's use the first example of this chapter, and we will change the `root` property (data) as follows:

```
root: {
  text: 'My Application',
  expanded: true,
  checked:false,
  children: [{
    text: 'app',
    checked:false,
    children:[
    { leaf:true, text: 'Application.js', checked:false }
    ]
  },{
    text: 'controller', expanded: true, children: [],
    checked:false
  },{
```

```
    text: 'model', expanded:true, checked:false,
    children: [
      {leaf:true, text: 'clients.js', checked:false},
      {leaf:true, text: 'providers.js', checked:false},
      {leaf:true, text: 'users.js', checked:false}
    ]
  },{
    text: 'store', checked:true,
    children: [
      {leaf:true, text: 'clients.js', checked:false},
      {leaf:true, text: 'providers.js', checked:true},
      {leaf:true, text: 'users.js', checked:false}
    ]
  },{
    text: 'view', checked:false,
    children: [
      {leaf:true, text: 'BasicTreePanel.js', checked:false},
      {leaf:true, text: 'TreeStorePanel.js', checked:false}
    ]
  },{
    text: 'resources', checked:false,
    children: [
      {text: 'images', checked:false},
      {text: 'css', checked:false,
    children: [
      {leaf:true, text: 'main.css', checked:false},
      {leaf:true, text: 'clients.css', checked:false}
    ]
  }
  ]
  }]
}
```

In order to make this work properly, you need to ensure that each node has the checked property (`true` or `false`), otherwise the checkboxes may not appear.

So, after the change, let's run our file in the browser. We will see something like this:

The tree grid panel

The tree grid panel has the power of the tree, mixed with the flexibility of the grid panel. This tree configuration is very handy when we want to show more information in our tree panel. As a matter of fact, the tree grid is an `Ext.tree.Panel` with its columns configuration being the same as in the grid. It also needs some dependencies (Ext JS require) from the grid component, such as columns and others.

You can use the same column types as in the grid component (date, checkbox, template, widgets, and so on). For this example, we need to create the column definitions that our tree panel will be using. It is the same process as is used when we define columns for a grid component.

In this example, we are going to list our Menu (the previous example's data) bar in an extended way, like a permission assignment for the user profile

First, we will create our data model to specify fields that are not considered for a tree data model:

```
Ext.define('Myapp.model.Tree', {
  extend: 'Ext.data.Model',
  fields: [
    {name: 'description', type: 'string'},
    {name: 'level', type: 'int'},
    {name: 'allowaccess', type: 'boolean'}
  ]
});
```

Now, taking the second code example file as the code base, let's modify it and change
it like this:

```
Ext.onReady(function(){

  Ext.tip.QuickTipManager.init();
  var MyTreeStore = Ext.create('Ext.data.TreeStore',{
    autoLoad: true,
    model: 'Myapp.model.Tree',
    storeId: 'myTreeStoreDS',
    proxy:{
      type: 'ajax',
      url: 'serverside/menu_extended.json'
    }
  });
  var MyTreePanel = Ext.create('Ext.tree.Panel',{
    title: 'User profile - Select access for user...',
    width: 670,
    height: 430,
    frame: true,
    store: MyTreeStore,
    columns:[{
      //column provide tree structure
      xtype: 'treecolumn',
      text: 'Module',
      dataIndex:'text',
      flex: 1,sortable: true
    },{
      xtype: 'templatecolumn',
      text: 'Module description',
      flex: 2,
      sortable: true,
      dataIndex:'description',
      align: 'left',
      tpl: Ext.create('Ext.XTemplate',
      '<div class="levelcolor_{level}">{description}</div>')
    },{
      xtype: 'checkcolumn',
      header: 'Allow access',
      dataIndex: 'allowaccess',
      width: 100,
      stopSelection: false,
      menuDisabled: true
    }
    ],
    renderTo:'myPanel'
  });
});
```

As you can notice, this code is essentially the same as our second code example in this chapter, but the differences are as follows:

- We added a data model to the TreeStore
- We added the `columns` configuration to the tree panel definition

So now, let's run our example. We will have something like this:

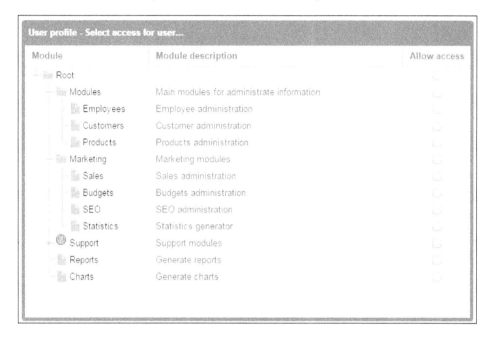

As you can see, the tree grid component and the grid component are very similar in columns (visual result and behavior) selection. You can create as many columns as you want (remember that they must be considered in the model).

Summary

In this chapter, you learned the basics of creating tree panels and the available variants of the way in which we can use tree components.

The Ext JS library has implemented a very robust component that supports all the common configurations we need when developing our applications to fit the customer's needs. As with all components in the library, it is very important to know in which situation we should use which component and the style of the component.

Remember that when developing an Ext JS application, we don't need to know all the properties of the classes by memory. We can always go and search in the API documentation.

In the next chapter, we are going to see the Ext JS Architecture and you will learn more about the MVC and MVVM patterns. Also, we will see data binding (view models), routers, and so on, which are used to create a more robust application.

10
Architecture

In order to create a better code and organization structure, improve teamwork, and also reduce the amount of code to be written, the MVC pattern was first introduced in Ext JS 4. To go further, Ext JS 5 introduced the MVVM pattern, which is another pattern to be used for our applications.

These patterns are quite similar, but the difference is that MVVM introduces a feature called **view model** (**VM**) that manages the changes between models' data. Also, the view's representation (by data bindings) gives developers the ability to reduce the code even further, which is occasionally hard to manage for some and a tedious task for others.

In the third code example in *Chapter 9*, *The Tree Panel*, we used the MVC pattern to give you an idea of what will be coming in this chapter. Now we can go further by covering these topics:

- MVC and MVVM patterns
- Creating a more robust application – our first application using both patterns
- Adding interaction (controllers) and making use of data binding (**ViewModel**)
- Using routers (a new feature in version 5)

Keep in mind that the discussion on MVC and MVVM varies depending on the coding languages and frameworks, among others. So, when we talk about Ext JS's MVC or MVVM, we will also see how Sencha Ext JS handles these patterns.

The MVC and MVVM patterns

If you are new to these patterns, this section will tell you how the patterns work so that you can get an idea on what to expect. So, let's start with the general concepts:

- **Model**: The collection of fields and data. This is used with stores to present data, use it with our components, or interact with our code. Refer to *Chapter 4, It's All about the Data*, for more details.

- **View**: This is the visual part where the end user will be interacting. Types of container components—grids, panels trees and so on—are all views.

- **Controller**: These are special containers (classes) where we will put the code that makes our application work (handles events and methods). This will be like an intermediary between the model and the view.

- **ViewController**: This is a controller that will be attached to a specific view instance and will manage that specific view and its child components. Each time a view is created, a new instance of the ViewController will be created for that specific view.

- **ViewModel**: This is a class that handles a data object and lets us bind its data to our view making changes and interactions with the view. Also, the ViewModel acts in way similar to the ViewController (new instance is created for the new instance of the view).

Model-View-Controller (MVC)

MVC is and architectural pattern. This pattern is divided into three parts, allowing us to organize the base code into logical representations, depending on their functions. The following diagram shows a basic schema of how this pattern works:

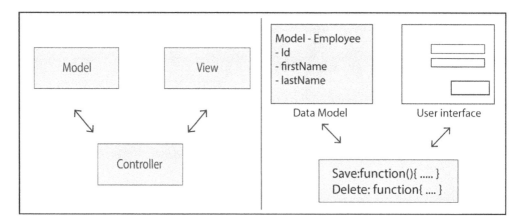

Model-View-ViewModel (MVVM)

MVVM is the new architectural pattern introduced in this version. The idea of this pattern is to provide additional advantages of data binding. In this way, the model and the framework internally interact more, with the idea of minimizing the application logic for manipulation of the view. Despite the name Model-View-ViewModel, the **MVVM** pattern may still utilize controllers (this is, kind of, confusing sometimes because some developers may choose to call it an *MVC + VM* architecture).

This diagram shows a basic schema of how this pattern works:

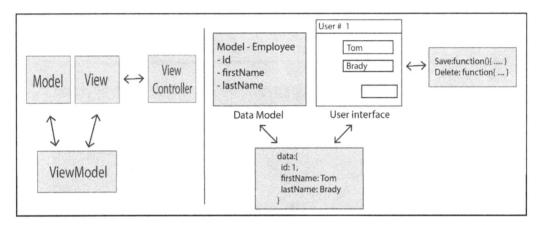

As an example, the idea behind the ViewModel is to bind the data with the text fields within the form so that we won't have to code the way in which those fields will be populated. Instead setting data binding to the fields, make it easier for us to fill in the fields.

It's important to mention that Sencha always recommends the latest features so that you can take advantage of the framework. However, remember that you can always use the architecture you want (individual, mixed, and so on). Also by using these patterns — MVC or MVVM — it's going to be easier to share code with others, understand other people's code, and integrate code by new developer (or developers) into our project. For more information about MVC and MVVM patterns, you can always check out the related documentation and articles at `http://www.sencha.com/blog` or `http://docs.sencha.com/`.

Creating our first application

So far, all the chapters in this book have given an understanding of the basics in Ext JS. Now we are going to apply this knowledge to create our application. Let's start by opening our console tool (this depends on the operating system you are using: Windows, OS X, or Linux), and we will use the Sencha CMD tool. Create a folder inside your web server (XAMPP or WAMP) called `myApp` and type the following command:

```
sencha -sdk /path/to/ext generate app myApp /path/to/myApp
```

Change the paths to the proper locations of your SDK (Ext JS's folder) and the folder the application will be in. After executing the command, you will see something like this (for Windows):

```
Administrator: cmd - Shortcut

K:\x_extjsdev\app_test>sencha-5.1.1.39 -sdk K:\x_extjsdev\ext-5.1.1\ generate ap
p myapp K:\x_extjsdev\app_test\myapp
Sencha Cmd v5.1.1.39
[INF] Processing Build Descriptor : default
[INF] Loading app json manifest...
[INF] Appending content to K:\x_extjsdev\app_test\myapp/bootstrap.js
[INF] Writing content to K:\x_extjsdev\app_test\myapp/bootstrap.json


K:\x_extjsdev\app_test>
```

 When you have multiple versions of the Sencha CMD tool, if you type `sencha`, then the last version will be used. If we want to use a previous version, then we have to type `sencha-x.x.x.x`, where `x.x.x.x` is the version of the Sencha CMD tool we are going to use. As you can notice in the previous image we used `sencha-5.1.1.39`.

Now, let's check out the folder. You will see the following output inside the folder:

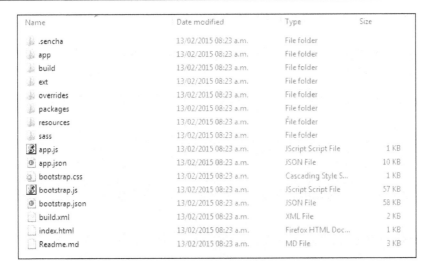

The Sencha CMD tool has created a basic application skeleton, from which we will start working. Now let's test it; open `index.html`. You should see something similar to this screenshot:

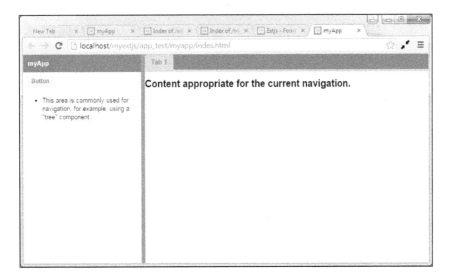

 Remember to use the proper Sencha CMD tool to check compatibility between the Ext JS framework's versions. Refer to `http://docs.sencha.com/cmd/5.x/compatibility_matrix.html` for more information about which framework's version the CMD tool supports.

So now, we are ready to begin working on our application.

 At this point, you can use the example code of this chapter. Copy or replace the files from the code inside the basic skeleton generated and run it in your browser.

The views

Now that we have created the initial skeleton, let's proceed to create our initial view in the application. Inside the app/view folder, we remove all existing files (the initial skeleton), and proceed to create the initial view our application will have. Let's start with the myViewport.js file, with the following code:

```
Ext.define('myApp.view.myViewport', {
    extend: 'Ext.container.Viewport',
    alias: 'widget.myviewport',
    requires: [
        'myApp.view.appZone',
        'Ext.panel.Panel'
    ],
    layout: 'border',
    items: [{
        xtype: 'panel',
        region: 'north',
        height: 76,
        itemId: 'appHeader',
        bodyPadding: 0,
        cls: 'appheaderbg',
        title: '',
        header: false,
        html: '<div class="appheader appheaderbg"><img src=
            "resources/images/myapp_logo.png"/></div>',
    },{
        xtype: 'appzone',
        region: 'center',
        itemId: 'myappZone'
    }]
});
```

Here, we are creating the basic layout of the viewport. It will have a **border layout** and contain two components; the header will be a panel (region: 'north'), and the main zone (region: 'center') will be a component with xtype: 'appzone'. This will be a new view, or class, that we will create. Again, in the app/view folder, create a new file called appZone.js and place the following code in it:

```
Ext.define('myApp.view.appZone', {
  extend: 'Ext.panel.Panel',
  alias: 'widget.appzone',
  // Alias property let us define the xtype to appzone on the
    viewport previously

  requires: [
    'myApp.store.modulesTreeDs',
    'Ext.tab.Panel',
    'Ext.tab.Tab',
    'Ext.tree.Panel',
    'Ext.tree.View'
  ],
  layout: 'border',
  header: false,
  title: '',
  items: [{
    xtype: 'tabpanel',
    region: 'center',
    itemId: 'mainZone',
    header: false,
    title: '',
    items: [{
      xtype: 'panel',
      itemId: 'startappPanel',
      title: 'Dashboard',
      bodyPadding: 5,
      html:'myApp Dashboard',
      region: 'center'
    }]
  },{
  xtype: 'panel',
  itemId: 'accessPanel',
  region: 'west',
  split: true,
  width: 180,
  layout: 'fit',
  title: 'App modules',
  items: [{
    xtype: 'treepanel',
    header: false,
    title: 'My Tree Panel',
    store: Ext.create( 'myApp.store.modulesTreeDs', {
      storeId: 'accessmodulesDs'
}), //'modulesTreeDs'
```

```
            rootVisible: false
        }]
    }]
});
```

In this file, we create a panel with a layout border, and it contains two components. The first component is a tab panel component, where we will place our module's contents, such as tabs.

The second component is a tree panel component from where we will have access to the application modules. As we explained in *Chapter 9, The Tree Panel*, the component will require a tree store and a data model. So now, we need to create the files for this task.

In the app/model folder, create the modulesModel.js file and place the following code in it:

```
Ext.define('myApp.model.modulesModel', {
    extend: 'Ext.data.Model',
    requires: [
        'Ext.data.field.String',
        'Ext.data.field.Boolean',
        'Ext.data.field.Integer'
    ],
    fields: [
        {type: 'string', name: 'description'},
        {type: 'boolean', name: 'allowaccess'},
        {type: 'int', name: 'level'},
        {type: 'string', name: 'moduleType', defaultValue: ''},
        {type: 'string', name: 'moduleAlias', defaultValue: ''},
        {type: 'string', name: 'options'}
    ]
});
```

Then, in the app/store folder, create the modulesTreeDs.js file, as follows:

```
Ext.define('myApp.store.modulesTreeDs', {
    extend: 'Ext.data.TreeStore',
    requires: [
        'myApp.model.modulesModel',
        'Ext.data.proxy.Ajax'
    ],
    constructor: function(cfg) {
        var me = this;
        cfg = cfg || {};
```

```
    me.callParent([Ext.apply({
      storeId: 'mymodulesTreeDs',
      autoLoad: true,
      model: 'myApp.model.modulesModel',
      proxy: {
        type: 'ajax',
        url: 'serverside/data/menu_extended.json'
      }
    }, cfg)]);
  }
});
```

The store is using the new model we created (**'myApp.model.modulesModel'**), and also you can see the URL on the `proxy` configuration object. This means that inside our application folder (root level) we need to create a new folder called **'serverside/data'** and place the **menu_extended.json** file created/used in *Chapter 9, The Tree Panel*, in it.

Now let's add an image for use as a logo in our header to the `resources/images` folder, or copy the image located in the example code in the `shared/images/logo` folder. Create a new CSS file called `style.css` inside the `resources/css` folder, and place the following code in it:

```
.appheader {width:100%; padding:5px;}
.appheaderbg {background-color:#CCC;}
.appheader img {width:185px;}
```

Let's link the CSS file in the index.html file, and we will get this:

```
<!DOCTYPE HTML>
<html manifest="">
<head>
<meta http-equiv="X-UA-Compatible" content="IE=edge">
<meta charset="UTF-8">
<title>myApp</title>
<!-- The line below must be kept intact for Sencha Cmd to build your
application -->
<script id="microloader" type="text/javascript" src="bootstrap.js"></
script>
  <link rel="stylesheet" type="text/css" href="resources/css/style.
css">
</head>
<body></body>
</html>
```

Finally, let's open the app.js file (the root level of our application) and change it as follows:

```
Ext.Loader.setConfig({});
Ext.application({
  name: 'myApp',
    views: [
        'myViewport',
        'appZone'
    ],
    launch: function() {
        Ext.create('myApp.view.myViewport');
    }
});
```

In the Ext.application configuration, the launch function will be called automatically when the page (index.html) has completely loaded. As you may have noticed in the previous examples, we had used the Ext.onReady method, so now Ext.application works in a similar fashion, but this method is the main entry point for applications.

Also, it's important to set the name of the application with the name: 'myApp' property. This will set the workspace we have been using with the classes in order to make Ext JS load the files properly. At this point, we are ready to make the initial launch in our browser. We run the index.html file in our browser, and we may get the following output:

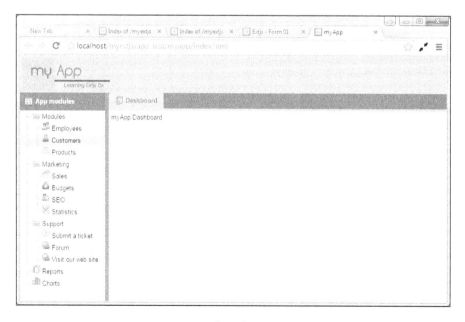

This process can also be made in Sencha Architect 3.x, and there are some initial templates with similar layouts. However, the main purpose of this book is not to describe Sencha Architect. Rather, it is about you learning how to work from scratch.

The controller

Now that we have the initial part, we are going to begin adding the interaction code to the tree panel. For this, we are going to create a basic controller (MVC-style) in order to control access to the app's modules.

Let's create a new file called `app.js` inside the `app/controller` folder and place the following code in it:

```
Ext.define( 'myApp.controller.app' , {
extend: 'Ext.app.Controller',
requires: [
  'myApp.view.appZone',
  'myApp.view.myViewport'
],
config: { },
init: function() {
console.log ('app controller init');
}
});
```

In this code, we extend the `Ext.app.Controller` class. This class contains several methods that will help us listen to events and save references. Basically, we are going to add our logic in here.

As for the second step, we have defined a method called `init`. This method will be executed when our controller is created. This method is like a constructor for our class; it will be the first code executed in our controller. In here, we usually create the listeners.

Now we have an empty controller that only shows a message on the JavaScript console. We need to add this controller to our application definition. Open the app.js file at the root level and make the following change:

```
Ext.application({
  name: 'myApp',
  controllers: ['app'],
    views: [
        'myViewport',
```

```
        'appZone'
    ],
    launch: function() {
        Ext.create('myApp.view.myViewport');
    }
});
```

Here we are setting the controllers that are used in the application.

Listening to events

Once we have our controller in place, let's add some actions to our view. We will need to open modules when the user double-clicks on any child node (leaf:true) in the access panel. Now what we need to do is add a listener to the itemdblclick event that belongs to the tree panel.

We do that using the control method that is defined in the Controller class that we are extending. Let's change the controller code as follows:

```
Ext.define('myApp.controller.app', {
    extend: 'Ext.app.Controller',
    requires:[
        'myApp.view.appZone',
        'myApp.view.myViewport'
    ],
    config:{
        refs:{
            myappzone:{
                selector:'appzone',
                xtype:'appzone',
                autoCreate:false
            }
        }
    },
    init: function() {
        console.log('app controller init');
        var me=this;
        this.control({
            'appzone #accessPanel treepanel' :{
                itemdblclick: me.handleAccess
            }
        });
    },
```

```
handleAccess:function (cmpView, record, itemx, index, evt, eOpts ){
    console.log('handle access for: ' + record.data.text );
    var me=this, moduleData = record.data;
    if (moduleData.hasOwnProperty('moduleType')){
      var typeModule = moduleData.moduleType;
      if (typeModule==''){
        return;
      } else if (typeModule=='link'){
        me.executeLink(moduleData);
      } else if (typeModule=='window'){
        me.runWindow(moduleData);
      } else if (typeModule=='module'){
        me.addModule(moduleData);
      }
    }
  },
  addModule:function(Data){
    console.log('Adding Module: ' + Data.options);
  },
  runWindow:function(Data){
    console.log('Execute window: ' + Data.options );
  },
  executeLink:function(Data){
    console.log('launch Link: ' + Data.options );
  }
});
```

First we set a `refs` property inside the configuration object in order to set a reference name for our view (in this case, the **appzone** class) so that the controller will recognize the view by the name of **myappzone**.

In the `init` function, we set the controller's `control` configuration. The `control` property will set event listeners to the referenced elements and makes use of a selector (see the `Ext.ComponentQuery` documentation for more details), `appzone #accessPanel treepanel` in this case.

Ext JS will know that it has to add the event listener for the `itemdblclick` event to the `treepanel` component inside the `appzone` view, and also inside the component with the `itemId` property with the value of `accessPanel`.

Now, in our JSON file called menu_extended.json inside the serverside/data folder, let's make changes on some elements:

1. Find the node element for Customers and set it as follows:

```
{
    "leaf": true,
    "text": "Customers",
    "allowaccess": false,
    "description": "Customer administration",
    "level": 3,
    "moduleType": "module",
    "options": "myApp.view.modules.customers"
}
```

2. Then, find the node element for "Submit a ticket", and set it like this:

```
{
"leaf": true,
"text": "Submit a ticket",
"allowaccess": false,
"description": "Submit support tickets",
"level": 3,
"moduleType": "window",
"options": "myApp.view.ticket"
}
```

3. As the last step, find the Forum element and make the following changes:

```
{
"leaf": true,
"text": "Forum",
"allowaccess": false,
"description": "Go to Forum",
"level": 3,
"moduleType": "link",
"options": "http://www.sencha.com/forum/"
}
```

Onto these three elements/nodes inside our JSON file, we added some new properties in order to control the behavior of the access modules. Let's run our application in the browser and also open the developer tools/console to check the behavior of the listener. Click on the **Customers** node, then on **Submit a ticket**, and finally on the **Forum** node. Our console/developer tools will look like what is shown in the following screenshot:

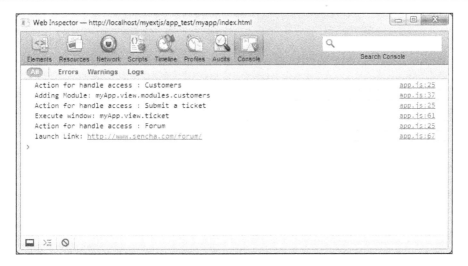

We can see that the listener is responding properly according to each type of module we are going to control inside the app.

Opening modules

Now that we have the listener working, we will create the code for meant for opening each of the modules (even though we haven't yet created each module; we will do this later). So, let's change the controller file again. Change the `addModule`, `runWindow`, and `executeLink` functions as follows:

```
addModule:function(data){
  console.log('Adding Module: ' + data.options);
  var me=this;
  var myZone = me.getMyappzone();
  var ModulesTab = myZone.query('tabpanel #mainZone')[0];
  var existModule= false;
  for (var i=0;i<ModulesTab.items.items.lenght;i++){
    if (ModulesTab.items.items[i].xtype==data.moduleAlias){
      existModule= true;
      break;
    }
  }
  if (existModule){
    ModulesTab.setActiveTab(i);
    return;
  } else {
    var mynewModule = Ext.create(data.options);
    ModulesTab.add(mynewModule);
```

```
        ModulesTab.setActiveTab((ModulesTab.items.items.lenght -1));
        return;
      }
    },
    runWindow:function(data){
      console.log('Execute window: ' + data.options );
      Ext.Msg.alert("Window module", "here we show window:<b>" +
        data.text+ "</b>");
    },
    executeLink:function(data){
      console.log('launch Link: ' + data.options );
      window.open(data.options);
    }
}
```

This previous code will provide us with functionality for accessing our modules. Now, let's begin creating the view for the customer's module.

Creating a module

Before we create the customer module, we are going to reuse the code written in *Chapter 7, Give Me the Grid.* To be more precise, we are going to use the code made in example 07 and make slight changes. First, for the model, we'll use the following code:

```
Ext.define(' myApp.model.Customer',{
    extend: 'Ext.data.Model',
    requires:  ['myApp.model.Contract'],
    idProperty: 'id',
    fields: [
    {name: 'id', type: 'int'},
    {name: 'name', type: 'string'},
    {name: 'phone', type: 'string'},
    {name: 'website', type: 'string'},
    {name: 'status', type: 'string'},
    {name: 'clientSince', type: 'date', dateFormat: 'Y-m-d H:i'},
    {name: 'country', type: 'string'},
    {name: 'sendnews', type: 'boolean'},
    {name: 'employees', type: 'int'},
    {name: 'contractInfo', reference: 'Contract', unique:true}
    ]
});
```

For the Customers file, add the following code:

```
Ext.define('myApp.store.Customers', {
    extend: 'Ext.data.Store',
```

```
requires: [
  'myApp.model.Customer',
  'Ext.data.proxy.Ajax',
  'Ext.data.reader.Json'
],
constructor: function(cfg) {
  var me = this;
  cfg = cfg || {};
  me.callParent([Ext.apply({
    storeId: 'Customers',
    autoLoad: true,
    model: 'myApp.model.Customer',
    proxy: {
      type: 'ajax',
      url: 'serverside/data/customers.json',
      actionMethods: {read:"POST"},
      reader: {
        type: 'json',
        rootProperty: 'records',
        useSimpleAccessors: true
      }
    }
  }, cfg)]);
  }
});
```

Remember that these two models need to be saved in the app/model folder. Now, we create the Grid panel (which will be a new view inside our application), save the file as customers.js in the app/view/modules folder, and write the code as follows:

```
Ext.define('myApp.view.modules.customers', { //step 1
  extend: 'Ext.grid.Panel',
  requires: [
    'myApp.view.modules.customersController',
    'Ext.grid.column.Number',
    'Ext.grid.column.Date',
    'Ext.grid.column.Boolean',
    'Ext.view.Table',
    'Ext.button.Button',
    'Ext.toolbar.Fill',
    'Ext.toolbar.Paging'
  ],
  xtype: 'customersmodule',  //step 2
  alias: 'widget.customersmodule',
  controller: 'customersmodule',
```

```
    frame: true,
    closable: true,
    iconCls: '',
    title: 'Customers...',
    forceFit: true,
    listeners: {//step 3
      'afterrender': {fn: 'myafterrender'},
      'render': {fn: 'myrenderevent'}
    },
    initComponent: function() { //step 4
      var me = this;
      me.store = me.createCustomersStore();
      me.columns = [/* columns definition here... */];
      me.dockedItems= [/* items here... */];
      me.callParent();
    },
    createCustomersStore:function(){
      return Ext.create('myApp.store.Customers');
    }
});
```

Let's understand the preceding code step by step:

1. First, we defined the `'myApp.view.modules.customers'` class. It extends the `Ext.grid.Panel` panel class.

2. Then, we defined the `xtype`, `alias`, and `controller` properties in order to make the application to recognize the type of component we are using"—customersmodule"—and also the controller (view controller) that this view will use.

3. We defined the grid listeners (render and afterrender) with the following code:

   ```
   listeners: { //step 3
     afterrender: {fn: 'myafterrender'},
     render: {fn: 'myrenderevent'}
   },
   ```

   So, these `afterrender` and `render` functions will be handled by the `ViewController`.

4. Finally, in the `initComponent` function, we define the other properties that our view will have (this is useful when we have to set the properties based on configuration or special permissions) or some parts (child components of the view that could change).

Now, the columns configuration for our view is the following:

```
me.columns =[{
  xtype: 'rownumberer',
  width: 50,
  align:'center'
},{
  xtype: 'numbercolumn',
  width: 70,
  dataIndex: 'id',
  text: 'Id',
  format: '0'
},{
  xtype: 'templatecolumn',
  text: 'Country',
  dataIndex: 'country',
  tpl: '<div><divclass="flag_{[values.country.toLowerCase()]}">' +
    ' </div>  {country}</div>'
},{
  xtype: 'gridcolumn',
  width: 210,
  dataIndex: 'name',
  text: 'Customer name'
},{
  xtype: 'datecolumn',
  dataIndex: 'clientSince',
  width: 120,
  text: 'Client Since',
  format: 'M-d-Y',
  align:'center'
},{
  xtype: 'booleancolumn',
  dataIndex:'sendnews',
  width: 100,
  align:'center',
  text: 'Send News?',
  falseText: 'No',
  trueText: 'Yes'
}];
```

The code for `dockedItems` is as follows:

```
me.dockedItems=[{
  xtype: 'toolbar', dock: 'top',
  items: [{
    xtype: 'button',
    text: 'New...',
    iconCls:'addicon-16',
    action:'newrecord',
    listeners: {click:'btnactionclick'}
  },{
    xtype: 'button',
    text: 'Edit...',
    iconCls:'editicon-16',
    action:'editrecord',
    listeners: {click:'btnactionclick'}
  },{
    xtype: 'button',
    text: 'Delete...',
    iconCls:'deleteicon-16',
    action:'deleterecord',
    listeners: {click:'btnactionclick'}
  },{
    xtype: 'tbfill'
  },{
    xtype: 'button',
    text: 'Help.',
    iconCls:'help-16',
    action:'showhelp'
  }]
}];
```

ViewController

As we talked before, the view controller needs to be attached to the view, and every time a new instance of the view is created, a new instance of the ViewController will also be created. In version 5, this new feature was implemented for the reason that sometimes, to create a module, developers used only one controller for many views (wrapping all as a module; this was a chaotic issue for maintaining code).

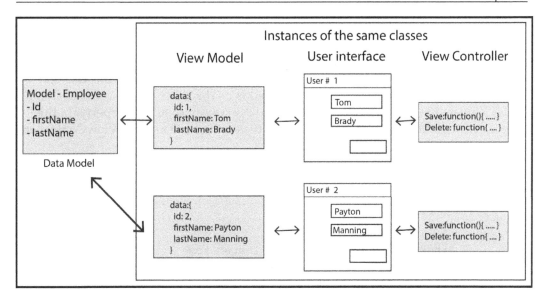

For this new module (customers) that we have created, we are going to use the view controller. Now, inside the app/view/modules folder, create another file called customersController.js (this will be the ViewController for the view), and place the following code:

```
Ext.define('myApp.view.modules.customersController', {
  extend: 'Ext.app.ViewController',
  alias: 'controller.customersmodule',
  config: {
    control: {
      // Other alternative on how to listen some events
      'customersmodule button[action=showhelp]': {
        click: 'btnactionclick'
            }
          }
    },
  init: function() {
    console.log('customers view controller init');
  },
  myrenderevent:function(cmpx, eOpts){
    console.log('Grid - customers render event');
  },
  myafterrender:function(cmpx, eOpts){
    console.log('Grid - customers afterrender event');
  },
  btnactionclick:function(btnx, evt, eOpts){
    console.log('Button clicked : ' + btnx.action);
```

```
    }
  });
```

In this code, we defined the ViewController for our customer's view. Check out the name; it is `myApp.view.modules.customersController`, and it extends the `Ext.app.ViewController` class. The alias we used is `controller.customersmodule`, and it is related to our view's `controller: 'customersmodule'` property. In this way, Ext JS will know the proper relation between the view and the ViewController.

Also, you might have noticed that in the customers view, we have a toolbar (`dockeditems`), and we set on the first three buttons the listeners for each button, but on the help button, we didn't. Now, inside the ViewController, we place this code:

```
config:{
  control: {
    // Other alternative on how to listen some events
    'customersmodule button[action=showhelp]': {
      click:'btnactionclick'
    }
  }
},
```

This code will be will be listening/waiting for the Help button to be clicked on to run the `btnactionclick` function defined in the view. So, as of now, our code must work, run the app in our browser, and access the **Customers** module. We will see something like this:

Now, click on the buttons inside the new module and check the console output (using developer tools/Firebug). You may see this:

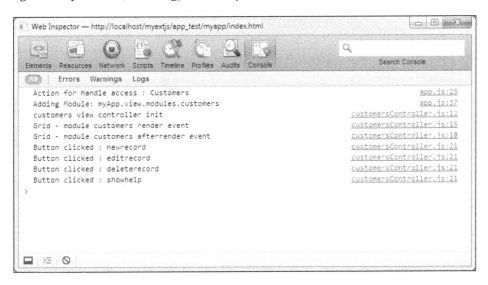

We can see that our view and its ViewController are linked correctly and responding as we need. Now, let's create the form responsible for adding new customer records. On this new form, we will implement the ViewModel, linking its data and the form's behavior by the use of data bindings.

ViewModel

The **ViewModel** in Ext JS is a class that manages a data object. It will monitor changes and interact with those interested in its data. This class is also able to link to a parent ViewModel (the hierarchy in components/views), which means that it allows child views to inherit the data of the parent ViewModel.

In version 5, components have a new config property called `bind`, and this allows us to associate any configuration with the data coming from the ViewModel.

As we talked previously, the ViewModel will create a new instance once its associated view instance is created. Now, create the ViewModel file for the **Customers** form, name it as `customerFormViewModel.js`, place it inside the `app/view/forms` folder, and add the following code in it:

```
Ext.define('myApp.view.forms.customerFormViewModel', { //step 1
extend:'Ext.app.ViewModel',
alias:'viewmodel.customerform',
data:{  //step 2
```

```
            action: 'add',
            ownerCmp: null,
            rec: null
    },
    formulas:{ //Step 3
        readOnlyId:function(get){
            return (get('action')!=='add');
        },
        ownerNotNull:function(get){
            var cmpx = get('ownerCmp');
            return (cmpx!==null && cmpx!==undefined);
        },
        refName:function(get){
            var value='';
            if (get('action')!=='add'){ //Edit action
                var id = get('rec.id'), custname =get('rec.name');
                if (custname===''){ custname ='(not defined)'; }
                    value = 'Editing : ' +  id + ' - ' + custname + "..." ;
                } else {
                    value = 'New customer...';
                }
                //Step 4
                var xtypeOwner= this.getView().ownerCt.getXType();
                if (xtypeOwner=="customerwindow"){
                    this.getView().ownerCt.setTitle(value);
                }
                Return value;
            }
        }
    }
});
```

Let's explain the preceding code step by step:

1. We defined the class extending `Ext.app.ViewModel,` and also set the `viewmodel.customerform` alias so that we can later reference this ViewModel as `customerform`.

2. We set the default `data` configuration object. It will be overwritten when we create our new (view).

3. We set the `formulas` property inside the configuration of ViewModel. The `formulas` object is an object that defines named values whose value is managed by functions, so we can manipulate the values. In this case, we set three new properties, named `readOnlyId,` `ownerNotNull,` and `refName.`

4. If you look carefully at the `formulas.refname` function, you will notice that we are using `this.getView()`. This method allows us to access our (linked) view class/instance and manipulate it.

Binding and data binding

In Ext JS 5, one new addition in the components is the `bind` config, which allows us to associate data from the ViewModel. So, using bind, we can bind the appropriate/desired configuration, and whenever the bound value changes, this config will automatically be updated.

To refer to the proper data inside the model, we need to use bind descriptors:

- **Direct bind**: This value is passed directly without changes, like this for example:

  ```
  bind:{ value: '{firstName}'}
  ```

- **Bind template**: We can produce customized strings as in `Ext.Template`. An example of this is shown here:

  ```
  bind:{ title: 'Hello {firstName} {lastName}..!'}
  ```

- **Boolean bind**: This is useful for binding a Boolean config, like this for example:

  ```
  {!isAdmin.checked}
  ```

 You can check out the Ext JS documentation to see all the available ways of binding data and more advanced examples.

Now, let's create the `view` file for the customers form, name it `customerForm.js` inside the `app/view/forms` folder, and place the following code in it:

```
Ext.define('myApp.view.forms.customerForm', { //Step 1
    extend: 'Ext.form.Panel',
    alias: 'widget.customerform',
    xtype: 'customerform',
    requires:[
        'Ext.form.field.Number',
        'Ext.form.field.Date',
        'Ext.form.field.ComboBox',
        'Ext.toolbar.Toolbar',
        'Ext.toolbar.Fill',
        'Ext.button.Button',
```

```
      'myApp.view.forms.customerFormViewController',
      'myApp.view.forms.customerFormViewModel',
      'myApp.model.Customer'
   ],
   controller: 'customerform', //Step 2
   ViewModel: {type: 'customerform' }, //Step 2
   bodyPadding: 6,
   header: false,
   title: 'Customer...',
   bind:{ title: '{refName}' }, //Step 3
   defaults:{
      labelAlign: 'right',
      labelWidth: 80,
      msgTarget: 'side',
      anchor: '-18'
   },
   items: [{
      xtype: 'numberfield',
      fieldLabel: 'Customer ID',
      name: 'id',
      anchor: '100%',
      maxWidth: 200,
      minWidth: 200,
      hideTrigger: true,
      bind:{ value:'{rec.id}', readOnly:'{readOnlyId}'}//Step 3
   },{
      xtype: 'textfield',
      fieldLabel: 'Name',
      name: 'name',
      bind: '{rec.name}' //Step 3
   },{
      xtype: 'textfield',
      fieldLabel: 'Phone',
      name: 'phone',
      bind: '{rec.phone}' //Step 3
   },{
      xtype: 'textfield',
      fieldLabel: 'Web site',
      name: 'website',
      bind: '{rec.website}' //Step 3
   },{
      xtype: 'datefield',
      anchor: '60%',
      fieldLabel: 'Client since',
```

```
          name:'clientSince',
          submitFormat: 'Y-m-d',
          bind:'{rec.clientSince}' //Step 3
      },{
        xtype: 'combobox',
        fieldLabel: 'Country',
        name: 'country',
        store: Ext.create('Ext.data.Store', {
          fields: ['id', 'name'],
          data : [
            {"id": "USA", "name": "United States of America"},
            {"id": "Mexico", "name": "Mexico"}
          ]
        }),
        valueField: 'id',
        displayField: 'name',
        bind:'{rec.country}' //Step 3
    },{
      xtype: 'combobox',
      fieldLabel: 'Status',
      name: 'status',
      store: Ext.create('Ext.data.Store', {
        fields: ['id', 'name'],
        data: [
          {"id": "Active", "name": "Active"},
          {"id": "Inactive", "name": "Inactive"},
          {"id": "Suspended", "name": "Suspended"},
          {"id": "Prospect", "name": "Prospect"},
        ]
      }),
        valueField: 'id',
        displayField: 'name',
        bind: '{rec.status}' //Step 3
    },{
        xtype: 'numberfield',
        anchor: '60%',
        fieldLabel: '# Employees',
        name:'employees',
        bind:'{rec.employees}' //Step 3
    },{
        xtype:'checkbox',
        fieldLabel: 'Send news ?',
        boxLabel:'check if yes/uncheck if no...!',
        name:'sendnews',
```

```
              inputValue:1,
              bind:'{rec.sendnews}' //Step 3
          }],
          dockedItems: [{
              xtype: 'toolbar', dock: 'bottom',
              items: [{
                  xtype: 'tbfill'
              },{
                  xtype: 'button',
                  iconCls: 'save-16',
                  text: 'Save...', action:'savecustomer'
              },{
                  xtype: 'button',
                  iconCls: 'cancelicon-16',
                  text: 'Close / Cancel',
                  action:'closeform',
                  bind:{ hidden:'{ownerNotNull}'}
              }]
          }],
          initComponent: function(){
              // place your code....
              this.callParent();
          },
          listeners:{ //Step 4
              'titlechange':{
                  fn:function( panelx, newtitle, oldtitle, eOpts){
                      if (panelx.rendered){
                          panelx.ownerCt.setTitle(newtitle);
                      }
                  }
              },
              'afterrender':{
                  fn:function( panelx, eOpts ){
                      panelx.ownerCt.setTitle(panelx.title);
                  },
                  single:true
              }
          }
      });
```

Here is a step-by-step explanation of the preceding code:

1. We created the class extending `Ext.form.Panel` because this component/class will be reused in the *Chapter 12, Responsive Configurations and Tablet Support.*

2. We defined the controller and the ViewModel with the `{type: 'customerform'}` code, which references the ViewModel.

3. With the `bind` property, we linked all other properties inside the `customerForm` configuration as well as the form's fields. Also, we checked all the bindings we are making, and we can use a string or an object to define. In the case of strings, the default bind for some components (example fields) will be the `value` property.

4. Notice that we set the `bind` config on the close button as `bind : {hidden: '{ownerNotNull}'}`. This will ensure that if `formPanel` has an owner container or was set in the configuration, then the button will appear, otherwise it won't.

5. We used some event listeners to monitor title changes in our extended form panel. You can notice that in the configuration, we set `header:false`, but we bind the title of `formPanel` to be changed by the ViewModel. So when the title changes, thanks to the ViewModel, our `ownerCt` component (if it exists and is set to a value) will change the title.

Finally, create the file named `customerFormViewController.js` inside the `app/view/forms` folder and add the following code to it:

```
Ext.define('myApp.view.forms.customerFormViewController', {
    extend: 'Ext.app.ViewController',
    alias: 'controller.customerform',
    config: {
      control: {
        'customerform button[action=savecustomer]': {
          click:'saveCustomer'
        },
        'customerform button[action=closeform]': {
          click:'formClose'
        }
      }
    },
    init: function() {
      console.log('customers form view controller init');
    },
    formClose: function(cmpx, eOpts){
      console.log('Closing Form');
      var closeCmp= this.getViewModel().get('ownerCmp');
```

```
    if(closeCmp!==null && closeCmp!==undefined){
      var xtypeUsed = closeCmp.getXType();
      if (xtypeUsed ==='panel' || xtypeUsed ==='gridpanel' ||
        xtypeUsed ==='window' || xtypeUsed ==="customerwindow"){
        closeCmp.close();
      }
    }
    return;
  },
saveCustomer:function(btnx, evt, eOpts){
  var action= this.getView().getViewModel().get('action');
  console.log('Performing action in form : ' + btnx.action);
  if(action=='add'){
    if( this.getView().getForm().isValid() ) {
      var newCustomerData =this.getView().getForm().getValues();
      var mycustomer = Ext.create('myApp.model.Customer',
        newCustomerData );
      this.getView().gridModule.getStore().add(mycustomer);
      Ext.Msg.alert('Ok', 'New customer added successfully..!');
      this.formClose();
    } else {
      Ext.Msg.alert('Error!', 'There are' + 'some errors in the
        form , please check' + ' the information!');
      return;
    }
  } else { //Edit action
    if ( this.getView().getForm().isValid()){
      var newCustomerData = this.getView().getForm().
        getValues();
      var Record = this.getView().gridModule.getStore().getById(
        newCustomerData.id);
      var editResult = Record.set(newCustomerData);
      if (editResult!=null){
        Record.commit();
        Ext.Msg.alert('Ok', 'Customer edited successfully.!');
        this.formClose();
      } else {
        Ext.Msg.alert('Error.!', 'Error updating customer.!');
        return;
      }
    } else {
      Ext.Msg.alert('Error..!', 'There are some errors in the
        form, please check the information..!');
      return;
    }
```

The controller file will add the save and close functionality to our form's buttons, so let's save our files. Now we are going to create a new view that will act as a wrapper for our `customerForm` view. So now, create the `customerWindow.js` file inside the `app/view/forms` folder and place the following code in it:

```
Ext.define('myApp.view.forms.customerWindow', { //Step 1
    extend: 'Ext.window.Window',
    alias: 'widget.customerwindow',
  xtype: 'customerwindow',
    requires: [
'myApp.view.forms.customerWindowViewController',
        'myApp.view.forms.customerForm'
    ],
  controller: 'customerwindow',   //Step 2
height: 368,
width:  489,
iconCls: 'customer-16',
layout:'fit',
  closable:true,
  minimizable:true,
  title: '',
  tools:[{ //Step 3
    type:'restore',
    tooltip: 'Restore window...',
    handler: function(event, toolEl, panelHeader) {
      var cmpx=panelHeader.up('window');
      if (cmpx.collapsed){
        cmpx.expand();
      }
    }
  }],
  initComponent: function() {
    var me=this;
//Step 4
var myForm =Ext.create('myApp.view.forms.customerForm',{
    gridModule: me.gridModule,
    ViewModel:{
      data:{
        action:me.action,
        ownerCmp: me,
        rec:  me.record || null
```

```
                }
              }
            });
            me.items=[myForm];
            me.callParent(arguments);
        }
    });
```

Let's understand the preceding code step by step:

1. In Step 1, we defined our class.

2. Then, we defined the controller.

3. We created a tool for handling the code for restoring the window after it is minimized.

4. Inside the initComponent function, we created an instance of the customerForm class, which this window will contain. You might see that inside the configuration object, we set ViewModel and its data. This will make Ext JS create an instance of the customerForm ViewModel and apply this data.

Finally, here's the controller for our window class:

```
Ext.define('myApp.view.forms.customerWindowViewController', {
    extend: 'Ext.app.ViewController',
    alias: 'controller.customerwindow',
    config: {
     control:{
        'customerwindow':{
            'minimize':'mywindowMinimize',
            'expand':'myExpand'
         },
      }
    },
    mywindowMinimize:function(cmpx, eOpts){
     console.log('customerWindow minimizing..!');
     cmpx.collapse();
         cmpx.alignTo(Ext.getBody(),'tr-tr');
     },
    myExpand:function(cmpx, eOpts){
     cmpx.center();
     }
    });
```

Basically, this controller will control when the window minimizes and when it is restored. It will center the window in our web page or browser document.

> It's important to be careful with the names and typos (uppercase and lowercase letters), because a bad typo will represent a JS error. This is because Ext JS will not recognize the names in our MVC or MVVM architecture correctly.

At this point, we can run our application. Open the customer's module, select a record, and then click on the **Edit** button. You will see something similar to the following screenshot:

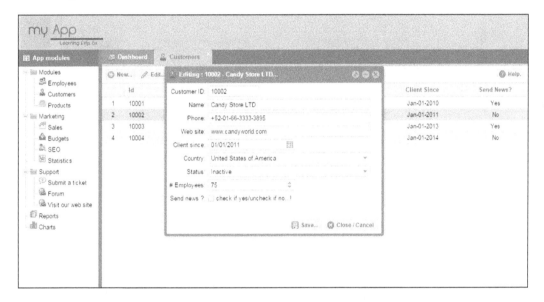

Notice that the fields were correctly filled in with the data from our Store and model (record) inside the form. Try to write something in the **Customer ID** field and you will see that it is read-only. Now let's make a change in the customer's name field. You will see this:

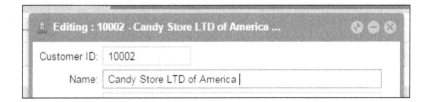

Did you see how the window's title changes as the value of the **Name** field changes? If you empty the **Name** field, you will see (not defined), because you set this inside the code of `refName` on the `formulas` configuration in the ViewModel.

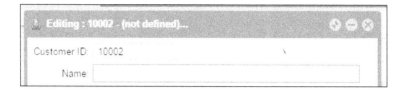

Now minimize the window and edit another record. This is what you will see:

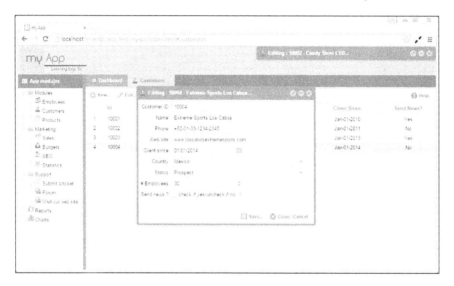

Check out how the minimized window went to the top-right corner of the window/document. Also, we have another window editing another record. Here, each window (instance of the `customerWindow` class) is an individual instance that contains its own ViewModel and ViewController, and they do not mess with each other.

Remember that you can mix MVC, MVVM, or MVC + VM in the same application. It's up to you to decide which one suits your needs best according the modules or requirements that you have to work on. The main idea is to reduce code as much as possible. Also, these code examples have not very complex, so you get an idea and understanding of what Ext JS can offer you with respect to architecture.

Router – implementing and using

Another new addition in version 5 is the use of routers in our application. Routing can be used to track an application's state through the use of the browser history stack. It also allows deep linking into the application, which allows a direct link to a specific part of your application. As an example, open the **Kitchen Sink** example (Sencha's own examples), as shown here:

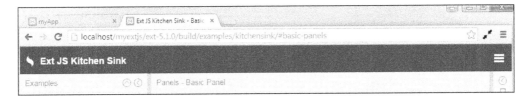

The **#basic-panels** part of the URL is called the **hash** or **fragment identifier**. The browser fires an event, called `hashchange`, that is recognized by our application, and we can use it and react according to the value (or values) assigned to it.

So, in this URL example, if you copy the URL, close the browser, reopen it, and paste the URL, the application will open with the last module (view) you were in. In this case, it is the `basic-panels` example.

To implement this in our application, let's make some slight changes to the `app.js` file. At the end of the file (code), insert the following code:

```
init:function() {
    this.setDefaultToken('');
}
```

The `setDefaultToken` method will set `defaultToken` to be used when the application launches, if one is not present. Now, in the `app/controller/app.js` file, make the following changes to the `handleAccess` function:

```
handleAccess: function(cmpView, record, itemx, index, evt, eOpts ){
    console.log('Action for handle access : ' + record.data.text);
    var me=this, moduleData = record.data;
    if (moduleData.hasOwnProperty('moduleType')){
        var typeModule = moduleData.moduleType;
        if (typeModule==''){
            return;
        } else if(typeModule=='link'){
            me.executeLink(moduleData);
        } else if (typeModule=='window'){
            me.runWindow(moduleData);
        } else if  (typeModule=='module'){
```

```
                //Change to be made for router
                if (moduleData.options=="myApp.view.modules.customers"){
                    this.redirectTo('customers', true);
                    return;
                } else {
                    me.addModule(moduleData);
                }
            }
        }
    },
```

The `redirectTo` method will update the hash. By default, it will not execute the routes if the current token and the token passed are the same. We pass the `customers` parameter and `true`. The first parameter will set the hash string, and the second will force the update of the hash regardless of the current token. In the same file, update the `config` property to the following:

```
    config:{
        refs:{
            myappzone:{
                selector:'appzone',
xtype:'appzone',
autoCreate:false
            }
        },
        routes:{
                ':id': {
                    action: 'handleRoute',
                    before: 'beforeHandleRoute'
                }
            }
    },
```

Here, we set the `routes` methods for each event (`before` and `action`). At the end of this file, we insert the functions we set the `handleRoute` and `beforeHandleRoute` routes:

```
    beforeHandleRoute: function(id, action) {
        if (id!='customers'){
            Ext.Msg.alert("Route error", "invalid action...!");
            action.stop();
        } else {
            action.resume();
        }
    },
    handleRoute: function(id) {
```

```
if (id=='customers'){
  var myStore=this.getMyappzone().query('treepanel')[0].
    getStore();
  var myRecord = myStore.findNode('text', 'Customers');
  if (myRecord!=undefined){
    this.addModule(myRecord.data);
  } else {
    Ext.Msg.alert("Route error", "error getting customers data
      access...!");
  }
}
}
```

The `beforeHandleRoute` method is executed before doing anything (if there is a **hash**), so if everything is okay, we need to call the `action.resume()` function to let Ext JS to continue executing the route. Otherwise, with `action.stop()`, the router will do nothing.

The `handleRoute` function will get the record data from the tree panel (access modules) and will launch the `addModule` function to create the desired module (in this case, the `Customers` module).

So now, run the application and open the customer module. You will see that the hash has been updated. After being updated the hash reloads the web page. Then, see the results, as follows:

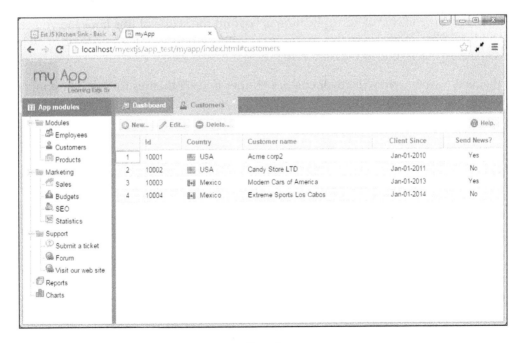

Also, it's important to mention that routes can be configured to accept more parameters, and we can set conditions to validate hash values in order to add a bit more security to our application.

Summary

It's recommended to have good architecture so that you can easily manage and maintain the code, and generate good teamwork, if the case applies. Developers build architectures in their own personalized taste and fashion, so following an architecture pattern can be easier when involving new developers in your project.

Remember to analyze the requirements you have so that you can properly choose the pattern that suits you the most, otherwise you are likely to write more code than you need.

You can check out more information at the Sencha documentation or blog to understand more advanced topics about controllers, viewModel, data binding, and view Controllers, among others. The link to visit is `http://docs.sencha.com/extjs/5.1/application_architecture/application_architecture.html`.

From the pages of this chapter, you learned how to organize your code using classes and following the MVC, MVC, MVVM, or MVC + VM pattern to assign the right task to each class. Using a controller to write our logic for the views and giving life to our components is a great way to keep our code clean and organized.

Demonstrating the complete application is beyond the scope of this book, so you can try adding other modules to this example on your own using the same logic or steps, and adapting each module as required.

In the next chapter, we will cover custom themes and UI themes for our components, and give them a different look.

11
The Look and Feel

One of the challenges in Ext JS applications is to create a specific look and feel, for example, branding or setting the company's or the client's desired colors into the application. Usually, the Ext JS UI is known for its classic light blue theme. In Ext JS versions older than version 4, it was difficult to customize and create themes due to the theme's architecture.

Since version 4, a new architecture/base code was implemented, which gave us the ability to change colors, gradients, fonts, and so on in the Theme globally and per component. Now we can also create different styles for the same component using the `ui` property.

In this chapter, you are going to learn how to create new themes. We will create a theme for the main application that we have been working on since the previous chapter.

We will cover the following topics in this chapter:

- CSS, Compass, and SASS
- Advanced theming
- Different styles on the same component
- Support for legacy browsers

Setting up our environment

Before we start creating our new theme and UIs, we need to install some tools onto our computer. These tools will help us write our theme in Ext JS, because we are going to use Compass and SASS to generate our CSS code and give a new feel to our application.

SASS, also known as **Syntactically Awesome Style Sheets** (http://sass-lang.com/), is an extension of CSS that allows us to use variables, nested rules and mixins, and it's more thoroughly compatible with CSS syntax. This will allow us to create style sheets with less effort.

COMPASS (http://compass-style.org/) is a SASS framework designed to make more work more smooth and efficient. Let's call it a library of tools and the best practices for manipulating SASS. In the end, the compiled output will be CSS files.

In order to use both tools (SASS and Compass), we need to have Ruby installed on our computer. Ruby is a dynamic language and is popular among web developers worldwide. For the moment, don't worry if you are not familiar with using this language, because we are not going to write apps or code with it. It is needed so that Compass and SASS can work properly in our OS.

So let's download and install Ruby. If you are using Windows, you ought to know that there are installers specific for this, and they make it easier to get started. We can find installers and downloads of Ruby at https://www.ruby-lang.org/en/downloads/. If you are using Mac, you will need to install XCode, Ruby, and all its dependencies. Also, you can use the RVM project to install any version of Ruby on the same machine; this works for Linux systems as well.

At the time of writing this book, the latest version of Ruby is 2.2.1, but on Windows, I have found that version 1.9.3p448 works fine. Install Ruby, and once it is installed, usually on Windows OS 7 or greater, you may need it to set up the PATH environment variable. After doing this on Windows OS 7 or greater, restart Windows so that PATH can work properly.

Now let's open a terminal (on Windows, go to **Start** | **All Programs** | **Accessories** | **Command Prompt**). A window will open, and you have to type the following command:

```
$ruby -v
```

This command should give us the version of Ruby already installed. We should see something like this:

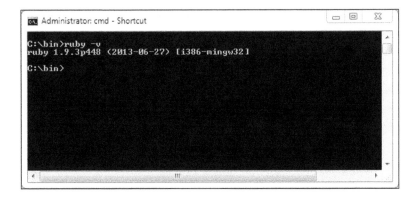

Now, Ruby comes with a package (command) tool called **gem**. We are going to use this tool to install Compass. In our terminal (Command Prompt), we execute the following command:

```
$gem install compass
```

This command downloads and installs all of the software and dependencies required in order for it to work properly, as in this case as Compass needs SASS this will be installed too. After finishing the installation, run the following commands:

```
$compass -v
```

```
$sass -v
```

If everything goes correctly, we will see the version of each gem (package) installed on our system. So now, we are ready to start working with our custom theme (the first theme for some people).

The packages folder

As we've seen in *Chapter 1, An Introduction to Ext JS 5*, we talked about the folder structure in version 5. We also said that the resources folder disappeared, and in its place, we have now the packages folder. This folder contains many subfolders that are used to build our application and also contains theme folders (CSS, images, SASS, and so on).

Theme folders were reorganized in this version in order to provide a cleaner and organized way to create new themes. Also, we can say that themes were hierarchically constructed. This means that Ext JS themes extend a package in order to be created.

Look at the following diagram to understand how the hierarchy is set for themes:

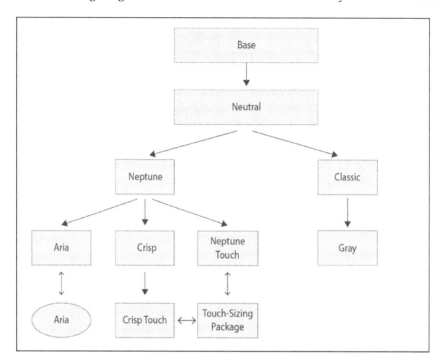

So, after showing this hierarchy, it's advisable to say that **Neptune** and **Classic** are the most frequent themes to be extended to create a custom theme. This is because both of these themes contain all of the necessary code for creating new themes.

Extending the **Neutral** theme can be considered a very abstract theme, and will require much work, such as adding many variable overrides code. Nevertheless, it can be extended.

So, to create our first theme, first of all, we need to open our console (Command Prompt), and go to our application's directory (the app workspace) inside the myapp/ folder. Once we are there, we type the following command:

```
sencha -sdk [path to SDK] generate theme -extend ext-theme-neptune my-
custom-theme
```

As we are creating our custom theme for our application, the path to the SDK will be the ext/ folder inside our workspace (the myapp/ext folder). Now type this:

```
sencha -sdk ext generate theme -extend ext-theme-neptune my-custom-
theme
```

After the command completes, we will see the `ext/packages` folder (inside the `myapp/` folder) with a new structure, like this:

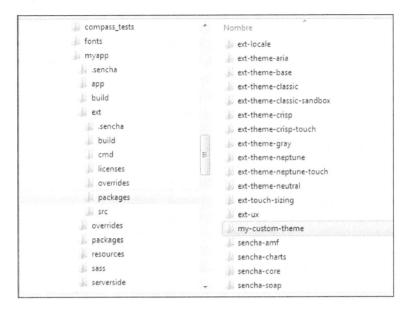

 It's always recommended to generate and use the application's workspace to create a new theme, and always avoid using the Ext JS framework's folder.

Now that we have our initial theme base, let's update some application files in order to use the new theme inside our application. In the root of our application folder, we search for the `app.json` file and locate the following line:

```
"theme": "ext-theme-neptune",
```

Change it to this one:

```
"theme": "my-custom-theme",
```

Then save the changes. So far, we have made the settings for our application to use the theme named `my-custom-theme`. If we run the application, it will look like we are using the Neptune theme. This is because our new theme so far is exactly the same as the Neptune theme and doesn't have any changes. For the moment, we are ready to proceed and we can begin working with our new theme.

Variables

In Ext JS themes, there are a lot of variables that we can change to customize our theme, such as variables for colors, fonts, margins, borders, and many more things. To change and add variables, we need to use the Compass code syntax.

In Compass, we can define variables using the dollar ($) sign. Every time we find a word that starts with the dollar sign, it means that it's a variable that we can read or assign a value to. The following lines of code show some examples of variables:

```
$background-color: #f3f3f3;
$font-size: 1.5em;
$header-height: 45px;
$custom-text: 'This is a text value';
```

As shown in the previous code, we can assign a value using a colon (:). We can also use colors, sizes, or texts as values. We need to use a semicolon (;) every time we end a statement.

As we are extending the Neptune theme, so far, our theme has no variables set. Ext JS uses the Neptune theme's values until we define our own variables in our theme. For the theme's variables, we have two types:

- **Global variables**: These will be values used throughout the theme.
- **Component-specific variables**: These variables will be used at a component-specific level. But be aware that if a component is extending another, then the values will be shared. For example, we change the variable values for `Ext.panel.Panel`. This means that `Ext.grid.Panel`, which is extending `Ext.panel.Panel`, will then inherit the changes we made to the theme.

In the Ext JS documentation, we can find the global variables at `http://docs.sencha.com/extjs/5.1/5.1.1-apidocs/#!/api/Global_CSS`.

For specific components, we can find them at the locations marked here:

Now, to set our global variables, let's go to the `ext/packages/my-custom-theme/sass/var` folder, and create a new file called `Component.scss`. Inside this file, we are going to write the following code:

```
/* My Custom Theme SCSS Component file */
$color: #6d6d6d !default;
$base-color: #0d7179 !default;
```

Here, we are setting two variables: `$color` will be the font/text color used throughout the theme, and `$base-color` will be the color base for almost all our components. Save the file, and in your console tool, go to the theme's folder (`ext/packages/my-custom-theme/`). Let's use the Sencha CMD tool and type the following:

```
sencha package build
```

This command will generate the `build` folder inside our theme folder. This new folder will contain the compiled CSS and resources ready to be used in our app. After executing this command, you will see something similar to the next screenshot:

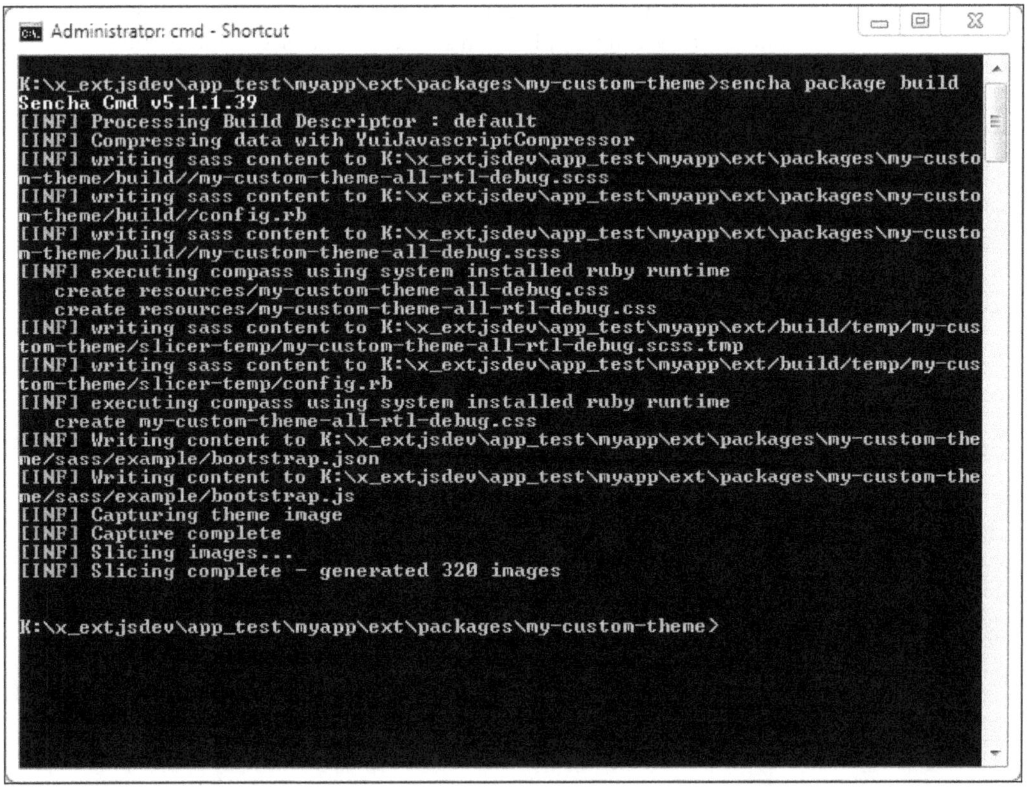

In Windows OS, this command sometimes hangs on the **[INF] Capturing theme image** line, so be sure that you are using the correct **Java Runtime Environment (JRE)**, which needs to be version 1.7. Speaking from personal experience using other versions hangs indefinitely and needs to be stopped by pressing *Ctrl + C*.

Now, we need to apply the changes made in `app.json` to our app's root folder (`myapp/`). In order to fully use our new themes, let's go back to our root directory (application workspace root) and type this:

```
sencha app watch
```

This command is intended to monitor changes made in our app, refresh some/many files, and recompile as needed.

 When you change your theme's variables, it's recommended that you use some other instance of the console tool and recompile it. The `sencha app watch` command will be on the first instance, running and checking changes, and when a change occurs in the theme, the Sencha CMD tool will update the files of the application so that we can see the updated changes.

Now let's run the application. We may get the following result:

Notice the base color (blue is no longer used). Now it's using the color we set in the $base-color variable. Also, the black color used in text has changed to a gray color.

Note that we can use any color according to the design we want. At this point, you can start playing or experimenting with many or all variables, and see how the theme is affected.

Advanced theming

In this section, we will cover some common situations where we need to modify the original theme (the extended theme). This is frequently used for branding or visual purposes.

Changing the component's style

For this example, we are going to change the style of the Ext.toolbar.Toolbar component, so let's go to the ext/packages/my-custom-theme/sass/var/ folder and create a folder called toolbar. Inside this folder, create a file named Toolbar.scss and place the following code in it:

```
$toolbar-background-color: rgba(188,188,188,1);
$toolbar-background-gradient: recessed;
```

Save the file. Now, in your console tool, go to the ext/packages/my-custom-theme/ folder and compile your theme:

```
sencha package build
```

Next, let's refresh our app, open the **Customers** module, and check the changes, as shown here:

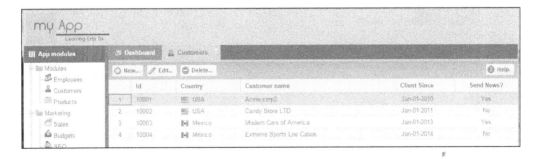

Notice that the toolbar's background color and gradient have changed in your app. This change, which we have already made, will be applied to all the toolbars and (components that extend toolbar class) in our custom theme.

To understand how to apply styles to other components, take a look at the **Neptune** theme inside the `sass/var` folder. You will notice that there is a folder structure and there are files for each component type, like this:

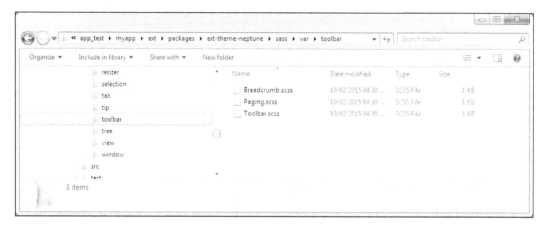

Adding new gradients

Sometimes, the default gradients set in Ext JS themes are not all of the ones we desire to be using. Even though there are some gradients defined in the theme variables, such as matte, glossy, bevel, recessed, and so on, these may not be the choices we want to include in our theme.

So, it's important to mention that we should not touch the `ext-theme-base` or `ext-theme-neutral`. This is because these are basic for other themes and we may compromise something critical. So, we can override these gradients inside our theme.

Therefore, we need to define a new type of gradient for our toolbar component, and it needs to be the one we are 100 percent sure we desire. To accomplish this task, we need to go into this directory:

```
/ext/packages/my-custom-theme/sass/etc/
```

In this folder, you will see a file with the name `all.scss`. Open it; it may be empty or blank. So, place the following code in it:

```
@import 'mixins';
```

This code will tell the compiler to use the `mixins` file. In this case, the theme compiler will look for the `mixins.scss` file located in the same folder. As this file does not exist yet, we proceed to create it and then place the following code:

```
@import 'mixins/background-gradient';
```

Once again, we are making a setting to ensure that another file will be used. Now this file needs to be named `background-gradient.scss`, but it has to be inside the `mixins` folder, so let's create the folder and the file. Once that is done, we place the following code:

```
@function linear-gradient-recessed ($direction, $bg-color) {
    @return linear-gradient(left, color_stops(#fbb040, #cccccc));
}
```

This last file has the purpose of overriding one of the default gradients set in Ext JS (theme base). You can see all the available gradients defined in Ext JS at `http://docs.sencha.com/extjs/5.1/5.1.1-apidocs/#!/api/Global_CSS-css_mixin-background-gradient`.

Remember that we are using the **ext** folder inside our application's workspace (the structure generated by the Sencha CMD tool and when we created the basic skeleton for our initial application in *Chapter 10, Architecture*). Save the file, then go to the `Toolbar.scss` file located in the `ext/packages/my-custom-theme/sass/var/toolbar/` folder, and make the following change:

```
/*$toolbar-background-color: rgba(188,188,188,1); */
$toolbar-background-gradient: recessed;
```

Save the file. In your console tool, go to the `ext/packages/my-custom-theme/` folder and compile your theme once again:

```
sencha package build
```

Now let's refresh and also wait for that `sencha app watch` command to detect changes (if not, then run it again to be sure of the changes made in your app, and refresh the browser). We may see the following result:

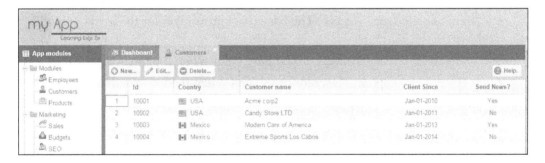

Notice that the gradient (customized for our needs) has been applied to the toolbar.

It's recommended that before you make these types of changes, and also if you are new to Compass and SASS, check out the documentation of both in order to know exactly what you are doing, and also to have the right syntax in the SCSS files. Some useful links about this theme are:

- `http://compass-style.org/reference/compass/css3/images/`
- `http://compass-style.org/examples/compass/css3/gradient/`

 The SASS documentation can be found at `http://sass-lang.com/documentation/file.SASS_REFERENCE.html`.

Styling the tabs

In our next exercise we will change the tabs' style. In fact, thanks to the new theme architecture in version 5, this will also be easy to do and it's a very similar process. Let's start creating a new folder called `tab` inside the `ext/packages/my-custom-theme/sass/var/` folder, and also create a new file called `Tab.scss`. Now place the following code inside this new file:

```
/* Tab Custom style for my-custom-theme */
$tab-base-color: #65a9e0;
$tab-base-color-active: #c5c5c5;
$tab-base-color-disabled: #597179;
$tab-color-active: #333333;
```

In this code, we are changing four properties:

- `$tab-base-color`: The base color of the tabs (normal appearance)
- `$tab-base-color-active`: The base (background) color the active tab will have
- `$tab-base-color-disabled`: The base color when the tab is disabled
- `$tab-color-active`: The color of the text when the tab is active

Save the file. Now we are ready to compile the theme again, so in our console tool, we go to the `ext/packages/my-custom-theme/` folder. Let's compile our theme again:

```
sencha package build
```

Also, remember to check the `sencha app watch` command if needed. Now let's take a look at our browser (refresh the page) and check the result, as follows:

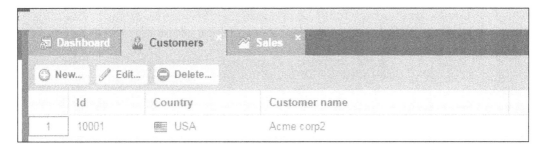

You can see that the *Active* tab has a gray color and the text color is dark gray. The *Normal* tabs have a blue color and a white text color (we didn't change this, so its color comes from the Neptune theme we extended). Now we check out the old version of our theme, as shown in the following screenshot, to see the difference:

Remember that you can use the DOM inspector to find the CSS class (or classes) that is used to add styles to an element or component that you want to modify. The Google Chrome or Safari developer tools are great for this. You can also use Firebug if you are more used to Firefox for development.

Adding custom fonts to our theme

Frequently, many developers and designers feel the need to change the font in the theme.

Also, this task has become part of the trend around web apps — using different font-face types to give a better look to screens and UIs. This task has become more popular nowadays.

So, we need a custom font. A popular place to get them is Google fonts or FONT Squirrel, so let's go to `http://www.fontsquirrel.com/fonts/open-sans` and download `@font-face kit`.

This font-face kit contains the font files and also the CSS files ready for embedding into web pages. Now let's extract the font in a temporary folder and create a new folder named `fonts`.

Inside the `ext/packages/my-custom-theme/resources` folder, create a folder named `open-sans` and copy the content from the `web fonts/opensans_regular_macroman` folder to the new folder. At this moment, you should have something similar to the following screenshot:

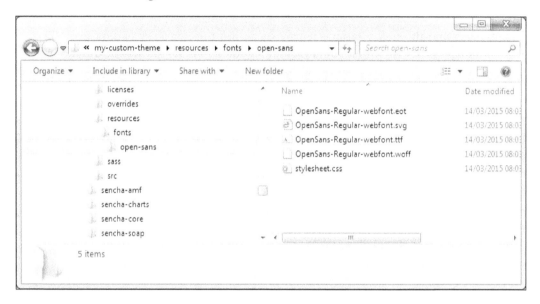

Now that we have our fonts, we open the `stylesheet.css` file and locate the following code:

```
@font-face {
  font-family: 'open_sansregular';
  src: url('OpenSans-Regular-webfont.eot');
  src: url('OpenSans-Regular-webfont.eot?#iefix') format(
    'embedded-opentype'),
  url('OpenSans-Regular-webfont.woff') format('woff'),
  url('OpenSans-Regular-webfont.ttf') format('truetype'),
  url('OpenSans-Regular-webfont.svg#open_sansregular') format(
    'svg');
  font-weight: normal;
  font-style: normal;
}
```

Copy this code and paste it at the beginning of the Component.scss file located in the ext/packages/my-custom-theme/sass/var/ folder. Also, add the following variable:

```
$font-family: open_sansregular;
```

In the end, the Component.scss file will look like this:

```
@font-face {
  font-family: 'open_sansregular';
  src: url('../resources/fonts/open-sans/
    OpenSans-Regular-webfont.eot');
  src: url('../resources/fonts/open-sans/
    OpenSans-Regular-webfont.eot?#iefix') format(
      'embedded-opentype'),
  url('../resources/fonts/open-sans/
    OpenSans-Regular-webfont.woff') format('woff'),
  url('../resources/fonts/open-sans/OpenSans-Regular-webfont.ttf')
    format('truetype'),
  url('../resources/fonts/open-sans/OpenSans-Regular-webfont.svg
    #open_sansregular') format('svg');
  font-weight: normal;
  font-style: normal;
}
$font-family: 'open_sansregular';
$color: #6d6d6d !default;
$base-color: #0d7179 !default;
```

Notice that we changed the URL in the @font-face styles. This is because when we compile the theme, the compiled CSS will be looking at the font in the path relative to the CSS file location. Also, we added a new variable called $font-family and set the value to open_sansregular so that the font family for all our themes will be the font-face value we added at the beginning.

Let's save the file and repeat the process of compiling the theme:

```
sencha package build
```

Also, remember to check the `sencha app watch` command, if needed. Now let's take a look at our browser (refresh the page) for the result, which should be like this:

Notice how the font family has changed in our theme (screen). Now, after carrying out these common tasks on themes, we are ready to advance to creating individual UIs for the same component.

Different styles for the same component

In an application, it's common to have different styles of buttons, windows, panels, and so on. For example, in our application, we can define different styles for a panel (according to the type of data we are going to show in there) and different styles for the toolbars inside panels, or for different types of buttons.

In this case, the `ui` property is essential for this kind of task. Every widget in Ext JS has a `ui` property, which contains prefixes for the CSS classes. In this way, we can define specific classes for every component. In the following exercise, we are going to create the dashboard for our application and give a custom `ui` property to each one of the panels inside the dashboard.

Our layout for the dashboard will be like this:

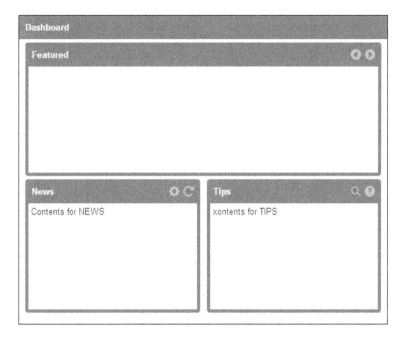

The idea is that we assign each panel a different style, so the **Featured** panel will be purple, the **News** panel will be dark blue, and finally **Tips** will be orange. Also, the title's text and the icons for the panel's tools need to change color. So let's start modifying the `app/view/appZone.js` file and change the `items` property so that it will look like the following code:

```
//...
items: [{
  xtype: 'tabpanel',
  region: 'center',
  itemId: 'mainZone',
  header: false,
  title: '',
  items: [{
    xtype: 'panel',
    itemId: 'startappPanel',
    title: 'Dashboard',
    iconCls: 'home-16',
    bodyPadding: 5,
    region: 'center', //html:'myApp Dashboard',
    layout: 'anchor',
    items:[{
```

```
        xtype: 'container',
        margin: '0px 5px 0px',
        layout: 'anchor',
        items: [{
          xtype: 'panel',
          frame: true,
          height: 200,
          margin: '0px 5px 0px 5px',
          title: 'Featured',
          bodyPadding: 4,
          html: 'Place contents for FEATURED zone',
          tools: [{
            xtype: 'tool',
            type: 'prev'
          },{
            xtype: 'tool',
            type: 'next'
          }]
        }]
      },{
      xtype: 'container',
      height: 200,
      layout: {
        type: 'hbox',
        align: 'stretch'
      },
      items: [{
        xtype: 'panel',
        flex: 2,
        frame: true,
        height: 150,
        html: 'Place contents for NEWS zone',
        margin: '0px 5px 0px 5px',
        bodyBorder: true,
        bodyPadding: 4,
        title: 'News',
          tools: [{
            xtype: 'tool',
            type: 'gear'
          },{
            xtype: 'tool',
            type: 'refresh'
          }]
        },{
```

```
            xtype: 'panel',
            flex: 2,
            frame: true,
            height: 200,
            html: 'Place contents for TIPS zone',
            margin: '0px 5px 0px 5px',
            bodyBorder: true,
            bodyPadding: 4,
            title: 'Tips',
            tools: [{
              xtype: 'tool',
              type: 'search'
            },{
              xtype: 'tool',
              type: 'help'
          }]
        }]
        }]
      }]
    },{
    xtype: 'panel',
    itemId: 'acessPanel',
    region: 'west',
    split: true,
    width: 180,
    iconCls:'app-modules',
    layout: 'fit',
    title: 'App modules',
    items: [{
      xtype: 'treepanel',
      header: false,
      title: 'My Tree Panel',
      store: Ext.create( 'myApp.store.modulesTreeDs',{
        storeId:'accessmodulesDs',
        rootVisible: false
      })
    }]
  }]
```

This code will create the layout we intend to use for our panels. So now, we are going to begin creating the UI (custom style) for each panel as we have previously discussed .

In the `ext/packages/my-custom-theme/sass/src` folder, let's create a new folder called `panel` and also create a `Panel.scss` file. Inside the `Panel.scss` file, let's place the following code:

```
@include extjs-panel-ui(
  $ui:'featuredpanel',
  $ui-header-background-color: #5e1b5e,
  $ui-border-color: #5e1b5e,
  $ui-header-border-color: #5e1b5e,
  $ui-body-border-color: #5e1b5e
);

@include extjs-panel-ui(
  $ui:'featuredpanel-framed',
  $ui-header-background-color: #5e1b5e,
  $ui-border-color: #5e1b5e,
  $ui-header-border-color: #5e1b5e,
  $ui-body-border-color: #5e1b5e,
  $ui-border-width: 5px,
  $ui-border-radius: 4px
);
```

Here, we defined two UIs: one for the framed version and the other for the non-framed version of the panel. Save the file and wait for `sencha app watch` to detect changes. If not, then compile the theme. Now, in the Featured panel's properties, set the `ui` property as shown in the following code:

```
xtype: 'panel',
ui:'featuredpanel',
frame: true,
```

This property, `ui`, will tell Ext JS to use/assign the CSS generated for that panel component. Also, because we have set `frame:true`, the CSS used will be for the framed version. Let's refresh the application, and we may get the following result:

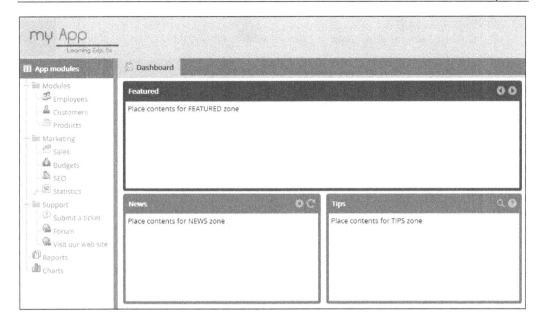

Notice that the **Featured** panel is now purple and the other panels are using the default color from the theme. This is because of the ui property we assigned and the CSS generated in the theme. Note that we used $ui:'featuredpanel-framed' in our .scss file. This created the CSS to be used when the panel has the frame property set to true.

If we change this property to false, then the visuals will not quite be correct. This means that we will have to create another set (UI) for the non-framed panels. Let's change our Panel.scss one more time, and we will add the pending UI sets for the other panels. At the end of the file, let's add this:

```
@include extjs-panel-ui(
  $ui:'newspanel',
  $ui-header-background-color: #003264,
  $ui-border-color: #003264,
  $ui-header-border-color: #003264,
  $ui-body-border-color: #003264
);

@include extjs-panel-ui(
  $ui:'newspanel-framed',
  $ui-header-background-color: #003264,
  $ui-border-color: #003264,
  $ui-header-border-color: #003264,
  $ui-body-border-color: #003264,
```

```
  $ui-border-width: 5px,
    $ui-border-radius: 4px
);


@include extjs-panel-ui(
  $ui:'tipspanel',
  $ui-header-color:#6d6d6d,
  $ui-header-background-color: #ff9900,
  $ui-border-color: #ff9900,
  $ui-header-border-color: #ff9900,
  $ui-body-border-color: #ff9900,
  $ui-tool-background-image:'tools/tool-sprites-purple');
@include extjs-panel-ui(
  $ui:'tipspanel-framed',
  $ui-header-color:#6d6d6d,
  $ui-header-background-color: #ff9900,
  $ui-border-color: #ff9900,
  $ui-header-border-color: #ff9900,
  $ui-body-border-color: #ff9900,
  $ui-tool-background-image:'tools/tool-sprites-purple',
  $ui-border-width: 5px,
  $ui-border-radius: 4px
);
```

In this code, we are adding the UI for the `newspanel` framed version and non-framed version, and also the `tipspanel` UI. Notice that in `tipspanel`, we added one more property/variable—`$ui-tool-background-image`. This property will set the image to be used for the tools.

Here, we can change the image to get a purple color. Place the image in the `resources/images/tools/` folder. Also, the image must be named `tool-sprites-purple.png`. Save the file. Now we need to set the `ui` property for each panel. For the **News** panel, set it like this:

```
xtype: 'panel',
ui: 'newspanel',
frame: true,
```

Use the following code for the **Tips** panel:

```
xtype: 'panel',
ui: 'tipspanel',
frame: true,
```

Save the changes and wait for the code to be refreshed by `sencha app watch`. If it is not refreshed, compile the theme. Refresh the browser and look at the output, which should be like this:

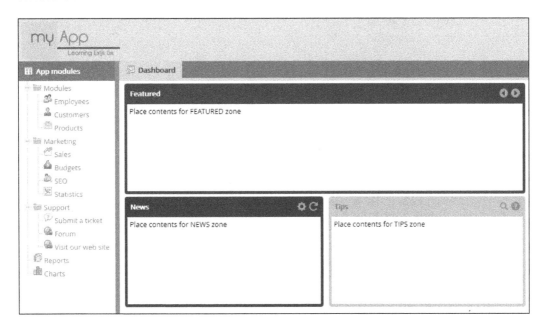

Now each panel will have its own color assigned according to the UI property set on it. In the **Tips** panel, check out how the tool's color has changed, as shown in the following screenshot, thanks to the new image we set:

It's important to notice that at this moment, each panel has the `frame: true` property, so we need to test a non-framed panel in this case as we set the code for `newspanel` (framed and non-framed), let's use this for our test. Change the code for the **Tips** panel as follows:

```
{
    xtype: 'panel',
    ui:'tipspanel',
    frame: true,
    flex: 2,
    height: 200,
    margin: '0px 5px 0px 5px',
```

```
        bodyBorder: true,
        bodyPadding: 4,
        title: 'Tips',
        tools: [{
          xtype: 'tool',
          type: 'search'
        },{
          xtype: 'tool',
          type: 'help'
        }],
        layout:'fit',
        items:[{
          xtype: 'panel',
          ui: 'newspanel',
          title: 'Sub panel using UI newspanel',
          html: 'this is a non framed panel..!<br/>
            Place contents for TIPS zone',
          border: true,
          bodyBorder: true
        }]
    }
```

Now check out the output. It should be like this:

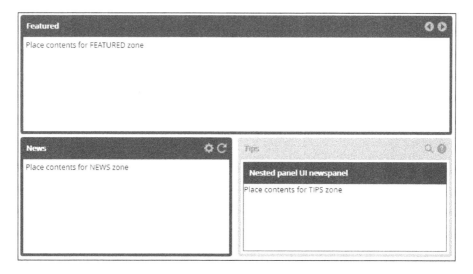

Notice that the subpanel is using the newspanel UI and it is nested inside a panel with another custom UI. The procedure for creating custom UIs for components/ widgets we have worked on applies to other components as well.

It's important to mention that, as we create more UIs, the output CSS file (or files) for our theme will keep growing. So, it's important to use only the UIs necessary for your applications.

Supporting legacy browsers

So far, we have created a theme that looks nice on most modern browsers, such as Google Chrome, Firefox, Opera, and Safari, but there is a chance that we want to support Internet Explorer. At this moment, if we open our application using IE, the theme may not work well. This is because IE doesn't support many of the new goodies of CSS3.

So, we need the Sencha CMD tool when compiling or building the theme makes sliced images for our custom theme. In this way, older IE versions or browsers that not support CSS3's new goodies will then be able to look almost the same, thanks to the use of images. To do this, let's open the `my-custom-theme/sass/example/custom.js` file. Now you will see this line commented:

```
//Ext.theme.addManifest();
```

Change it to the following:

```
Ext.theme.addManifest(
    {
        xtype: 'widget.panel',
        ui: 'featuredpanel'
    },
    {
        xtype: 'widget.panel',
        ui: 'newspanel'
    },
    {
        xtype: 'widget.panel',
        ui: 'tipspanel'
    }
);
```

In this code, we are specifying which widgets in our custom theme will be sliced (for images). Now we need to build the theme once again with this line:

```
sencha package build
```

When the process completes, we have to verify that it worked. Go to the `my-custom-theme/build/resources/images/panel` path, which is a new folder created by the compilation process. You will see something like this:

Now let's rebuild our application in order to get the latest resources in it:

```
sencha app build development
```

An alternative can be this:

```
sencha app build production
```

Then load the page in IE 8, or if you have the latest version, you can use developer tools and emulate the page to serve as IE 8 or less. You will get the following result:

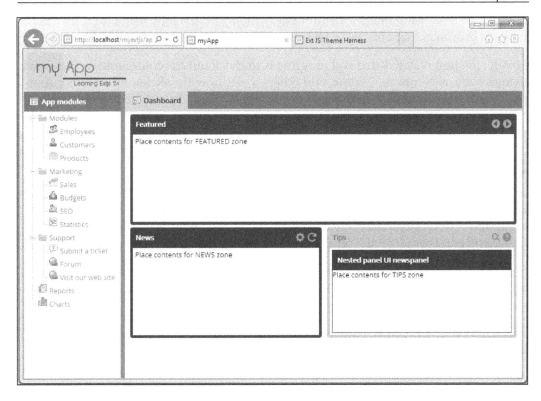

If you check out the developer tools (**Network**), you may find something like this:

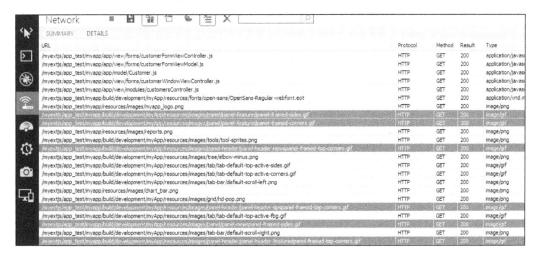

Notice that IE is using images for rounder corners and the look is the same as it is in modern browsers that only use CSS3.

Finally, the best way to learn and progress is to check out the configuration files inside themes such as **Neptune**, **Classic**, and others to see how the skeleton is created. Also, see the configuration files. In this way, you can get more ideas about achieving other things you may want to perform.

Summary

In this chapter, you learned how to create new themes. We can create complex designs and even completely change the look and feel of the default theme used in our application. Don't be afraid to change original files to fit your needs or to play with them. You can always get the original back from the SDK package of the Ext JS library.

One of the great things here is that we can create new themes and change values according to our needs. We also have the `ui` property and many looks for the same component.

In the next chapter, you will learn about responsive configurations and table support in Ext JS 5, which is a nice feature added in version 5x.

12

Responsive Configurations and Tablet Support

Ext JS version 5 now gives support for touch screen devices, such as tables, touch screen laptops, and other devices. This can be implemented with a little effort. As we saw in *Chapter 11*, *The Look and Feel*, Ext JS 5 introduced more themes to the framework. Two of these new themes are called **Neptune Touch** and **Crisp Touch**. Some of the themes can be seen in the following image:

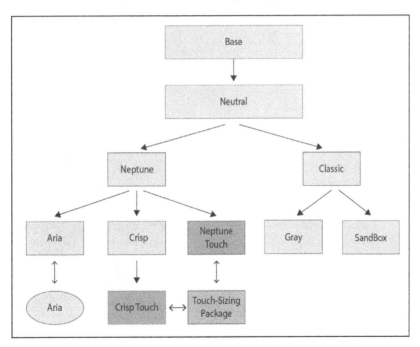

These new themes will be the base for handling touch screen input from the user. They have touch-friendly dimensions in their design.

In this chapter, we will cover these topics:

- **An overview of touch support**. Under this, we will cover Touch-screen-friendly themes and Neptune Touch and Crisp Touch.

- How to **implement responsive configurations**.

Overview

By using Event normalization, Ext JS 5 is able to run itself on touch screen devices. This normalization runs in an invisible way that translates mouse events into their equivalent functionality for the touch device. Consider the following example:

```
myDivElement.on('mousedown', function(e) {
    // event handling logic here
});
```

This is translated to the following:

```
myDivElement.on('touchstart', function(e) {
    // event handling logic here
});
```

Alternatively, it can be translated to this:

```
myDivElement.on('pointerdown', function(e) {
    // event handling logic here
});
```

These translations will be made depending on how the device supports each of them. It's important to mention that Ext JS cannot translate all touch interactions, so the events that are not translated must be covered on an individual basis.

 If you are new to mobile development or touch screen devices, you can learn more about them at http://www.html5rocks.com/en/mobile/touch/ and http://developer.android.com/design/patterns/gestures.html.

Elements can fire synthesized "gesture" events. So, as Ext JS contains a part of Sencha touch as the basis for the event system, it's possible to handle gestures. For some examples of gestures, look at the following diagram:

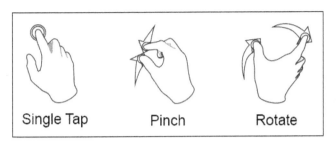

For browsers, there are three basic events (Start, Move, and End), and for each of these events there are three types of pointers, touch, and mouse events as described in the table:

Event	Touch	Pointer	Mouse
Start	touchstart	pointerdown	mousedown
Move	touchmove	pointermove	mousemove
End	touchend ·	pointerup	mouseup

Events such as drag, swipe, long press, pinch, rotate, and tap can be listened to like any other event in Ext JS 5; here is an example:

```
Ext.get('myDivElement').on('pinch', doSomething);
```

This means that Ext JS 5 will allow any gesture to respond to any type of input. So as an example, single-point gestures, such as Tap and Swipe, can be triggered using a mouse as well.

Now, some important points we need to highlight about this topic are as follows:

1. Ext JS 5 does not perform normalization on events such as mouseover, mouse out, mouse enter, and mouse leave, so when developing applications, we need to look for alternative events to implement these interactions.

2. If you intend to create a custom component that provides touch screen support for end users, then you need to adjust some events as needed.

3. At the time of writing this book, Ext JS 5 only has support for Safari, Chrome, and IE10+. The Android browser is not supported. Although this much is the only support described by Sencha, Firefox supports it in smooth way.

New themes

As we have mentioned, Ext JS 5 contains new themes (touch friendly). These themes have custom CSS and some JS overrides that are meant to create a friendly touch device theme and let the user have better control.

Using themes such as Classic, Gray, Neptune, or Crisp in a device such as a tablet or touch device can be quite a painful experience, because users need to zoom into the web document in order to make elements (buttons, icons and so on) bigger so that they can make a touch action properly. Also, the components may not respond to these events.

So, a distinctive feature is that these new themes have bigger fonts and icon sizes in order to handle touch actions easily and give the user a friendlier experience.

If you are creating a new theme for touch screen support, it is recommended that you use Neptune touch or Crisp touch.

Neptune touch and Crisp touch

The **Neptune Touch** and **Crisp Touch** themes extend the **Neptune** base theme, and also have the touch-sizing package as the base.

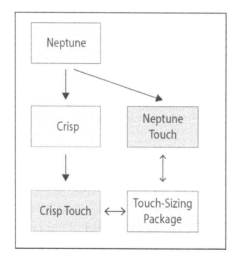

Note; the difference between Neptune touch and Crisp touch is the visual style, but they both work in the same way and keep the same touch-friendly dimensions. Now let's take a look at the difference between **Neptune** and **Neptune touch**, as shown here:

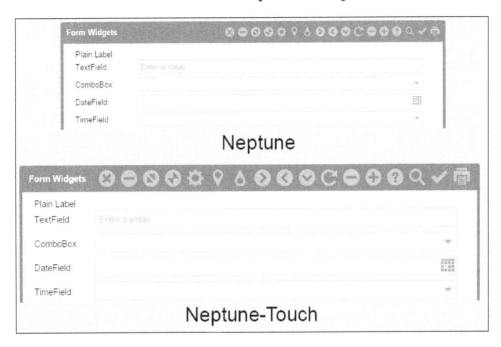

Notice how the size of the touch theme increases, allowing end users to be able to select, tap (click), and so on, in an easy way. On the other hand, Neptune becomes quite hard to handle in touch screen devices.

Implementing responsiveness to the application

For implementing responsiveness in our applications we have two fundamental classes in Ext JS, and those are:

- `Ext.plugin.Responsive`
- `Ext.mixin.Responsive`

These two classes work in the same way but there is a difference, as follows:

- `Ext.plugin.Responsive` must be used for already created components
- `Ext.mixin.Responsive` must be used for classes or components that we create or extend

Creating responsiveness

Let's create a simple HTML file, name it `responsive_01.html`, and add the
following content:

```
<!doctype html>
<html>
<head>
<meta charset="utf-8">
<title>Responsive - 01 - basic sample</title>
  <link rel="stylesheet" type="text/css" href="../ext-5.1.1/packages/
ext-theme-neptune-touch/build/resources/ext-theme-neptune-touch-all.
css">
  <script src="../ext-5.1.1/build/ext-all.js"></script>
  <script src="../ext-5.1.1/packages/ext-theme-neptune-touch/build/
ext-theme-neptune-touch.js"></script>
  <script src="responsive_01.js"></script>
</head>
<body>
</body>
</html>
```

Now let's create the `responsive_01.js` file and place the following code in it:

```
Ext.Loader.setConfig({
    enabled: true
});
Ext.onReady(function(){
    Ext.create('Ext.container.Viewport',{
      padding:'0px',
      layout:'border',
      items: [{
        xtype: 'panel',
        title: 'North Region',
        header: false,
        region: 'north',
        split: false,
        minHeight: 75,
        maxHeight: 75,
        plugins: 'responsive',
        html:'<div>Content of Header Zone ( W >800 ) ..!</div>',
        responsiveConfig: {
         'width < 800': {
            hidden:true
         },
         '(desktop && width >= 800)':{
```

```
         bodyStyle: {
           'background-color':'#f1f1f1','color': '#277cc0'
         },
           hidden:false
         },
           '(tablet || phone )': {
           hidden:true
       }
     }
   }
},{
    xtype: 'panel',
    title: 'Main Menu', //region:'west',
    header: false,
    bodyPadding: '5px',
    collapsible: false,   // make collapsible
    region: 'north',
    hidden: true,
    split: false,
    minHeight: 75,
    maxHeight: 75,
    bodyPadding: '10px',
    bodyStyle: {
      'background-color':'#fbb040',
      'color':'#663399',
      'font-weight':'bold',
      'font-size':'1.25em'
    },
    html:'<div>My Menu (w < 800) Zone..!</div>',
      plugins: 'responsive',
      responsiveConfig: {
        'width < 800': {
          hidden:false
        },
        '(desktop && width >= 800)': {
          hidden:true
        },
        '(tablet || phone)': {
          hidden:false,
          html:'<div>My Menu (phone or table) Zone..!</div>',
        }
      }
},{
  xtype: 'panel',
  title: 'West Region', //region:'west',
```

```
  bodyPadding: '5px',
  width: 300,
  collapsible: true,    // make collapsible
  region: 'west',
  split: true,
  html: '<div>Content of WEST Zone..!</div>',
  plugins: 'responsive',
  responsiveConfig: {
    '(desktop && width < 800)': {
      hidden:true
    },
    '(desktop && width >= 800)': {
      hidden:false
    },
    '(phone)': {
      hidden:true
    },
    '(tablet && width < 800)': {
      hidden:true
    },
    '(tablet && width >= 800)': {
      hidden:false
    }
  }
},{
  title: 'Center Region',
  region: 'center',
  html: '<b>Main content</b> goes here',
  plugins: 'responsive',
  responsiveConfig:{
    'desktop':{
      title: 'Center Region - Desktop'
    },
    '!(desktop) && (tablet)':{
      title: 'Center Region - Tablet'
    },
    '!(desktop) && (phone)':{
      title: 'Center Region - phone'                 }
  }
},{
  xtype: 'panel',
```

```
        title: 'South Region is resizable',
        header: (Ext.platformTags.phone ||
          Ext.platformTags.tablet)?false:true,
        region: 'south',
        bodyPadding: '5px',
        height: 200,
        split: true ,
        html: '<div>Content of South Zone..!</div>',
        plugins: 'responsive',
        responsiveConfig: {
        '(desktop && width < 800)': {
          hidden: true,
          header: false,
          title: '',
          height: 100,
          maxHeight: 175
        },
        '(desktop && width >= 800)': {
          hidden:false,
          header:true,
          title: 'South Region is resizable',
          height: 120 ,
          maxHeight: 175
        },
        '!(desktop)': { // Tablets and phones (will work)
          hidden: false,
          header: true,
          minHeight: 75,
          maxHeight: 75,
          height: 75,
          bodyStyle: {'background-color':'#66cc99','color': '#333333'}
            }
          }
      }]
    });
  });
```

Save the file (or files). For now, let's run the code and see the output in our browser. We should get something like the following output:

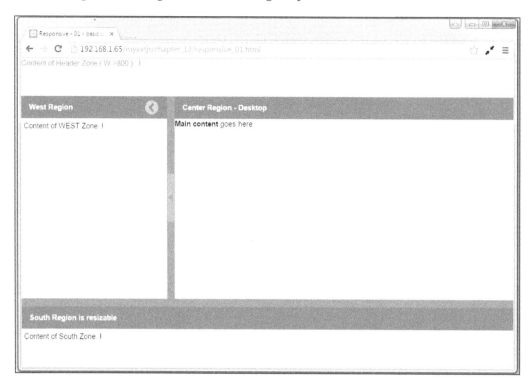

Investigating the output

As you can see we set an initial viewport, and it contains a panel in the border layout with **North**, **West**, **Center**, and **South** regions.

Now, in the `responsive_01.js` file, you can notice that in some items (mostly panel components), we set two new properties to these:

```
plugins: 'responsive',
responsiveConfig: {
    ....
}
```

First, as we are using direct components (not extending) as in Ext.panel.Panel, we use the Ext.plugin.Responsive class by its abbreviation, responsive. Then we set the responsiveConfig property (object). This object will contain some keys/conditions that will be applied to the component when the condition is met. Let's check the first item (the panel for the **North** region):

```
plugins: 'responsive',
responsiveConfig: {
    'width < 800': {
    hidden: true
    },
    '(desktop && width >= 800)':{
    bodyStyle: {'background-color':'#f1f1f1','color': '#277cc0'},
    hidden: false
    },
    '(tablet || phone )': {
    hidden: true
    }
}
```

We can see that the following:

1. The first criteria, width < 800, ensures that if the document has a width less than 800, then the component will be hidden.

2. The second condition, (desktop && width >= 800), ensures that if the platform we are running the app on is a desktop and the width of the page/document is greater than or equal to 800, then the component will be shown (not hidden), and the bodyStyle attribute will have some background color and text color.

3. The third condition, (tablet || phone), ensures that if the platform running the code is a tablet or phone, then the component will be hidden.

For a list of other values considered in the scope of the book, and for more documentation, see http://docs.sencha.com/extjs/5.1/5.1.1-apidocs/#!/api/Ext.plugin.Responsive.

For a property to be part (inside) of `responsiveConfig`, the `hidden` property in this case, you must be sure that the component has a setter method. Now let's resize the browser, make the size (width) less than 800 pixels, and see how it changes, like this:

Notice that now the first panel's (inside the panel with the border layout) criteria, `width < 800`, has been met, so the header is hidden. The second panel's criteria, which is the same (`width < 800`), also met the requirement, but the second panel has become visible. Also notice that the south panel has become hidden (not visible). This was because the criteria in its `responsiveConfig` property, (`desktop && width < 800`), was met.

Checking all panels

An important question that you might be asking yourself is: where are the desktop, phone, and tablet defined? The answer is that these values are set in `Ext.platformTags`, which is an object containing information about the current device/platform where the code is running.

It's important that you don't forget to set the plugin property on each of the items (direct components), otherwise the responsive changes you desire, won't work.

Now let's look at the **South** panel's responsiveConfig property:

```
plugins: 'responsive',
responsiveConfig: {
  '(desktop && width < 800)': {
    hidden: true,
    header: false,
    title: '',
    height: 100,
    maxHeight: 175
  },
  '(desktop && width >= 800)': {
    hidden: false,
    header: true,
    title: 'South Region is resizable',
    height: 120 ,
    maxHeight: 175
  },
  '!(desktop)': { // Tablets and phones (will work)
  hidden: false,
  header: true,
  minHeight: 75,
    maxHeight: 75,
    height: 75,
    bodyStyle: {
      'background-color':'#66cc99',
      'color': '#333333'
    }
  }
}
```

In this case, notice that responsiveConfig has three criteria, and all of these share common properties, such as hidden, header, title, height, and maxHeight. But the third criterion has two other properties that are not shared in the first two, which are bodyStyle and minHeight.

In this situation, we must be careful because when the third criteria is met, bodyStyle and minHeight will become permanent property values for the component, even if they satisfy other criteria. So, it's important to change the same properties to restore the previous state of the properties.

Notice the third criteria is `!(desktop)`. So, this will be applied to tablets, phones, or other devices that are not considered as *desktop*. Look at the following screenshot taken from the Xcode iOS emulator (iPhone):

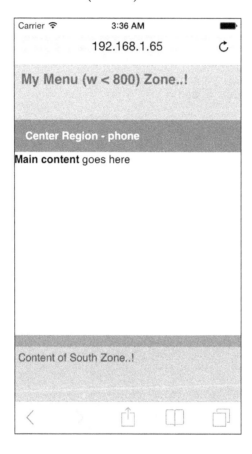

Now take a look at a screenshot of a tablet in landscape orientation:

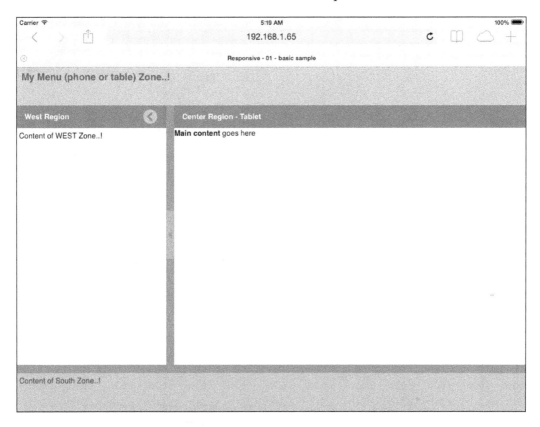

One important thing to look at is the following code in the south panel. Initially, in the configuration we set the following parameter:

```
header: (Ext.platformTags.phone || Ext.platformTags.tablet)?
   false:true,
```

In this case (`header`), is initially set in the creation object by the platform, because this property cannot change dynamically due to responsive changes made to the component by the framework. If we don't set this property, we will get something like this:

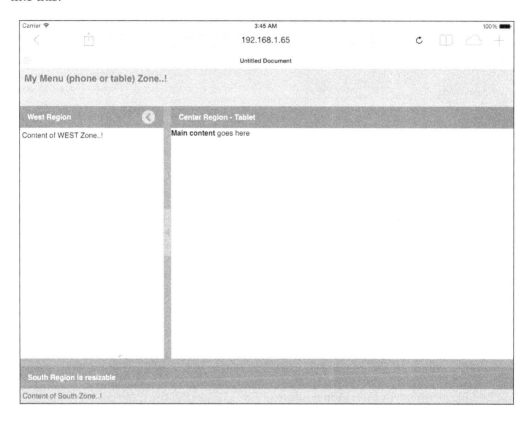

So far, the way we worked with `responsiveConfig` using `Ext.plugin.Responsive`, is similar to the way we had worked with `Ext.mixin.Responsive`. Look at the following code:

```
Ext.Loader.setConfig({
    enabled:true
});
Ext.define('Myapp.sample.customPanel',{
  extend: 'Ext.panel.Panel',
  alias: 'widget.customPanel',
  title: 'my Extended Panel',
  header: true,
```

```
    html: '',
    mixins: ['Ext.mixin.Responsive'],
    responsiveConfig: {
      '(tablet)': {
        html: 'my panel (desktop) content here..!',
        bodyStyle: {
'background-color':'#6d6d6d',
'color': '#ffffff'
}
      },
      '(desktop)':{
        html: 'my panel (desktop) content here..!',
        bodyStyle: {
'background-color':'#c4801c',
'color': '#ffffff'
}
      },
      '(phone)': {
        html: 'my panel (phone) content here..!',
        bodyStyle: {
'background-color':'#5e1b5e',
'color': '#ffffff'
}
      }
    }
});
Ext.onReady(function(){
  Ext.create('Ext.container.Viewport',{
    layout:'fit',
    items: [{
      xtype: 'customPanel',
      title: 'my Sample Panel',
      html:'<div>Content Panel</div>'
    }]
  });
});
```

Notice that we are extending the `Ext.panel.Panel` class, so we set the `mixins` property with the `Ext.mixing.Responsive` value, and then set the `responsiveConfig` property in the class, as in the first example. We set the conditions for responsiveness/platform. Now let's run the code in the phone (emulator) or desktop. We may get the following result:

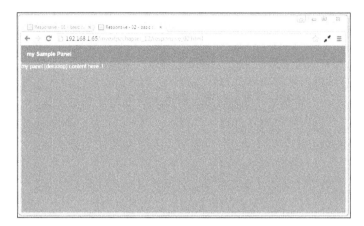

Then, on the phone, we will get the following screen:

So basically, Ext JS handles responsiveness in a very easy, and not too complicated, way. Also remember that we must use the simple `responsiveConfig` property. Don't try to add too advanced code or implement functions for mobile phones. Also, it's important to point out that Ext JS is not made for phones. On phones, we must use Sencha touch. Ext JS is intended to be good-looking and functional for tablets.

Summary

In this chapter, you learned the importance of themes, that is, Neptune touch and Crisp touch, which are the base themes for tablets and touch screen devices. You can create other new themes based on these themes, as we saw in *Chapter 11*, *The Look and Feel*.

Also, you learned how to apply responsive configurations to components in an easy way using criteria, or conditions, and `platformTags` (`Ext.platfomTags`) such as desktop, tablet, and phone.

Remember that for tablets or other touch screen devices, it's important to set the CSS properly in order to get a good look and also nice functionality such as font size, icon sizes (24 x 24 is the recommended size), and other styles for improvement and creating a better user experience. Ext JS 5 is not intended for phones, but can work nicely on tablets.

You can try adding responsive configurations to the basic application made in *Chapter 10*, *Architecture*. If you do this, remember to change the theme to Neptune touch or Crisp touch in order to test the application on tablets and other touch screen devices. Also remember that you can try or play as many criteria, or conditions, in order to make this concept clearer.

In the next chapter, we will see the basis for creating charts in Ext JS 5.

13
From Drawing to Charting

Ext JS offers a complete drawing library just as it did in its previous version. This drawing library is intended to be used with the chart components. However, the Sencha team has not only focused on the charting components, but has also decided to implement a more versatile set of tools that form the core of the charting library.

This means that we can use the drawing package to implement cross-browser custom graphics. The drawing package contains an `Ext.draw.Surface` class that abstracts graphics implementation and enables the developer to create arbitrarily shaped sprites that respond to the user. It also provides a rich set of animations.

The topics we are going to cover in this chapter are as follows:

- Basic drawing
- Adding interactions
- Charts (we will cover types such as legend, axis, gradients, and series)
- Series examples (in this section, Bar, Pie, and 3D bars will be described)

Now, before we begin, it's important to mention that Draw and Chart classes are not part of the Ext JS 5 framework as basic classes; they are included as two packages:

- **ext-charts** (charts and draw classes): This is a legacy package compatible with version 4, and is located in the `ext-5.x.x/packages/ext-charts` folder
- **sencha-charts** (charts and draw classes): This is a brand new package specific for Ext JS 5, and is located in the `ext-5.x.x/packages/sencha-charts` folder

We will see later how to include these classes in our code and our application.

If you are new to SVG and VML, check out these resources so that you can understand what we are talking about a bit more:

- `http://www.w3schools.com/svg/`
- `http://www.w3.org/Graphics/SVG/`
- `http://www.w3.org/TR/NOTE-VML`
- `https://msdn.microsoft.com/en-us/library/ee384217%28v=vs.85%29.aspx`

Basic drawing

Ext JS handles drawing by the use of SVG and Canvas (this depends on the browser capabilities). It's important to mention that Canvas is actually the default engine.

If you are migrating your code from Ext JS version 4 to 5, it's important that you check out the changes and notes about upgrading, because they are not the same. Also, the source code of charts and draw classes (properties, methods, and so on) is quite different. You can read more about this at `http://docs.sencha.com/extjs/5.1/whats_new/5.0/charts_upgrade_guide.html`.

Let's create our first code. It will draw some shapes and sprites, and we will see how the `draw` package works. Create the initial HTML file with the following code:

```
<!doctype html>
<html>
<head>
<meta charset="utf-8">
<title>Draw - 01 - basics</title>
   <link rel="stylesheet" type="text/css" href="../ext-5.1.1/packages/
ext-theme-neptune/build/resources/ext-theme-neptune-all.css">
   <script src="../ext-5.1.1/build/ext-all.js"></script>
   <script src="../ext-5.1.1/packages/ext-theme-neptune/build/ext-
theme-neptune.js"></script>
   <script src="draw_01.js"></script>
</head>
<body>
</body>
</html>
```

Now, let's create the `draw_01.js` file and place the following code in it:

```
Ext.Loader.setConfig({
  enabled: true,
  paths: {
    'Ext.draw': '../ext-5.1.1/packages/ext-charts/src/draw'
  }
});
Ext.require([
  'Ext.*',
  'Ext.draw.*'
]);
Ext.onReady(function(){

  var myDrawCmp = Ext.create('Ext.draw.Component', {
    viewBox: false,
    itemId:'mypaneldraw',
    items:[{
      type: 'circle',
      radius: 8,
      x: 250,
      y: 18,
      fill: 'blue',
      zIndex: 2
    },{
      type: 'rect',
      x: 0,
      y: 69,
      width: 200,
      height: 6,
      fill: 'blue'
    },{
      type: 'ellipse',
      cx: 265,
      cy: 215,
      rx: 40,
      ry: 25,
      fill: '#66cc33',
      globalAlpha: 1,
      stroke : '#993399',
      'stroke-width':2
    },{
      type: "path",
```

```
              path: "M 230 110 L 300 110 L 265 190 z",
              globalAlpha: 1,
              fill: '#16becc',
              lineWidth: 2
          },{
              type: 'text',
              x: 50,
              y: 50,
              text: 'Sencha',
              'font-size':'38px',
              fillStyle: 'blue'
          },{
              type: "image",
              src: "images/apple-touch-icon.png",
              globalAlpha: 0.9,
              x: 205,
              y: 20,
              height: 100,
              width: 100,
              listeners: {
                  dblclick: function(){
                      Ext.Msg.alert('Logo',
                      'event dblclick on Sencha logo');
                  }
              }
          }]
      });
      Ext.create('Ext.Window', {
          title:'drawing components',
          closable:true,
          resizable:false,
          width: 600,
          height: 300,
          layout: 'fit',
          items: [myDrawCmp]
      }).showAt(30,50);
  });
```

Notice that in this example (the basic Ext JS code style), we set the loader properties in the following code:

```
paths: {
    'Ext.draw': '../ext-5.1.1/packages/ext-charts/src/draw'
}
```

Also notice that in these draw examples, we are using a legacy package (it is compatible with Ext 4). Here, we are telling Ext JS that the namespace called `Ext.draw` will have the following location, or path.

This is done so that Ext JS (`Ext.Loader`) knows where the classes that belong to the `Ext.draw` namespace are located, and it loads all the classes needed/involved. Also, in the `require` section, we set this:

```
Ext.require([
    'Ext.*',
    'Ext.draw.*'
]);
```

This code means that Ext JS needs to load all the `Ext.draw` classes so that it can work properly. Another alternative is to set specific classes, as is shown in the following example:

```
Ext.require([
    'Ext.*',
    'Ext.draw.Container',
    'Ext.draw.Surface',
    'Ext.draw.sprite.Sprite',
    'Ext.draw.sprite.Rect'
]);
```

Now, let's save the file and run our example in our browser. We may get the following result:

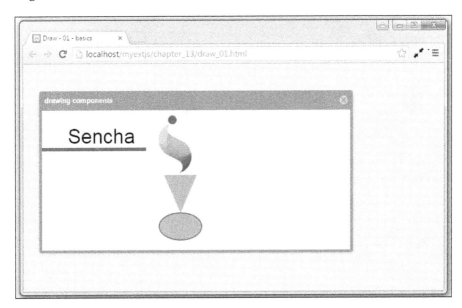

In the preceding screenshot, we can see our elements (sprites), created for you to understand a bit more. Now, look at this diagram:

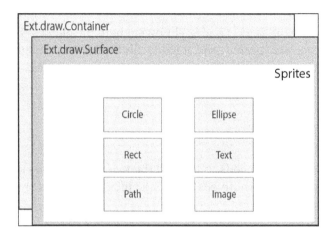

In order to create elements (sprites), Ext JS needs to create a surface element. This surface element needs to be contained within Ext.draw.Container. So, in the end, the elements (sprites) are rendered (created) inside the surface element.

In the preceding example, we defined an instance of Ext.draw.Component that contains six sprite elements:

- circle: To draw circles, you can change the radius with the radius property.
- rect: To draw rectangles, set the width and height properties in the configuration object.
- ellipse: To draw ellipses, you have to set these four properties:
  - The cx attribute defines the *x* coordinate of the center of the ellipse
  - The cy attribute defines the *y* coordinate of the center of the ellipse
  - The rx attribute defines the horizontal radius
  - The ry attribute defines the vertical radius
- path: This is one of the most powerful sprite types. With it, you can create arbitrary shapes using the SVG path syntax.
- text: This creates text elements as sprites. The font/font size can be set using the font property, or font-size: '38px', as shown in the preceding example.
- image: This type renders images as sprites. You need to set the source path with the src property. Also, width and height can be important.

As we said before, **sprites** are elements rendered on a drawing surface. Depending on the type of sprite, the properties can be different. You can refer to http://www.w3schools.com/svg/ and http://www.w3.org/Graphics/SVG/ to learn more about them.

It is very important that you be careful about which package you include in the app or code, and based on that, play with the properties of each sprite in order to get a good result.

Also keep in mind that Draw components were created in order to be the drawing engine for Charts, so if you plan to create a game or SVG animation, you can use other libraries or frameworks that are intended specifically for those purposes.

Adding interaction

We can add events, animation, and custom behavior to sprites. The main feature of this class is that we aren't tied to a specific shape or structure, and it is browser and device agnostic.

In the previous example, you might have noticed that we have the following code:

```
{
  type: "image",
  src: "images/apple-touch-icon.png",
  globalAlpha: 0.9,
  x: 205,
  y: 20,
  height: 100,
  width: 100,
  listeners: {
    dblclick: function(){
        Ext.Msg.alert('Logo', 'event dblclick on Sencha logo');
    }
  }
}
```

So, we can add or attach listeners to our sprite elements and add interaction. Let's create a new example—first, the HTML page:

```
<!doctype html>
<html>
<head>
```

```
<meta charset="utf-8">
<title>Draw - 02 - Interactivity</title>
  <link rel="stylesheet" type="text/css" href="../ext-5.1.1/
    build/packages/ext-theme-neptune/build/resources/
      ext-theme-neptune-all.css">
  <script src="../ext-5.1.1/build/ext-all.js"></script>
  <script src="../ext-5.1.1/build/packages/ext-theme-neptune/
    build/ext-theme-neptune.js"></script>
  <script src="draw_02.js"></script>
</head>
<body>
</body>
</html>
```

And now, let's place the following code in the draw_02.js file:

```
Ext.Loader.setConfig({
  enabled: true,
  paths: {
    'Ext.draw': '../ext-5.1.1/packages/ext-charts/src/draw'
  }
});
Ext.require([
  'Ext.*',
  'Ext.draw.*'
]);
Ext.onReady(function(){
  var myDrawCmp = Ext.create('Ext.draw.Component', {
    viewBox: false,
    itemId:'mypaneldraw',
    style:'background-color:#999999',
    items: [{
      type: 'text',
      x: 10,
      y: 10,
      text: 'My Pac-Man',
      'font-size':'18px',    //fontSize: 38,
      fillStyle: 'blue'
    },{
      type: 'rect',
      x: 0,
      y: 45,
      width: 600,
```

```
        height: 60,
        fill: '#ffffff',
        zIndex: 1
    },{
        type: "image",
        src: "images/inkyghost.gif",
        x: 100,
        y: 50,
        height: 50,
        width:  50,
        zIndex: 2
    }
    ]
});

    var myWindow = Ext.create('Ext.Window', {
        title: 'drawing components',
        closable: true,
        resizable: false,
        width: 600,
        height: 300,
        layout: 'fit',
        items: [myDrawCmp]
    });

myWindow.on({
afterRender{
    fn:function(cmpx, eOpts){
    var myPacman = Ext.create('Ext.draw.Sprite', {
        type: "image",
        src: "images/pacman02.gif",
        x: 10,
        y: 50,
        height: 50,
        width:  50,
        zIndex: 3
    });
    myDrawCmp.surface.add([
      myPacman,{
        type: "image",
        src: "images/inkyghost.gif",
        x: 160,
        y: 50,
```

```
          height: 50,
          width:  50,
          zIndex: 2
       }
    ]);
    myDrawCmp.surface.renderAll();
    var runner = new Ext.util.TaskRunner();
    var task = runner.newTask({ //start a task
      run:function() {

      var xp=0;
      var itemPacman= myDrawCmp.surface.items.items[4];
      var itemGhost= myDrawCmp.surface.items.items[2];
      var itemGhostB= myDrawCmp.surface.items.items[3];
      var xp =itemPacman.attr.x; xp+=4;
      if (xp>=600){ xp= (-200); }
      var xg =itemGhost.attr.x; xg+=4;
      if (xg>=600){ xg= (-150); }
      var xgg =itemGhostB.attr.x; xgg+=4;
      if (xgg>=600){ xgg= (-100); }
      itemPacman.setAttributes({x:xp}, true );
      itemGhost.setAttributes({x:xg}, true );
      itemGhostB.setAttributes({x:xgg}, true );

      },
      interval: 30,
      scope: this
    });
    task.start(); // start the task
    },
    delay: 400,
    scope: this
  }
});
  myWindow.showAt(30,50);
});
```

Here, in this code, we created a drawing surface and added four sprites (one text and three image type sprites). If we run our code, we may see something like this:

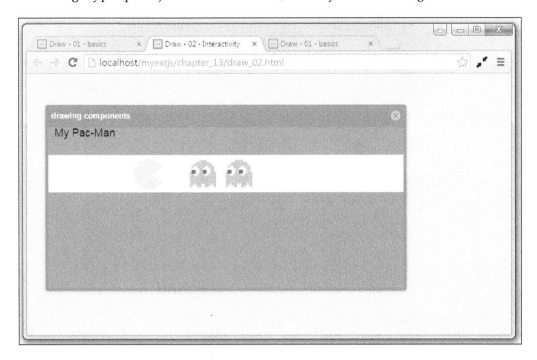

We used Ext.util.TaskRunner to move the image sprites (Pac-Man and the ghosts) on the drawing surface at an interval of 30 milliseconds. Once the sprites get out of bounds (zone), the images will start over from the beginning.

Charts

Now that you have an idea of how the drawing package works, you are ready to see how the Ext JS library uses package capabilities in the chart package.

The chart package is a set of classes that define a chart container to manage axes, legends, series, labels, tips, Cartesian and radial coordinates, and specific series, such as Pie, Area, Bar, Radar, Gauge, and so on.

As we have said before, charts is a package inside the framework and doesn't come as part of the core or widgets, so we need to define it on Ext.Loader, and also inside our application's app.json file (we will cover this later).

It's important to mention that every chart must have three components: data, axes, and a series. These components can be seen in the following diagram:

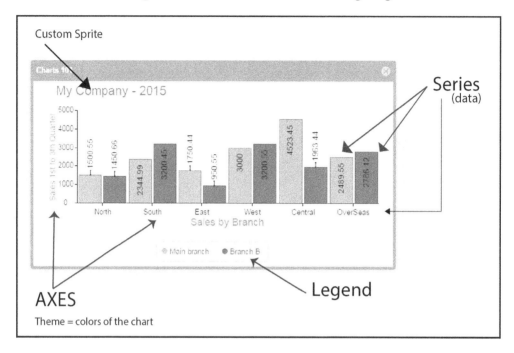

In the previous figure, you can see the basic parts of a chart and some custom elements.

Legend

The chart configuration object accepts a legend parameter to enable legend items for each series and set the position of the legend, as follows:

```
legend: {
   docked: 'left' // possible values are left, top, bottom, right
}
```

Axis

The axis package contains an abstract axis class that is extended by the `Axis` and `Radial` classes. There are axes for categorical information (**Category axis**) and axes for quantitative information, such as a **numeric axis**. There is also a **time axis** that is used to render information over a specific period of time.

Series

A `series` class is an abstract class extended by Line or Scatter visualizations. This class contains code that is common to these series, such as event handling, animation, shadows, gradients, common offsets, and so on. A `series` class will contain an array of items, with information about the positioning of each element. It also contains a shared `drawSeries` method that updates all positions for the series and then renders the series.

Themes

Ext JS 5.1.1 shipped charts with several built-in themes that you could select for your charts. However, building custom themes was not a documented process. With this release, we have been provided with the ability to make our own color palettes, and much more. A theme for charts is a class derived from `Ext.chart.theme.Base` and given an alias that starts with the following:

```
"chart.theme."
```

A basic theme can be as simple as this:

```
Ext.define('App.chart.theme.Awesome', {
    extend: 'Ext.chart.theme.Base',
    alias: 'chart.theme.awesome',
    singleton: true,
    config: {
      baseColor: '#4d7fe6'
    }
});
```

From here on, you can add any number of other configurations to style your series, axes, and markers. To see all the options, check out the `Ext.chart.theme.Base` reference for the available configurations at `http://docs.sencha.com/extjs/5.1/5.1.1-apidocs/#!/api/Ext.chart.theme.Base`.

To use the preceding theme, you have to simply set the `theme` configuration in your charts:

```
theme: 'awesome'
```

Series examples

Now we will see some of the basic charts in the Ext JS framework. Remember that we cannot cover all of them here, but those that we won't see are quite similar in configuration and behavior.

Bar charts (building our first chart)

Bar charts are easy to understand. That's why they are commonly used to display categorical data. Let's create our chart using the basic way (not inside the application). So, let's create our HTML file, name it `chart_01.html`, and add the following code:

```
<!doctype html>
<html>
<head>
<meta charset="utf-8">
<title>Chart - 01 - basics</title>
    <link rel="stylesheet" type="text/css" href="../ext-5.1.1/build/
packages/ext-theme-neptune/build/resources/ext-theme-neptune-all.css">
    <link rel="stylesheet" type="text/css" href="../ext-5.1.1/
packages/sencha-charts/build/neptune/resources/sencha-charts-all.css">
    <script src="../ext-5.1.1/build/ext-all.js"></script>
    <script src="../ext-5.1.1/build/packages/ext-theme-neptune/build/
ext-theme-neptune.js"></script>
  <script src="chart_01.js"></script>
</head>
<body>
</body>
</html>
```

Notice that inside the HTML file, we are adding a new resource—`sencha-charts.all.css`. These files will provide us with the necessary CSS classes for the charts. Now, let's make the JavaScript code for the `chart_01.js` file:

```
Ext.Loader.setConfig({
  enabled: true,
  paths: {
    'Ext.chart': '../ext-5.1.1/packages/sencha-charts/src/chart',
    'Ext.draw': '../ext-5.1.1/packages/sencha-charts/src/draw'
  }
});

Ext.require([
  'Ext.*',
```

```
    'Ext.draw.*',
    'Ext.chart.*'
]);


Ext.onReady(function(){

  var myChartStore = Ext.create('Ext.data.ArrayStore',{
    storeId:'salesStore',
    fields:[
      {name: 'id', type: 'int'},
      {name: 'region', type: 'string'},
      {name: 'sales', type: 'float'} ,
      {name: 'salesb', type: 'float'}],
    data:[
      [10001 ,"North", 1500.55 , 1450.66 ],
      [10002 ,"South", 2344.99 , 3200.45 ],
      [10003 ,"East",  1750.44 , 950.55 ],
      [10004 ,"West",  3000.00 , 3200.55 ],
      [10005 ,"Central", 4523.45 , 1963.44 ],
      [10006 ,"OverSeas", 2489.55, 2786.12 ]
    ]
  });

  var mychart= Ext.create('Ext.chart.CartesianChart', {
    store: myChartStore,
    insetPadding: {
      top: 50,
      left: 25,
      right: 25,
      bottom: 15
    },
    interactions: 'itemhighlight',
    axes: [{
      type: 'numeric',
      position: 'left',
      title: {
        text: 'Sales 1st to 3th Quarter',
        fontSize: 14,
        fillStyle:'#0d7179'
      },
      fields: 'sales'
    }, {
      type: 'category',
      position: 'bottom',
```

```
        title: {
          text: 'Sales by Branch',
          fontSize: 18,
          fillStyle:'#277cc0'
        },
        fields: 'region'
      }],
      series: {
        type: 'bar',
        title:['Main branch','Branch B'],
        xField: 'region',
        yField: 'sales',
        style:{
          strokeStyle: '#999999',
          fillStyle: '#cccc99'
        },
        highlight:{
          strokeStyle: '#990000',
          fillStyle: '#ffcc66',
          lineDash: [5, 3]
        },
        label: {
          field:'sales',
          display:'insideEnd'
        }
      },
      sprites: {
        type: 'text',
        text: 'My Company - 2015',
        fontSize: 22,
        fillStyle: '#993366',
        width: 100,
        height: 30,
        x: 40, // the sprite x position
        y: 25 // the sprite y position
      }
    });

Ext.create('Ext.window.Window', {
  title: 'Charts 101',
  closable:true,
  resizable:true,
  height: 400,
  width: 650,
```

```
    layout: 'fit',
    html:'My Chart',
    items:[mychart]

    }).show();

});
```

Here is the explanation of the preceding code:

1. The first step is to set the paths for the classes in `Ext.Loader.setConfig` so that Ext JS recognizes where to get information.

2. We set in the `Ext.require` code what we require (classes) so that those classes are loaded before executing our code.

3. Then, we create a data store (`Ext.data.ArrayStore`) with some dummy data that our chart will be using.

4. We create the `mychart= Ext.create('Ext.chart.CartesianChart' ....` variable.

The explanation of the configuration object (`mychart`) is as follows: first, we set the store (data). Then, we define some properties, such as `insetPadding` and interactions. The `insetPadding` is the internal padding on the drawing surface of the chart.

Interactions are optional modules that can be plugged into a chart to allow the user to interact with the chart and its data in special ways. The current supported interaction types include the following:

- `Panzoom`: This allows pan and zoom of axes
- `Itemhighlight`: This allows highlighting of series data points
- `Iteminfo`: This allows displaying of details of a data point in a pop-up panel
- `Rotate`: This allows rotation of pie and radar series

We set the axes with an object. The first object is the `numeric` type and this axis will be the representation in the left position for the `sales` field. The second axis will be the representation for the `region` field (North, West, and so on). Notice that for each object, inside the `axes` property, we added something like this:

```
title: {
  text: 'Sales 1st to 3th Quarter',
  fontSize: 14,
  fillStyle:'#0d7179'
},
```

This code is meant for setting the style and properties on the Axis. If you check it out, you will realize that it is like setting the properties for a **text** type sprite (drawing part).

We set the series for the chart. First, we specified the type as `bar`, and set the `xfield` and `yfield` properties so that the chart will know how to arrange its information.

The `style` property lets us change the appearance of the series (colors). If we don't set this property, Ext JS will handle the default theme (colors for the chart). The `highlight` property decides how the style will be for the bar when it receives the user interaction.

In the `label` property, we set the manner in which the values will appear on each bar element inside the chart. In this case, they will be inside the bar at the end. However, if the value is greater than the bar, it will be placed outside. See the following screenshot:

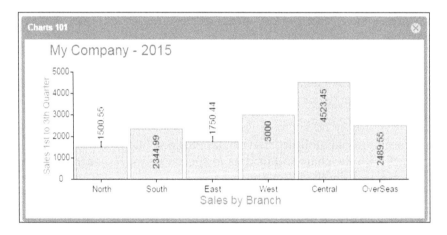

Observe how the first and third bars in the chart display the values outside themselves. This is because the space is not enough to display them inside the bar. But if we resize the window, then the appearance of those bars will change.

Finally, we set the property sprites with one element, as follows:

```
sprites: {
  type: 'text',
  text: 'My Company - 2015',
  fontSize: 22,
  fillStyle: '#993366',
  width: 100,
  height: 30,
  x: 40,
```

```
        y: 25
    }
```

This will create a static `text` sprite inside the chart so that we can have a title. Also, we create an instance of the `Ext.window.Window` class that will be the container for our chart.

Let's run the example in our browser and see the results, as shown here:

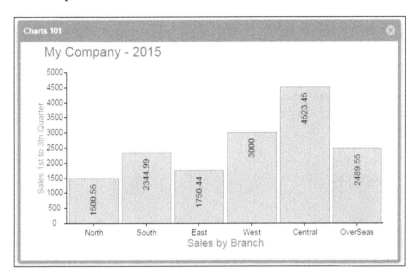

This process will apply to other types of charts as well, but it's important that according to the type of chart we are generating, we are able to modify the `axes` and `series` properties to display our data inside the chart correctly. You can see the **Charts kitchen sink** example to understand more about other types of charts.

Pie charts

Pie chart visualization is a very common visualization for displaying quantitative information of different categories. Like other charts, configuring a pie chart is very fast and simple. We only need to know how the series work in this type of chart.

Let's make a duplicate of the previous example and change the following code:

```
Ext.onReady(function(){

    var myChartStore = Ext.create('Ext.data.ArrayStore',{
        storeId:'salesStore',
        fields:[
            {name: 'id', type: 'int'},
```

```
        {name: 'region', type: 'string'},
        {name: 'sales', type: 'float'}
      ],
      data:[
        [10001 ,"North", 15.55],
        [10002 ,"South", 23.99],
        [10003 ,"East",  17.44],
        [10004 ,"West",  30.00],
        [10005 ,"Central", 4.1],
        [10006 ,"OverSeas", 2.55]
      ]
});

var mychart= Ext.create('Ext.chart.PolarChart', {
   store: myChartStore,
   insetPadding: {
      top: 50,
      left: 25,
      right: 25,
      bottom: 15
   },
   innerPadding: 20,
   interactions: ['rotate', 'itemhighlight'],
   theme: 'default-gradients',
   legend: {docked: 'bottom'},
   series: {
      type: 'pie',
      angleField:'sales', // xField
      label: {
         field:'region',
         calloutLine: {
         length: 60,
         width: 3
      }
   },
   highlight: true,
   tooltip: {
      trackMouse: true,
      renderer: function(storeItem, item) {
         this.setHtml(storeItem.get('region') + ': ' +
            storeItem.get('sales'));
      }
   }
},
```

```
    sprites: {
      type: 'text',
      text: 'My Company - 2015',
      fontSize: 22,
      fillStyle: '#993366',
      width: 100,
      height: 30,
      x: 40, // the sprite x position
      y: 25 // the sprite y position
    }
});

Ext.create('Ext.window.Window', {
  title: 'Charts 101',
  closable:true,
  resizable:true,
  height: 400,
  width: 650,
  layout: 'fit',
  html:'My Chart',
  items:[mychart]

}).show();
```

Now, let's run our browser and see the result, as follows:

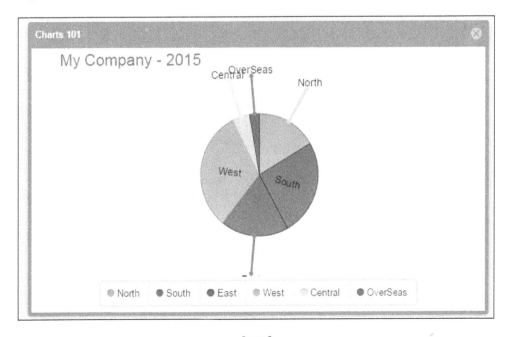

Refer to the highlighted code to see the difference:

- The `mychart` variable was set as a polar chart component with: `Ext.create('Ext.chart.PolarChart'`...

- We added the `theme` property on the charts to `default-gradients`. This property will give a gradient look to the pie elements (slices).

- In the `series` property, we changed the `type` to `pie` and set `angleField` to `sales` (`angleField` is an alias of the `xField` property). We also set the `tooltip` property such that when the mouse is over a slice, the tooltip (for that slice) will appear, as shown in the following screenshot:

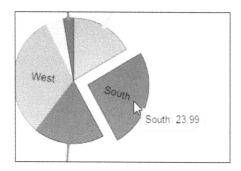

- Interactions for the chart are set to `interactions:['rotate', 'itemhighlight'],`. With this new interaction type, `rotate`, we can rotate the pie chart, like this:

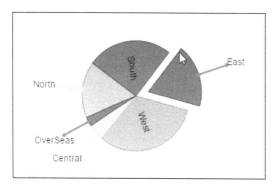

More charts

So far, we have seen the bar and pie charts (Cartesian and polar charts), but Ext JS comes with many more chart types. One nice introduction in version 5.1 is the 3D chart, which looks like this:

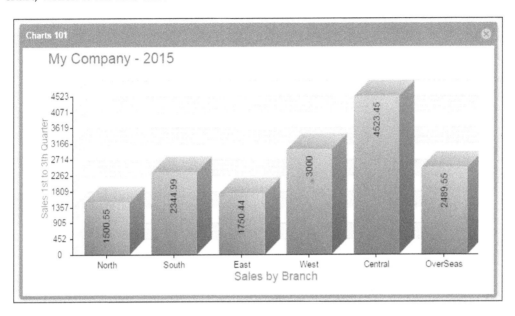

Some more chart types that we can generate are as follows:

- 3D Category: Pie 3D and Bar 3D
- Normal charts: Area, Bar, CandleStick, Gauge, Line, Polar, Radar, Scatter, Stacked and Cartesian

You can see all the types in the Charts Kitchen Sink example. In the beginning, when you use the charts or try to create new charts, it can be an overwhelming task, so check out the documentation. Also, I recommend that you take a look at the source code (ext-charts and sencha-charts) to understand how charts work.

Introducing chart themes

Chart themes are classes that contain preconfigured looks for our charts. This one has been added to the Ext JS framework since version 5.0.1. So, for you to get a clearer idea, let's take a look at the `ext-5.x.x/packages/sencha-charts/src/chart/theme` folder. You will see many files, as shown here:

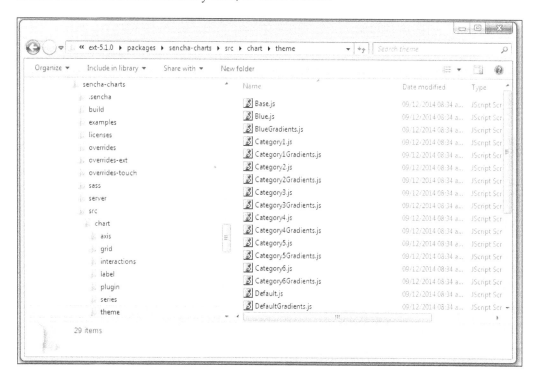

These files or themes (classes) extend the `Ext.chart.theme.Base` class. Also, these classes are singleton (`singleton:true`) in order to use the same instance when referenced. As an example, let's make a duplicate of the first code example (bar chart):

1. Define a new chart theme as follows:

```
Ext.require([
  'Ext.*',
  'Ext.draw.*',
  'Ext.chart.*'
]);

Ext.define('Ext.chart.theme.myChartTheme', {
    extend: 'Ext.chart.theme.Base',
    singleton: true,
    alias: [
```

```
        'chart.theme.mychartTheme',
        'chart.theme.myChartTheme'
    ],
    config: {
        baseColor: '#65a9e0',
        gradients: {
            type: 'linear',
            degrees: 90
        }
    }
});
```

```
Ext.onReady(function(){
  // CODE...
```

You can see that inside the code, we defined a new class extending `Ext.chart.theme.Base`. We also set two different values in the `alias` property just in case a bad typographical error (uppercase or lowercase) occurs. Inside the configuration object, we set the `baseColor` and `gradient` properties.

2. Now, in the `chart` config object, we need to add this property:

```
theme: {
  type: 'mychartTheme'
},
```

3. Remove previously defined styles so that the theme won't be overridden. Save the file and run in the browser to see the result, like this:

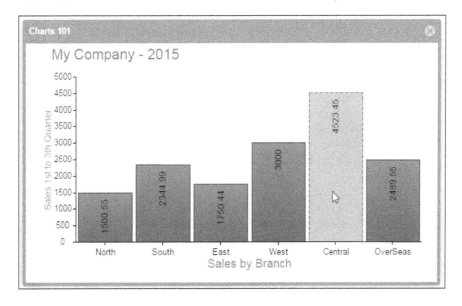

Notice how the blue color (the base color) and gradient configurations in our chart theme were applied to each bar. The highlighted property was set in the chart configuration. So, themes can be quite useful when we are using many charts in our applications. This will avoid setting code for every chart every time, and we will be reducing much of our code.

Enhancing our application with charts

The examples covered so far were in traditional code (basic examples using the Ext JS framework directly), but what happens when we want to embed the charts in an MVC or MVVM app? Well! First of all, we need to add a reference to the proper code package that we want to use:

1. So, let's begin by opening the app.json file (the application code used in chapters 10, 11, and 12) and locating this code:

    ```
    "requires": [
     ],
    ```

2. For use in Ext JS charting, let's change it to this:

    ```
    "requires": [
    "sencha-charts"
     ],
    ```

    Or for legacy charts (Ext JS 4), change to:

    ```
    "requires": [
    "ext-charts"
     ],
    ```

3. After this change, save the file. Now, let's use the Sencha CMD tool. Open the CMD tool and type this:

    ```
    sencha app build
    ```

4. By using this command, we ensure that our code as well as Ext JS and the Chart package are included in our application. So, after the build ends, let's monitor the changes in our application using this line:

    ```
    sencha app watch
    ```

    This procedure will make sure that the desired package is included in our application. So, now, let's create the view for our chart inside the app (we will reuse part of the code from our previous examples).

5. Let's create the file (view) called `myChartSample.js` in the folder `app/view`, and place the following code:

```
Ext.define('myApp.view.myChartSample',{
  extend: 'Ext.panel.Panel',
  alias: 'widget.myChartSamplePanel',
  xtype: 'mychartPanel',
  requires: [
    'Ext.draw.*',
    'Ext.chart.*'
  ],
  bodyPadding: 5,
  iconCls: 'chartx-16',
  closable: true,
  title: 'My Chart',
  layout: 'fit',
  initComponent: function() { //step 4
    var me= this;
    var myChartStore= Ext.create('Ext.data.ArrayStore',{
      storeId: 'salesStore',
      fields:[
        {name: 'id', type: 'int'},
        {name: 'region', type: 'string'},
        {name: 'sales', type: 'float'},
        {name: 'salesb', type: 'float'}
      ],
      data:[
        [10001 ,"North", 1500.55 , 1450.66 ],
        [10002 ,"South", 2344.99 , 3200.45 ],
        [10003 ,"East",  1750.44 , 950.55 ],
        [10004 ,"West",  3000.00 , 3200.55 ],
        [10005 ,"Central", 4523.45 , 1963.44 ],
        [10006 ,"OverSeas", 2489.55, 2786.12 ]
      ]
    });
    var mychart= Ext.create('Ext.chart.CartesianChart', {
      store: myChartStore,
      insetPadding: {
        top: 50, left: 25,
        right: 25, bottom: 15
      },
      interactions: 'itemhighlight',
      axes: [{
        type: 'numeric',
```

```
      position: 'left',
      title: {
        text: 'Sales 1st to 3th Quarter',
        fontSize: 14,
        fillStyle: '#0d7179'
      },
      fields: 'sales'
    }, {
      type: 'category',
      position: 'bottom',
      title: {
        text: 'Sales by Branch',
        fontSize: 18,
        fillStyle: '#277cc0'
      },
      fields: 'region'
    }],
    series: {
      type: 'bar',
      title: ['Main branch','Branch B'],
      xField: 'region',
      yField: 'sales',
      style:{
        strokeStyle: '#999999',
        fillStyle: '#cccc99'
      },
      highlight:{
        strokeStyle: '#990000',
        fillStyle: '#ffcc66',
        lineDash: [5, 3]
      },
      label: {
        field: 'sales',
        display: 'insideEnd'
      }
    },
    sprites: {
      type: 'text',
      text: 'My Company - 2015',
      fontSize: 22,
      fillStyle: '#993366',
      width: 100,
      height: 30,
```

```
        x: 40, // the sprite x position
        y: 25 // the sprite y position
      }
    });
    me.items = [mychart];
    me.tbar = ['->', {
      text: 'Download',
      handler: function() {
        var chart = me.down('cartesian');
        chart.download({
          filename: 'MyCompany_chart2015'
        });
      }
    }];
    me.callParent();
  }
});
```

So, this is our View file. Now notice that we added a toolbar and a button whose handler function gets the chart component by its alias (xtype) and calls the download function. This will cause the chart to be exported as an image file (PNG format by default).

> For more information on this, navigate to the documentation page at **Ext.chart.CartesianChart** to check out the full list of possible configurations.

1. Now, open the app/controller/app.js file and add the new view to the requires property, like this:

    ```
    requires:[
      'myApp.store.modulesTreeDs',
      'myApp.view.appZone',
      'myApp.view.myViewport',
      'myApp.view.myChartSample'
    ],
    ```

2. Then, open the serverside/data/menu_extended.json file and set the access for the view:

    ```
    {
      "leaf": true,
      "text": "Charts",
      "allowaccess":false,
      "description":"Generate charts",
    ```

```
        "level":2,
        "moduleType":"module",
        "iconCls":"charts-16",
        "options":"myApp.view.myChartSample",
        "moduleAlias":"myChartSamplePanel"
    }
```

3. Now we are ready to run our application, so let's open it in the browser and see the result, as follows:

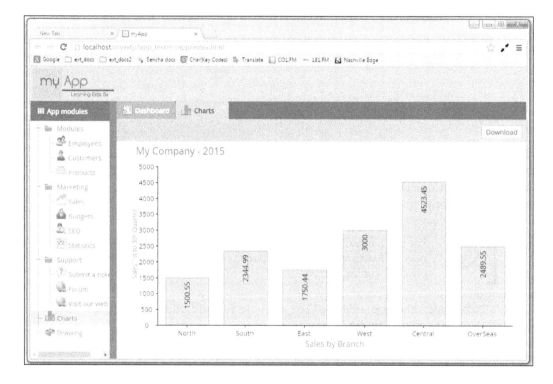

4. Finally, click on the **Download** button, save the image in your hard drive, and see the file.

As you can see, implementing charting in our application is not as hard as it looks. Now it's up to you to create real-world charts (and also to get the data for them). In these examples, we used an Array store, but remember that as it's a data store, you can always get information (data) from JSON and XML as well.

Summary

In this chapter, you learned the basics of drawing and applying properties to sprites (elements), and also the fundamentals of creating basic charts. We saw how chart themes can be quite useful for applying styles to our charts, and also how to integrate `ext-charts` and `sencha-charts` into our applications.

Remember to check out the SVG documentation and not to confuse **Legacy charts** with **Sencha charts**; you may get confused and use the wrong one, but don't despair. And remember to use these resources if something is not working properly with the `draw` or `chart` options.

In the next chapter, we will see how to complete our application and prepare it for deployment.

14
Finishing the Application

Since Ext JS version 4, we can compile our application using the Sencha CMD tool. This compilation gathers the required classes/JavaScript code and necessary resources in order to build our application for a production environment.

It's better to compile the code in order to protect the source code, and also minimize the size of the JS files, so that it will optimize the loading speed for our application. Also, while compiling the code, we must ensure that we have the necessary JavaScript classes and code in order to run our app, and also to avoid uploading the entire Ext JS framework on the server.

In this chapter, you are going to learn the basics of how to prepare our application and deploy it in a production environment. But before going further, please check the following properties in your application:

- Make sure that the code has the correct code syntax. Be aware of trailing commas (,) and also have the semicolon (;) properly set in the JavaScript instructions. We need to have good code quality in order to compile the code.

- If you are on a Windows OS, it's recommended that you have several versions of Sencha CMD installed, because not all Sencha CMD versions compile the code with the proper character encoding. So, if you are using special characters (Latin or others), this may be a major factor, because it can change the encoding of the strings in your application. For this, you will need to test and see which version suits your needs.

Also, it's important to mention that part of the build process (that is, some files, especially XML) are files that are to be used by Apache Ant. So, if you want to create advanced builds then it's important that you know a bit more about Apache Ant from http://ant.apache.org.

Preparing for deployment

So far, we have seen how to architect our JavaScript code, created classes and layers for specific tasks, and written maintainable and scalable code; but we need to prepare our application for a production environment.

In *Chapter 2*, *The Core Concepts*, we talked about the loader system in Ext 4, and you learned that classes have dependencies, and these dependent classes can be loaded automatically when requiring the main class.

In *Chapter 10*, *Architecture*, we created a basic application skeleton and also most of our application. So far in this chapter, our application is in the development environment, and also this environment made sure that Ext JS classes (also our own classes) were dynamically loaded when the application required to use them. In this environment, it's really helpful to load each class in a separate file. This will allow us to debug the code easily, and find and fix bugs.

In *Chapter 11*, *The Look and Feel*, and *Chapter 12*, *Responsive Configurations and Tablet Support*, we enhanced our app a bit more.

Now, before we start compiling, we must know the three basic parts of our application, as marked here:

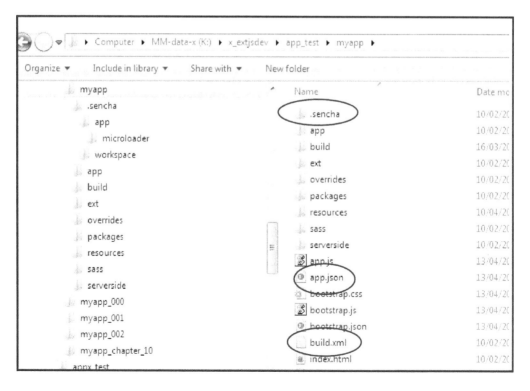

- `app.json`: This file contains specific details about our application. Also, Sencha CMD processes this file first.

- `build.xml`: This file contains a minimal initial Ant script, and imports a task file located at `.sencha/app/build-impl.xml`.

- `.sencha`: This folder contains many files related to, and are to be used for, the build process.

The app.json file

As we said before, the `app.json` file will contain information about the settings of our application. Open the file and take a look. In previous chapters, we made changes to this file, such as the theme that our application is going to use:

```
"theme": "my-custom-theme-touch",
```

Alternatively, we can use the normal theme:

```
"theme": "my-custom-theme",
```

The other change we made in previous chapters was this:

```
"requires": [
  "sencha-charts"
],
```

This was to specify that we are going to use the charts / draw classes in our application (the chart package for Ext JS 5). Now, at the end of the file, there is an ID for the application:

```
"id": "7833ee81-4d14-47e6-8293-0cb8120281ab"
```

After this ID, we can add other properties. As an example, suppose our application will be generated for Central and South America. Then we need to include the locale (ES or PT), so we can add the following:

```
,"locales":["es"]
```

We can also add multiple languages:

```
,"locales":["es","pt","en"]
```

This will cause the compilation process to include the corresponding locale files located at `ext/packages/ext-locale/build`.

However, this book can't cover each property in the file, so it's recommended that you take a deep look into the Sencha CMD documentation at: `http://docs-origin.sencha.com/cmd/5.x/microloader.html` to learn more about the `app.json` file.

The Sencha command

To create our production build, we need to use the Sencha Command. This tool will help us in our purpose.

 If you are running Sencha CMD on Windows 7 or Windows 8, it's recommended that you run the tool with "administrator privileges".

So let's type this in our console tool:

```
[path of my app]\sencha app build
```

In my case (Windows OS 7; 64-bit), I typed:

```
K:\x_extjsdev\app_test\myapp>sencha app build
```

After the command runs, you will see something like this in your console tool:

```
[INF] merging 315 input resources into K:\x_extjsdev\app_test\myapp\build\produc
tion\myApp\resources
[INF] merged 0 resources into K:\x_extjsdev\app_test\myapp\build\production\myAp
p\resources
[INF] merging 0 input resources into K:\x_extjsdev\app_test\myapp\build\producti
on\myApp
[INF] merged 0 resources into K:\x_extjsdev\app_test\myapp\build\production\myAp
p
[INF] writing sass content to K:\x_extjsdev\app_test\myapp/build/temp/production
/myApp/sass/myApp-all.scss.tmp
[INF] appending sass content to K:\x_extjsdev\app_test\myapp/build/temp/producti
on/myApp/sass/myApp-all.scss.tmp
[INF] appending sass content to K:\x_extjsdev\app_test\myapp/build/temp/producti
on/myApp/sass/myApp-all.scss.tmp
[INF] executing compass using system installed ruby runtime
Cannot determine the opposite position of: to
Cannot determine the opposite position of: to
overwrite myApp-all.css
[INF] writing sass content to K:\x_extjsdev\app_test\myapp/build/temp/production
/myApp/slicer-temp/myApp-example.scss.tmp
[INF] executing compass using system installed ruby runtime
Cannot determine the opposite position of: to
Cannot determine the opposite position of: to
identical myApp-example.css
[INF] Writing content to K:\x_extjsdev\app_test\myapp/sass/example/bootstrap.jso
n
[INF] Writing content to K:\x_extjsdev\app_test\myapp/sass/example/bootstrap.js
[INF] Capturing theme image
[INF] Capture complete
[INF] Slicing images...
[INF] Slicing complete - generated 387 images
[INF] Copying page resources to K:\x_extjsdev\app_test\myapp\build\production\my
App
[INF] Writing content to K:\x_extjsdev\app_test\myapp/build/production/myApp/app
.json
[INF] Writing content to K:\x_extjsdev\app_test\myapp/build/production/myApp/mic
roloader.js
[INF] Appending content to K:\x_extjsdev\app_test\myapp/build/production/myApp/m
icroloader.js
[INF] Building output markup to K:\x_extjsdev\app_test\myapp/build/production/my
App/index.html
[INF] Writing content to K:\x_extjsdev\app_test\myapp/build/production/myApp/ind
ex.html

K:\x_extjsdev\app_test\myapp>
```

So, let's check out the `build` folder inside our application folder. We may have the following list of files:

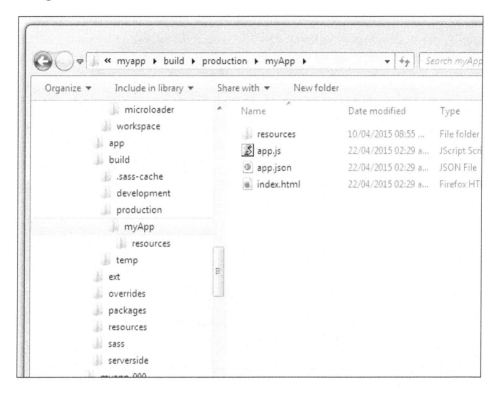

Notice that the build process has created these:

- `resources`: This file will contain a copy of our `resources` folder, plus one or more CSS files starting with `myApp-all`

- `app.js`: This file contains all of the necessary JS (Ext JS core classes, components, and our custom application classes)

- `app.json`: This is a small manifest file compressed

- `index.html`: This file is similar to our index file in development mode, except for the line:

```
<script id="microloader" type="text/javascript" src="bootstrap.
js"></script>
```

This was replaced by some compressed JavaScript code, which will act in a similar way to the micro loader.

Notice that the `serverside` folder, where we use some JSON files (other cases can be PHP, ASP, and so on), does not exist in the production folder. Well, the reason is that that folder is not part of what Sencha CMD and build files consider.

Normally, many developers will say, *"Hey, let's copy the folder and let's move on."* However, the good news is that we can include that folder with an Apache Ant task

Customizing the build.xml file

We can add custom code (Apache Ant style) to perform new tasks and things we need in order to make our application build even better. Let's open the `build.xml` file. You will see something like this:

```xml
<?xml version="1.0" encoding="utf-8"?>
<project name="myApp" default=".help">
<!-- comments... -->
<import file="${basedir}/.sencha/app/build-impl.xml"/>
<!-- comments... -->
</project>
```

So, let's place the following code before `</project>`:

```xml
<target name="-after-build" depends="init">
  <copy todir="${build.out.base.path}/serverside"
    overwrite="false">
  <fileset dir="${app.dir}/serverside" includes="**/*"/>
  </copy>
</target>
</project>
```

This new code inside the `build.xml` file establishes that after making the whole building process, if there is no error during the `Init` process then it will copy the (`${app.dir}/ serverside`) folder to the (`${build.out.base.path}/serverside`) output path. So now, let's type the command for building the application again:

```
sencha app build -c
```

In this case, we added `-c` to first clean the `build/production` folder and create a new set of files. After the process completes, take a look at the folder contents, and you will see this:

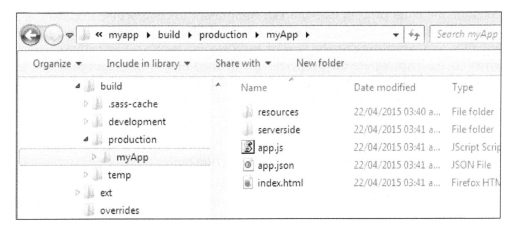

Notice that now the `serverside` folder has been copied to the production `build` folder, thanks to the custom code we placed in `build.xml` file.

Compressing the code

After building our application, let's open the `app.js` file. We may see something like what is shown here:

```
var Ext=Ext||{};if(!Ext.Toolbar){Ext.Toolbar={}}if(!Ext.app){Ext.app={}}if(!Ext.app.bind){Ext.app.bind={}}i
.matrix){Ext.data.matrix={}}if(!Ext.data.operation){Ext.data.operation={}}if(!Ext.data.proxy){Ext.data.prox
m.action={}}if(!Ext.form.field){Ext.form.field={}}if(!Ext.form.trigger){Ext.form.trigger={}}if(!Ext.fx){Ext
rrides.dom={}}if(!Ext.overrides.event){Ext.overrides.event={}}if(!Ext.overrides.event.publisher){Ext.overri
={}}if(!Ext.util.paintmonitor){Ext.util.paintmonitor={}}if(!Ext.util.sizemonitor){Ext.util.sizemonitor={}}i
ules={}}(function(F){var I,z=["constructor","toString","valueOf","toLocaleString"],E={},v={},G=0,y,B,t,D,J,
d[f]=c=e[f];c.$owner=a;c.$name=f}}},w=function(a){var e=function b(){return a.apply(this,arguments)||null}
for(f in a){if(a.hasOwnProperty(f)){c=a[f];if(c&&c.$isFunction&&!c.$isClass&&!==Ext.emptyFn&&c!==Ext.id
ame;if(ag.onCreated){ag.onCreated.call(e,a)}if(aa){t.triggerCreated(aa)}return e}.F.derive=u}(Ext.cmd={});
ettings||{});Ext.apply(Ext,{idSeed:0,idPrefix:"ext-",isSecure:/^https/i.test(window.location.protocol),enab
.now()}:(Date.now||(Date.now=function(){return +new Date()}),destroy:function(){var a=arguments.length,b,c
g(a)){return false}return t.test(a)},isObject:{v.call(null)==="[object Object]"?function(a){return a!==nul
a){if(!a||typeof a.length!=="number"||typeof a==="string"||Ext.isFunction(a)){return false}if(!a.propertyIs
if(Ext.isSandboxed){c=e.length;if(c>0){c--;e[c]="var Ext=window."+Ext.name+";"+e[c]}}a=e.join("");d=f[a];i
+=g}else{f+="()"}}if(a){f=f?(a+","+f):a}return f||g||""}Ext.Error=function(d){if(Ext.isString(d)){d={msg:d}
return d[a[h],a[g]]||(h-g)}};for(c=0;c<f;c++){b[c]=a[b[c]]}for(c=0;c<f;c++){a[c]=b[c]}return a}try{if(typeo
apply(a,A.call(arguments,1))},t=y?x:I,v=y?F:e,u=y?G:D,J={binarySearch:function(h,b,d,g,i){var c=h.length,f,
turn H.indexOf.call(a,b)!==-1:function(a,b){var d,c;for(d=0,c=a.length;d<c;d++){if(a[d]===b){return true}}
alse}}return true},clean:function(a){var d=[],f=0,b=a.length,c;for(;f<b;f++){c=a[f];if(!Ext.isEmpty(c)){d.p
],c,b;for(c=0,b=d.length;c<b;c++){a=a.concat(d[c])}return J.unique(a)},intersect:function(){var f=[],m=A.ca
g=0,c=a.length;g<c;g++){d=a[g]}if(b){if(b(f,d)===1){f=d}}else{if(d<f){f=d}}return f},max:function(a,b){var
```

By default, the build process uses the YUI compressor to compact the JS code (`http://yui.github.io/yuicompressor/`). Inside the `.sencha` folder, there are many files, and depending on the type of build we are creating, there are some files such as the base file, where the properties are defined in `defaults.properties`. This file must not be changed whatsoever; for that, we have other files that can override the values defined in this file. As an example for the production build, we have the following files:

- `production.defaults.properties`: This file will contain some properties/variables that will be used for the production build.

- `production.properties`: This file has only comments. The idea behind this file is that developers place the variables they want in order to customize the production build.

By default, in the `production.defaults.properties` file, you will see something like the following code:

```
# Comments ......
#  more comments......
build.options.logger=no
build.options.debug=false
# enable the full class system optimizer
app.output.js.optimize=true
build.optimize=${build.optimize.enable}
enable.cache.manifest=true
enable.resource.compression=true

build.embedded.microloader.compressor=-closure
```

Now, as an example of compression, let's make a change and place some variables inside the `production.properties` file. The code we will place here will override the properties set in `defaults.properties` and `production.defaults.properties`. So, let's write the following code after the comments:

```
build.embedded.microloader.compressor=-closure
build.compression.yui=0
build.compression.closure=1
build.compression=-closure
```

With this code, we are setting up the build process to use **closure** as the JavaScript compressor and also for the micro loader. Now save the file and use the Sencha CMD tool once again:

```
sencha app build
```

Wait for the process to end and 'take a look at `app.js`.

```
var Ext=Ext||{};Ext.Toolbar||(Ext.Toolbar={});Ext.app||(Ext.app={});Ext.app.bind||(Ext.app.bind={});Ext.app.
.data.operation={});Ext.data.proxy||(Ext.data.proxy={});Ext.data.reader||(Ext.data.reader={});Ext.data.schem
x={});Ext.fx.animation||(Ext.fx.animation={});Ext.fx.easing||(Ext.fx.easing={});Ext.fx.runner||(Ext.fx.runne
.overrides.plugin={});Ext.overrides.util||(Ext.overrides.util={});Ext.panel||(Ext.panel={});Ext.perf||(Ext.p
ndow||(Ext.window={});var ExtThemeNeptune=ExtThemeNeptune||{};ExtThemeNeptune.grid||(ExtThemeNeptune.grid={}
n&&!l.$isClass&&l!==Ext.emptyFn&&l!==Ext.identityFn?(m in n&&(l.$previous=n[m]),n[m]=l,l.$owner=j,l.$name=m)
ass&&M!==Ext.emptyFn&&M!==Ext.identityFn){L[k]=P=M,P.$owner=L,P.$name=k}L[k]=M}}}R.inheritableStatics&&(L.s
a=l<<b,B[C[a]=D[b]]=a}for(b in B){A|=B[b]}A=~A;Function.prototype.$isFunction=1;s=!(!x||!x.addAlias);w=Ext.C
s.$nullFn=q.$nullFn=s.$emptyFn=q.$identityFn=r.$nullFn=!0;r.$privacy="framework";Ext.suspendLayouts=Ext.resu
tring:new String,baseCSSPrefix:Ext.buildSettings.baseCSSPrefix,$eventNameMap:{},$vendorEventRe:/^(Moz.+|MS.+
=h)}}else{Ext.apply(g,f)}}}return g},valueFrom:function(e,d,f){return Ext.isEmpty(e,f)?d:e},isEmpty:functio
n !isNaN(parseFloat(b))&&isFinite(b)},isString:function(b){return"string"===typeof b},isBoolean:function(b){
pace,d;if(void 0===a){d=0;do{a="ExtBox"+ ++d}while(void 0!==v[a]);v[a]=Ext;this.uniqueGlobalNamespace=a}retu
ngth-1)&&0<j.length;){h=h+w+j.shift()}h=h.replace(l,w);k.push(h)}return k}})())});Ext.returnTrue.$nullFn=Ext.
XX");D=D+1!==C.length?!1:!0}else{D=!1}var C="indexOf" in F,B=!0;try{"undefined"!==typeof document&&E.call(dd
ion(j,h,p,n,m){var l=j.length,k;p instanceof Function?(m=p,p=0,n=l):n instanceof Function?(m=n,n=l):(void 0+
f(!b||!b.length){return[]}"string"===typeof b&&(b=b.split(""));if(B){return E.call(b,h||0,g||b.length)}var e
.indexOf(f,h)&&f.push(h)}return f},filter:"filter" in F?function(e,d,f){return e.filter(d,f)}:function(h,g,m
=i.unique(K);s(0,M,1);J=K.length;N=0.length;for(r=0;r<J;r++){I=K[r];for(p=G=0;p<N;p++){M=0[p];L=M.length;for
){j=h[l],g?-1===g(m,j)&&(m=j):j>m&&(m=j)}return m},mean:function(m){return 0<b.length?i.sum(b)/b.length:void
.sum;Ext.mean=i.mean;Ext.flatten=i.flatten;Ext.clean=i.clean;Ext.unique=i.unique;Ext.pluck=i.pluck;Ext.toArr
LowerCase(),e=e.toLowerCase()),g=0===f.lastIndexOf(e,0));return g},endsWith:function(f,e,h){var g=o(f,e);g&&
At(0).toLowerCase()+b.substr(1));return b||""},ellipsis:function(f,e,h){if(f&&f.length>e){if(h){h=f.substr(0
c=Array.prototype.slice.call(arguments,1);return d.replace(o,function(b,e){return c[e]})}var u,t=Date,s=/(
```

You can notice that the code is quite different. This is because the code compiler (closure) was the one that made the compression. Run the app and you will notice no change in the behavior and use of the application.

As we have used the `production.properties` file in this example, notice that in the `.sencha` folder, we have some other files for different environments, such as:

Environment	File (or files)
Testing	`testing.defaults.properties` and `testing.properties`
Development	`development.defaults.properties` and `development.properties`
Production	`production.defaults.properties` and `production.properties`

It's not recommended that you change the `*.default.properties` file. That's the reason of the `*.properties` file, so that you can set your own variables, and doing this will override the settings on default file.

Packaging and deploying

Finally, after we have built our application, we have our production build/package ready to be deployed. We will have the following structure in our folder:

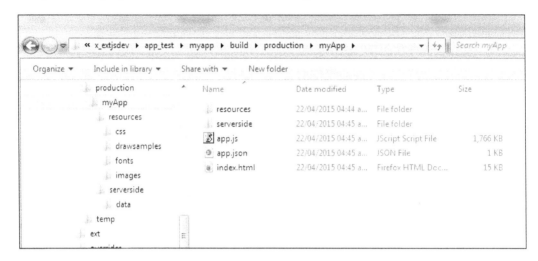

Now we have all the files required to make our application work on a public server. We don't need to upload anything from the Ext JS folder because we have all that we need in `app.js` (all of the Ext JS code and our code). Also, the resources file contains the images, CSS (the theme used in the app), and of course our `serverside` folder. So now, we need to upload all of the content to the server:

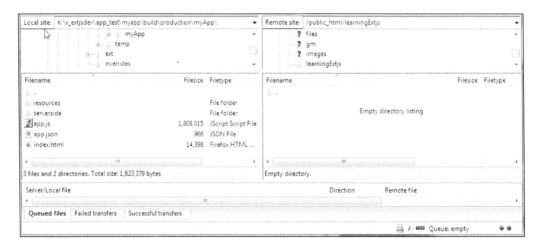

And we are ready to test the production in a public server.

Testing the application

Finally, after uploading the application to our server, we can begin testing, operating, and using it. Remember that the code is compiled, so it will be hard to debug. This is because we don't know the exact line of code, the complexity of the code, and so on. If there are any errors, it's important that you return to your development environment, fix the version, test again to see what the error was, recompile, and upload the new files or the entire package to the server.

Also, there are some considerations you must remember:

1. Try to use the Sencha CMD version that suits your needs. Some new versions may throw some warnings. For this, you may test whether the production build works properly and as expected.

2. Also check the output JS file and verify that the strings were properly treated and the encoding was not changed. If the encoding was changed, then try again with other Sencha CMD versions (this issue is mainly on Windows OS environments).

3. For more advanced topics and a full reference, check out the Sencha CMD documentation at `http://docs.sencha.com/cmd/5.x/`, and also the Apache Ant documentation at `https://ant.apache.org/manual/`.

4. Always keep good syntax in code and avoid errors.

5. Check the paths where you place the `Ext.ux` components and other required packages.

Summary

In this chapter, we talked about compiling and preparing our application for a production environment. This step has become quite important since version 4. Using Sencha CMD and also configuring JSON or XML files to build a project can sometimes be an overwhelming situation, but don't panic! Check out the documentation of Sencha and Apache.

Take a look at the JSON and XML files in examples, mainly in the kitchen sink example. This example has very complex JSON and XML files for building the application, which can give you some pointers to new ideas on how to work with it.

Also, remember that there's no reason to be afraid of testing and playing with the configurations. It's all part of learning and knowing how to use Sencha Ext JS.

15
What's Next?

Throughout this book, we have seen how to use the Ext JS framework version 5 and build rich Internet applications. However, you must remember that this book doesn't cover all the elements of the framework itself, so it's quite useful to know some resources, such as knowledge sharing sites. This chapter's main purpose is to give references to some resources and also to comment about some plug-ins, commercial and free.

Forums

The Sencha website is, in fact, the main resource for Ext JS and other Sencha products. Also this forum comes in Japanese and Portuguese.

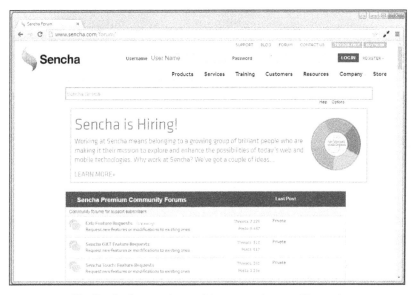

The Sencha forum at `http://www.sencha.com/forum/`

This is the main page for Sencha, and it has forums for all its products, and also new releases. Premium forums are only for those who have a support subscription. The difference between premium forums and plain forums is that premium forums have a short response time.

ExtMX – the Spanish-language community for the Ext JS framework (`http://extjs.mx/`)

ExtMX is a Spanish-language community for the Ext JS framework, where they host tutorials. They also provide resources for courses or training. To access more features, you may need to create a user account (it's free).

Resources

Also, there are other useful sites (resources) where you can find more information, tips, tutorials, and so on. Some of them are discussed in this section.

The **Learn from Saki** website contains many tutorials and code samples, and also offers commercial plug-ins for the framework's versions 4 and 5 (the prices are moderated). Registration is required, and some tutorials require membership in order for you to access them.

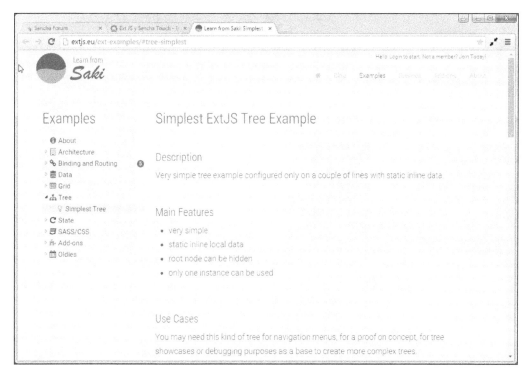

Learn from Saki at `http://extjs.eu`

Loiane Groner is a Brazilian author who is an expert in Ext JS and other technologies. She also has written many books about Ext JS. The following screenshot shows her website where she has discussed Ext JS:

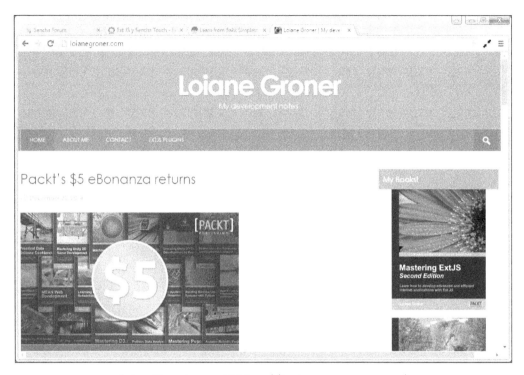

Loiane Groner's page at `http://loianegroner.com/`

Sencha Dev Tricks is another JavaScript experts' blog site. It has many good tutorials and tips.

The **Sencha Dev Tricks** page at `http://www.ladysign-apps.com/developer/`

Sencha has the following **vimeo** channel, with many videos about their products. There are also tutorials, videos about conferences, webinars, and so on. This is a nice resource for learning some tricks from the official developers.

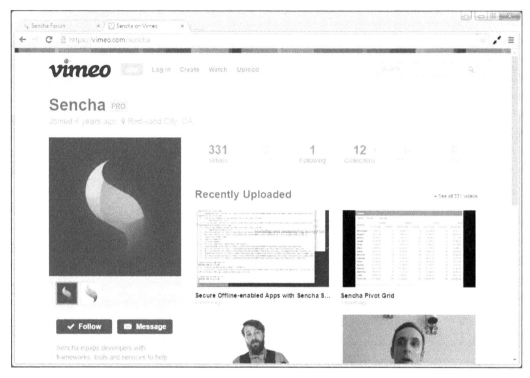

The **vimeo** page at `https://vimeo.com/sencha`

Third-party plugins (commercial)

The framework also comes with third-party components and plugins. Some of them are commercial, and are nice components that bring great power to applications. A few of them are described in this section.

Bryntum, shown as follows, has a very nice Gantt component and a scheduler component, among other products, such as Siesta (a JavaScript testing tool).

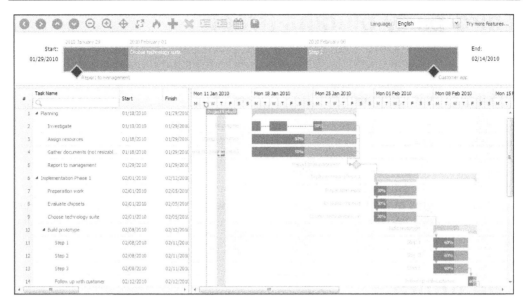

Bryntum at `http://www.bryntum.com`

Previously we mentioned the **Learn from Saki** website at `http://www.extjs.eu` as a useful resource for learning. Here, we are talking about the plugins and extensions it provides. This site has many plugins (mainly made for the Grid component) such as Multi search, Grid search, Multi sort, and Mini pager.

City	Country	Population	Latitude	Longitude	Elevation
	in CH,FR,IT	>=16000			>600
San Giovanni in Fiore	IT	18566	39.26330	16.69960	978
San Cataldo	IT	23154	37.48412	13.98542	647
Piazza Armerina	IT	21038	37.38595	14.36717	691
Enna	IT	28963	37.55885	14.28917	895
Bronte	IT	18512	37.78946	14.83418	836
Acri	IT	21891	39.49290	16.38379	733
Sankt Gallen	CH	70572	47.42391	9.37477	740
Littau	CH	16121	47.05000	8.25000	616
Le Châtelard	CH	23192	46.45000	6.91667	822
La Chaux-de-Fonds	CH	36825	47.09993	6.82586	1,034
Köniz	CH	37196	46.92436	7.41457	606
Gossau	CH	17043	47.41667	9.25000	669
Biel	CH	48614	47.13240	7.24411	668
Pontarlier	FR	20313	46.90347	6.35542	837
Le Puy-en-Velay	FR	22718	45.04366	3.88523	632

Page 1 of 2   Displaying 1 - 15 of 24

`http://extjs.eu`

Third-party plugins (free)

Also, the community across the world has published some free plug-ins and components. You can search for them primarily in the main forum on Sencha's website at `http://www.sencha.com/forum/`. However, Ext JS version 5 does not have many free plugins available.

Almost all the free plugins are/were made for version 4.x. Some of them may be compatible, while some others may not be, due to code changes from version 4 to 5. Still, some developers have made porting and compatible versions for Ext JS 5.

However, due the similarity of the framework's architecture, it's also possible to download plugins made for version 4 and give them a try in version 5. Yet, be aware that these plugins may require a few modifications in order to make them work on Ext JS version 5.

The future

As web technologies and new features become supported in browsers, sooner or later, the tendency and the direction of the Sencha company will be to merge Ext JS and Sencha Touch into a single framework. So, the most logical thing is to call it "Ext JS 6", but no worries! What you learn in this book will be very useful for the next version because Ext JS 4's and 5's classes, coding style, extending classes, and patterns such as MVC or MVVM will be available in version 6 as well. So, it will be much easier for you to understand what all this is about.

This is what you need to keep in mind:

- Wait for a stable release
- Check out the documentation for changes, new things, and what will be required for the migration of version 5 apps to version 6
- What Sencha CMD tool's version 6 can handle and what it cannot

Final thoughts

Ext JS 5 is a nice and powerful framework that can make powerful applications with no hard work. Worldwide, it's one of the most powerful frameworks for application development, and it will continue to be so for a long time. However, the tool will not do the work itself. We need to plan, design accurately, and understand how this framework works things out, so that it can make life easier for us and also speed up the development process.

As an example, you can combine other libraries, such as jQuery, with the same application. The trick is that you need to test and understand how these, being combined on the same application or web page, can coexist without conflicting with each other.

 Although, it is possible to use Ext JS and jQuery, it's not recommended to combine both, because Ext JS classes can produce the same functionality and results. So, there is no need to mix them, unless it's imperative for your project.

Summary

In this chapter, we talked a bit about some useful resources you can refer to learn more about Sencha Ext JS 5, and expand your knowledge about this framework. If you have understood the basics, you will manage to accomplish great things.

Keep in mind that this framework is not plain JavaScript but a mix of many things, such as HTML5, CSS, DOM manipulation, SASS, and so on. You also need to understand the basics in order to know how to manipulate things around the framework. You can create plugins, new components, and wrappers for other scripts, and do much more.

Personally, I recommend that you take a look at the source code in order to understand the internals and also see how things work so that you can build more advanced things. Compared to other frameworks (such as Angular JS), this one may be hard to understand at the beginning, but it's definitely more powerful. So keep practicing and testing, and happy Ext JS 5 coding!

Index

A

B

C

E

editors
  about 15
  Aptana 16
enhancements, Ext JS 5
  breadcrumb bars 21
  data package improvements 19
  event system 20
  form package improvements 21
  grids 20
  MVVM architecture 19
  New SASS Mixins 21
  new themes 19
  responsive configurations 19
  routing 19
  Sencha Charts 20
  Sencha Core package 22
  tablet support 19
  tab panels 20
  widgets 21
environment
  setting up 315-317
event-driven development 133-136
event normalization 344, 345
events
  handling, in DataView 247, 248
  listening to 288-291
Ext.Ajax-cfg-async
  URL 94
ext-charts package 363
Ext Charts Upgrade Guide
  URL 364
Ext.chart.theme.Base
  URL 375
Ext.data.BufferedStore
  URL 238
Ext.data.NodeInterface class 263
Ext.draw.Component
  sprite elements 368
Ext.enums.Widget
  URL 24
ext folder 325
Ext.form.Panel component 78

Ext.grid.feature.Feature class 224
Ext.grid.feature.Grouping 224, 226
Ext.grid.feature.GroupingSummary 226, 227
Ext.grid.feature.RowBody 228
Ext.grid.feature.Summary 229, 230
Ext.grid.Panel 223
Ext.grid.plugin.CellEditing 230-232
Ext.grid.plugin.RowEditing 233-235
Ext JS
  about 1, 2
  considering, for project 2
  downloading 4
  files 6, 7
  folders 6, 7
  layers 8
  URL, for downloading 4
  URL, for official website 3
Ext JS 5
  enhancements 19-21
  installing 5
  modified folders 7, 8
  setting up 5
Ext JS code
  writing 11
Ext JS, licenses
  commercial license 3
  commercial OEM 3
  open source license 3
ExtMX
  about 408
  URL 408
Ext.panel.Panel component 78
Ext.plugin.Responsive
  URL 353
Ext.tab.Panel component 78
Ext.Template
  about 248
  example 248, 249
Ext.tree.Panel class 257
Ext.Viewport component 78
Ext.window.Window component 78
Ext.XTemplate
  about 248
  example 250-252

W

WAMP
  about 15
  URL 15
Widget Column 214-218
Window component 81, 82

X

XAMPP
  about 15
  URL 15
XML reader 125, 126
xtype property
  about 75
  URL 75

Y

YUI compressor
  URL 402

Thank you for buying
Learning Ext JS
Fourth Edition

About Packt Publishing

Packt, pronounced 'packed', published its first book, *Mastering phpMyAdmin for Effective MySQL Management*, in April 2004, and subsequently continued to specialize in publishing highly focused books on specific technologies and solutions.

Our books and publications share the experiences of your fellow IT professionals in adapting and customizing today's systems, applications, and frameworks. Our solution-based books give you the knowledge and power to customize the software and technologies you're using to get the job done. Packt books are more specific and less general than the IT books you have seen in the past. Our unique business model allows us to bring you more focused information, giving you more of what you need to know, and less of what you don't.

Packt is a modern yet unique publishing company that focuses on producing quality, cutting-edge books for communities of developers, administrators, and newbies alike. For more information, please visit our website at www.packtpub.com.

Writing for Packt

We welcome all inquiries from people who are interested in authoring. Book proposals should be sent to author@packtpub.com. If your book idea is still at an early stage and you would like to discuss it first before writing a formal book proposal, then please contact us; one of our commissioning editors will get in touch with you.

We're not just looking for published authors; if you have strong technical skills but no writing experience, our experienced editors can help you develop a writing career, or simply get some additional reward for your expertise.

PUBLISHING

Mastering Ext JS

ISBN: 978-1-78216-400-5   Paperback: 358 pages

Learn how to build powerful and professional applications by mastering the Ext JS framework

1. Build an application with Ext JS from scratch.

2. Learn expert tips and tricks to make your web applications look stunning.

3. Create professional screens such as login, menus, grids, tree, forms, and charts.

Ext JS 4 Web Application Development Cookbook

ISBN: 978-1-84951-686-0   Paperback: 488 pages

Over 110 easy-to-follow recipes backed up with real-life examples, walking you through basic Ext JS features to advanced application design using Sencha's Ext JS

1. Learn how to build Rich Internet Applications with the latest version of the Ext JS framework in a cookbook style.

2. From creating forms to theming your interface, you will learn the building blocks for developing the perfect web application.

3. Easy to follow recipes step through practical and detailed examples which are all fully backed up with code, illustrations, and tips.

Please check **www.PacktPub.com** for information on our titles

Enterprise Application Development with Ext JS and Spring

ISBN: 978-1-78328-545-7   Paperback: 446 pages

Develop and deploy a high-performance Java web application using Ext JS and Spring

1. Embark on the exciting journey through the entire enterprise web application development lifecycle.

2. Leverage key Spring Framework concepts to deliver comprehensive and concise Java code.

3. Build a real world Ext JS web application that interacts with dynamic database driven data.

Oracle Application Express 4.0 with Ext JS

ISBN: 978-1-84968-106-3   Paperback: 392 pages

Deliver rich desktop-styled Oracle APEX applications using the powerful Ext JS JavaScript library

1. Build robust, feature-rich web applications using Oracle APEX and Ext JS.

2. Add more sophisticated components and functionality to an Oracle APEX application using Ext JS.

3. Build your own themes based on Ext JS into APEX - developing templates for regions, labels, and lists.

4. Create plug-ins in your application workspace to enhance the existing built-in functionality of your APEX applications.

Please check **www.PacktPub.com** for information on our titles